Boston
FOR
DUMMIES®
3RD EDITION

Marie Morris

WILEY

Wiley Publishing, Inc.

Boston For Dummies®, 3rd Edition

Published by
Wiley Publishing, Inc.
111 River St.
Hoboken, NJ 07030-5774
www.wiley.com

WILEY

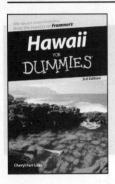
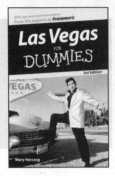

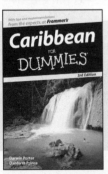
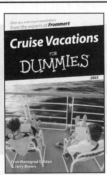

About the Author

Marie Morris grew up in New York City and graduated from Harvard, where she studied history. She has lived in the Boston area for most of the past two decades. Since 1997, she has written the *Frommer's Boston* travel guide and contributed to *Frommer's New England.* She is also the author of the latest edition of *Frommer's Irreverent Guide to Boston.* She has been, among other things, an assistant sports editor at the *Boston Herald* and an editor at *Boston* magazine. She enjoys cooking, entertaining, horse racing, and traveling. Marie lives in the North End, not far from the Freedom Trail, where she often encounters readers — bring along your copy of *Boston For Dummies,* and you might meet her there.

Publisher's Acknowledgments

We're proud of this book; please send us your comments through our Dummies online registration form located at www.dummies.com/register/.

Some of the people who helped bring this book to market include the following:

Editorial:

Editors: Jennifer Anmuth, Associate Editor, Kelly Ewing, Project Editor

Cartographer: Nicholas Trotter

Editorial Manager: Michelle Hacker

Editorial Supervisor: Carmen Krikorian

Senior Photo Editor: Richard Fox

Cover Photos: Front: © Frank Siteman Photography Back: © Walter Bibikow/AGE Fotostock, Inc.

Cartoons: Rich Tennant (www.the5thwave.com)

Composition Services

Project Coordinator: Michael Kruzil

Layout and Graphics: Carl Byers, Andrea Dahl,Lauren Goddard, Denny Hager, Joyce Haughey, Stephanie Jumper, Melanee Prendergast

Proofreaders: Leeann Harney, Jessica Kramer, Carl William Pierce, TECHBOOKS Production Services

Indexer: TECHBOOKS Production Services

Publishing and Editorial for Consumer Dummies

> **Diane Graves Steele,** Vice President and Publisher, Consumer Dummies
>
> **Joyce Pepple,** Acquisitions Director, Consumer Dummies
>
> **Kristin A. Cocks,** Product Development Director, Consumer Dummies
>
> **Michael Spring,** Vice President and Publisher, Travel
>
> **Kelly Regan,** Editorial Director, Travel

Publishing for Technology Dummies

> **Andy Cummings,** Vice President and Publisher, Dummies Technology/ General User

Composition Services

> **Gerry Fahey,** Vice President of Production Services
>
> **Debbie Stailey,** Director of Composition Services

Contents at a Glance

Maps at a Glance

Table of Contents

Part V: Living It Up after Dark: Boston Nightlife 237

Chapter 15: Applauding the Cultural Scene 239

Chapter 16: Hitting the Clubs and Bars 250

Part VI: The Part of Tens 259

Chapter 17: The Top Ten Ways Not to Look Like a Tourist 261

Introduction

The Big Dig — a highway-construction project that dominated downtown throughout the 1990s — is almost over. After 86 years, the Boston Red Sox finally won the World Series. One hundred and two days later, the Patriots won the Super Bowl — again, making this win its third in four years. The city is full of excitement and pride. What could be a better time to visit Boston than now? In this city, you notice the people, so many of them in their late teens and early twenties. Wow, Boston really is a college town! And that quintessential frat-boy fashion statement, the baseball cap, is everywhere. You see Red Sox caps on everyone from toddlers in strollers to residents of nursing homes. Soon you realize that some of the seniors have been rooting for their beloved team since *they* were in baby carriages. Everyone's still grinning over the Sox's 2004 World Series title.

The city's distinctive red-brick buildings surround lush parks and overlook a dazzling harbor. Most of the buildings and the parks stand on a landfill. And although it's hard to believe, the prettiest park (the Public Garden) is entirely manmade. Just two decades ago, pollution overwhelmed the harbor, and a federal judge ordered the massive cleanup that resulted in the entrancing body of water you see today.

In Boston, the past, present, and future collide. Right beside a 21st-century skyscraper will be a building that housed a turning point of colonial history. To reach a tempting boutique, you pass a street musician who turns out to be a student at one of the Boston area's world-class conservatories. Follow your nose to a tempting ethnic restaurant; immigrants have shaped Boston for nearly 400 years, and your tasty meal may come with an introduction to the latest newcomers.

The more time you spend in Boston, the more you understand, but even a one-day visit can give you a good sense of this multifaceted city.

About This Book

Remember that *Boston For Dummies,* 3rd Edition, is a reference book, not a "travel narrative." You don't need to read the chapters in order from front cover to back, and you don't need to remember everything you read. Just dip into the sections that particularly interest you. If you already know that you'll be staying on your friend's couch, for example, you can skip the accommodations information. If you're burning to do some serious shopping . . . well, you probably don't have your nose buried in the Introduction anyway.

Dummies Post-it® Flags

As you're reading this book, you'll find information that you'll want to reference as you plan or enjoy your trip — whether it be a new hotel, a must-see attraction, or a must-try walking tour. Mark these pages with the handy Post-it® Flags included in this book to help make your trip planning easier!

In assembling the information, suggestions, and listings in this book, I took a "greatest hits" approach. I present discriminating choices rather than encyclopedic directories. The focus is on what you need to know, not on "in case you were wondering" observations. Throughout the book, I offer plenty of insider advice to make you feel as comfortable as possible.

In addition, although I can't physically protect you every step of the way, your safety is important to me. I encourage you to stay alert and be aware of your surroundings. Keep a close eye on cameras, purses, backpacks, and wallets — all favorite targets of thieves and pickpockets.

Conventions Used in This Book

Like any reference book, *Boston For Dummies* uses some shorthand phrases and abbreviations. The most obvious are "Boston" and "the Boston area." Throughout eastern Massachusetts, you'll find people born in Newton, raised in Wellesley, educated in Cambridge, and living in Quincy who say they're "from Boston" without thinking twice. Rather than subject you to "Boston, Cambridge, sometimes Brookline, occasionally Somerville, and maybe a few other nearby suburbs," I use the shorter terms. When you need specifics (as in addresses), you get them.

Also note the "T" that appears in hotel, restaurant, and attraction listings. The T is the name of Boston's rapid transit system, and the listings include the name of the closest T stop.

I use the following credit card abbreviations in the text:

AE: American Express

DC: Diners Club

DISC: Discover

MC: MasterCard

V: Visa

I've divided the hotels into two categories — my personal favorites and those that don't quite make my preferred list but still get my hearty seal of approval. Don't be shy about considering these "runners-up" hotels if you're unable to get a room at one of my favorites or if your preferences differ from mine — the amenities that the runners-up offer and the services that each provides make all these accommodations good choices to consider as you determine where to rest your head at night.

I also include some general pricing information to help you as you decide where to unpack your bags or dine on the local cuisine (see Chapters 9 and 10). I use a system of dollar signs to show a range of costs for one night in a hotel (the price refers to a double-occupancy room) or a meal at a restaurant (included in the cost of each meal are an appetizer, main course, dessert, and nonalcoholic drink, not including tax and tip). The listings that come later in this book include exact prices for every establishment, attraction, and activity.

Check out the following table to decipher the dollar signs:

Cost	Hotel	Restaurant
$	Less than $125	Less than $20
$$	$125–$225	$20–$30
$$$	$226–$325	$31–$45
$$$$	$326 and up	$46 and up

Please be aware that travel information is subject to change at any time, and that this caveat is *especially* true of prices. I suggest that you surf, call, or write ahead for confirmation when making your travel plans.

For those hotels, restaurants, and attractions that are plotted on a map, a page reference is provided in the listing information. If a hotel, restaurant, or attraction is outside the city limits or in an out-of-the-way area, it may not be mapped.

Foolish Assumptions

As I wrote this book, I made some assumptions about you and what your needs might be as a traveler. Here's what I assumed about you:

- ✔ You may be an experienced traveler who hasn't had much time to explore Boston and wants expert advice when you finally do get a chance to enjoy the city.

- ✔ You may be an inexperienced traveler looking for guidance when determining whether to take a trip to Boston and how to plan for it.

✔ You're not looking for a book that provides *all* the information about Boston or that lists every hotel, restaurant, or attraction available to you. Instead, you're looking for a book that focuses on the places that will give you the *best* or most unique experience in Boston.

If you fit any of these criteria, then *Boston For Dummies* gives you the information that you're looking for!

How This Book Is Organized

This book consists of six parts that lead you through the process of arriving in and navigating the city, finding a great place to stay, searching out the restaurants that cater to your tastes, discovering the worthwhile attractions and shopping areas, perhaps taking a day trip, and generally having a great time.

Part 1: Introducing Boston

In this part, I acquaint you with a city that always seems familiar but never fails to surprise. You get an insider's view of Boston's top destinations and a quick look at the city's history. This part also includes the lowdown on the best times to visit.

Part 11: Planning Your Trip to Boston

Now you move from the theoretical to the specific. How much should you budget? How will you get to Boston? Where can families, seniors, travelers with disabilities, and gay and lesbian travelers find information tailored to them? What else do you need to know before you leave home? I answer it all in the chapters in this part.

Part 111: Settling Into Boston

In this part, I outline that final leg of your journey, from the airport to your hotel. I sketch the city's neighborhoods and explain how to get around and between them. You figure out which hotel is right for you, and you get the lowdown on Boston's diverse restaurant scene.

Part 1V: Exploring Boston

Here, I give you the scoop on the city's sights and attractions, from museums and historic buildings to tours and cruises. If those places sound too highfalutin, check out this part for my tips on sports and shopping. I also recommend some favorite itineraries and day trips.

Part V: Living It Up after Dark: Boston Nightlife

Boston makes up for its somewhat anemic nightlife with enough cultural offerings to class up a wrestling match — and enough bars and pubs to make up for early closing hours. You can't dance till dawn, but you can have a ball into the wee hours. I set the scene in this section.

Part VI: The Part of Tens

Veteran *For Dummies* readers know about The Part of Tens, and newcomers will recognize the value of the chapters here: interesting stuff that doesn't seem to fit anywhere else. I offer facts, pointers, and observations that complement the rest of this book. Enjoy!

Appendix: Quick Concierge

In the back of this book, I include an appendix — your Quick Concierge — containing lots of handy information you may need when traveling in Boston, such as phone numbers and addresses of emergency personnel or area hospitals and pharmacies, lists of local newspapers and magazines, protocol for sending mail or finding taxis, and more. Check out this appendix when searching for answers to lots of little questions that may come up as you travel. You can find Quick Concierge easily because it's printed on yellow paper.

Icons Used in This Book

In the margins of this book, six icons guide you toward information on your particular interests.

 Keep an eye out for the Bargain Alert icon as you seek out money-saving tips and great deals.

 Best of the Best highlights the best Boston has to offer in all categories — hotels, restaurants, attractions, activities, shopping, and nightlife.

 History flavors nearly everything you see and do in Boston. I use this symbol to single out particularly tasty morsels of information about the city's past.

 Watch for the Heads Up icon to identify annoying or potentially dangerous situations such as tourist traps, unsafe neighborhoods, budgetary rip-offs, and other things to be wary of.

 Look to the Kid Friendly icon for attractions, hotels, restaurants, and activities that are particularly hospitable to children or people traveling with kids. Boston is an exceptionally family-friendly city; this symbol flags the standouts.

 Find useful advice on things to do and ways to schedule your time when you see the Tip icon.

Where to Go from Here

For nearly 20 years, I've called Boston home. Friends puzzle over my refusal to relocate — until they hear me talk about my adopted hometown. I still can't get enough of Boston's sights and sounds, its history and geography, its walkability, and its proximity to the full range of New England's natural resources. From the salty ocean smell that comes in on the east wind to the flood of visitors that comes in with the autumn foliage, it's a thrill. And I'm thrilled to be able to share it with you.

Part I
Introducing Boston

The 5th Wave   By Rich Tennant

In this part . . .

*I*ntroducing a stranger to a new city is a bit like selling yourself to a job interviewer or a prospective blind date. You start with the high points — the fascinating history, the great shopping, and the lively dining scene. Maybe you touch on the hotels, but you don't dwell on how expensive they can be. And you'll have plenty of time later to mention the rotten traffic.

In this part, I introduce Boston by spotlighting my favorite experiences. I briefly explore the history of this fascinating city and give you an overview of its architecture, cuisine, and unique (to put it mildly) accent. Finally, I help you schedule your trip to coincide with interesting events, pleasant weather, and bargains on airfare and lodging.

Chapter 1

Discovering the Best of Boston

In This Chapter

▶ Searching out the city's best activities, sights, and experiences
▶ Finding the top places to stay, dine, and shop
▶ Seeing the most enjoyable local historical sites and attractions
▶ Discovering the best spots for kids to have fun

*P*eople from all over the world seem to feel a connection to Boston. Even if you haven't visited the city, you probably know something about it. Maybe your best friend went to college here, your internist did her residency at Massachusetts General, or your next-door neighbor woke up the whole block the night the Red Sox won the World Series. You see *Cheers* reruns and the Boston Pops' Fourth of July concert on TV, Fidelity manages your retirement savings, or you remember something about a tea party. You're thinking that Boston sounds like a fun place to visit. You're right.

The city's historic and cultural attractions, entertaining diversions, and manageable size make Boston a popular business, convention, and vacation destination. To help you plan the most enjoyable trip, in this chapter I let you in on my favorite places and activities.

 Throughout this book, the "Best of the Best" icon flags the establishments and experiences I like the most.

The Best Travel Experiences

If you want choices, Boston's got 'em. Whatever you prefer — strolling through gardens, exploring museums, watching live sports, sightseeing (in land and water), shopping, or wandering through historic neighborhoods — this city has something for you.

✔ Dotted with tulips, covered in snow, choked with tourists, or framing a wedding party, Boston's **Public Garden** is unforgettable in any season. The first botanical garden in the country, established in the mid–19th century, is also home to an admirably diverse collection of statuary. See Chapter 11.

✔ Two of the best art museums around are in Boston's Fenway neighborhood — they even share a T stop (cleverly named "Museum"). The **Museum of Fine Arts** offers an incredibly wide-ranging overview; the **Isabella Stewart Gardner Museum** focuses on European and American works beloved by its founder and eponym. See Chapter 11.

✔ A visit to **Fenway Park** incorporates the past, present, and future of baseball. The oldest park in the major leagues is home to the recent World Series champs. Maybe you heard that the 86-year title drought ended in 2004 — or maybe you heard the baseball fans of New England cheering (they were that loud). The team's visionary owners constantly introduce new features, from seating in unusual places (such as the top of the left-field wall called the Green Monster) to year-round tours. See Chapter 11.

✔ The Red Sox celebrated its big win with a huge parade on amphibious sightseeing vehicles, or "ducks." You can take the same ride. A **Boston Duck Tour** explores the city and then hops into the water for a cruise around the Charles River Basin. It's a unique perspective and an entertaining experience. (Singing "We Are the Champions" is optional — but please don't.) See Chapter 11.

✔ Shopping on **Newbury Street,** the "Rodeo Drive of New England," can cost as little or as very, very much as you like. Take the window-shopping and people-watching route or wear out your gold card at a dazzling variety of stores and boutiques. See Chapter 12.

✔ Sightseeing is great, but sometimes a little **loitering** can be even better. A picnic lunch near the river or the harbor, or an aimless walk through an unfamiliar neighborhood (try the North End or Beacon Hill), can show you aspects of Boston that a guided tour can't. Build a little down time into your travel schedule; you won't regret it.

The Best Hotels

All travelers have the same basic needs, but who wants to settle for basic? The following lodgings offer something extra for everyone from the jaded business traveler to the once-a-year vacationer. Splurge or save on your accommodations by choosing one of the fine establishments listed here. For more in-depth descriptions of these hotels and others, see Chapter 9.

✔ The **Four Seasons Hotel** isn't just the best hotel in Boston — it's the best hotel in New England. It offers top-of-the-line everything, from beds to spa treatments, plus service so good that you almost forget how much it's all costing.

✔ Spectacular water views literally set the scene at the outrageously plush **Boston Harbor Hotel.** Beautifully appointed rooms, a 60-foot lap pool, great business amenities, and easy access to the Financial District are a few of the features that make it the top downtown hotel choice.

✔ The **Marriott Residence Inn Boston Harbor** also overlooks the water. The views aren't as breathtaking as the Boston Harbor Hotel's vistas, but neither is the bill. Rates even include breakfast. Every spacious room has its own kitchen, and families can spread out in a one- or two-bedroom unit.

✔ The **Charlesmark Hotel** has its own version of a marvelous view: the Boston Marathon finish line. Just a block from Newbury Street, the hotel will leave plenty of money in your budget for shopping — the reasonable prices include such extras as local phone calls and continental breakfast.

✔ The **Midtown Hotel** is another great deal: Rates include parking (for one car), which saves you at least $25 a night in this convenient neighborhood. Kids enjoy the seasonal outdoor pool, and you can book them a connecting unit if you don't feel like sharing a room.

✔ The best lodging in Cambridge is the **Charles Hotel,** located in a prime spot between Harvard Square and the river. Luxurious but not frilly, it's a superb choice for travelers who need every business perk and vacationers who want to take advantage of the excellent spa, pool, and restaurants.

The Best Restaurants

In the name of research, I'm constantly trying out new places to eat — for better or (more often than you'd think) worse. My favorites are the restaurants I return to because I want to, not because I have to. From seafood to pizza and from high-end dining to neighborhood cafes, you'll have no trouble eating well in Boston. For more detailed listings of these and other eateries, see Chapter 10.

✔ The first two steps of the quintessential arrival in Boston are unpacking and ordering a lobster. The best place for lobster and anything else fishy is **Legal Sea Foods.** I know, I know — you're expecting to hear about a little place in a back alley, and I'm suggesting an internationally famous (oh, the horror) chain. Trust me.

✔ Speaking of alleys, **Casa Romero** is a place you could walk past a thousand times and never notice. In an alley a stone's throw from Newbury Street, this romantic hideaway serves flavorful traditional Mexican cuisine.

✔ In chain-store-choked Harvard Square, **Mr. Bartley's Burger Cottage** is a welcome slice of authenticity. A mom-and-pop place that serves yummy burgers (beef, turkey, and veggie) and phenomenal onion rings, it's a quirky delight.

✔ For fine dining in an elegant townhouse setting, try **Mamma Maria** — the best restaurant in the North End. It's a romantic special-occasion destination that deftly combines the traditional (great osso buco and short ribs) with super-fresh ingredients and creative techniques (excellent seafood specials).

✔ At the other end of the culinary spectrum but only a few blocks away, **Pizzeria Regina** is the classic North End pizza parlor. The ferocious brick oven produces superb crust that perfectly complements the tasty toppings. Just don't get in the way of the whirling-dervish waitresses.

The Best Stores

From cheap to chic, boho to bourgeois, the Boston area boasts consistently excellent shopping. For more information on these top retail destinations and others, see Chapter 12.

✔ Boston's excellent museums have excellent gift shops. (See Chapter 11 for more specific information on museums.) I particularly like the options at the **Museum of Science,** the **New England Aquarium,** and the **Children's Museum,** which feature educational but not homeworky toys and games. My favorite is the **Museum of Fine Arts,** which carries everything from jewelry based on pieces in the museum collections to a huge selection of books. The MFA's satellite locations, in Copley Place and Faneuil Hall Marketplace, offer a wide range of quality goods as well.

✔ **Filene's Basement** is the big name in New England discount shopping. The enormous selection and great prices bring out the hunter and gatherer in every bargain shopper who walks through the doors.

✔ The Newbury Street gallery scene isn't as intimidating as you might think; if you're curious, wander around. Whether the gallery's specialty is painting or photography, antique botanical prints or modern sculpture, dealers and other staff members are on hand and (usually) eager to explain why they fell for the work that's on display. Don't miss the **International Poster Gallery.**

✔ My idea of a great gift is something the recipient absolutely loves but would never think to buy for himself or herself. Of the dozens of worthy competitors in the Boston area, my top destination is **Joie de Vivre,** outside Cambridge's Porter Square. If you want to borrow my "one for them, one for me" rule, be my guest.

✔ The Boston area is blessed with a great selection of chain and independent bookstores. Every book lover has his or her favorite; mine are the **Harvard Book Store,** in Harvard Square, for new titles and remainders, and the **Brattle Book Shop,** near Downtown Crossing, for used volumes.

The Best Ways to Explore History

Colonial Boston is as tangible as the 21st-century city. In ways both big and small, all of New England preserves and celebrates the past, and the Boston area in particular has an especially rich legacy. I promise, walking around and seeing historic sites in person is more fun that reading about them. Here are some excellent places to investigate.

✔ The **Freedom Trail** may be a cliché, but like most clichés, the 3-mile path attained its status for a reason. I have two favorite ways to approach it: as a guide to downtown Boston's most interesting historic attractions and as the jumping-off point for innumerable entertaining detours. See Chapter 11.

✔ The most interesting stop on the Freedom Trail, the **Paul Revere House,** recalls the days when downtown was a nest of flammable wooden buildings. Built around 1680, the house stands within sight of downtown's glittering glass towers, allowing you to take in nearly 400 years of history without even taking a step. See Chapter 11.

✔ The main **Harvard University** campus captures more than 350 years of history in a couple of verdant quadrangles surrounded by brick and granite structures that no longer drip with ivy (it damages the building materials). Stroll around, imagining yourself walking in the footsteps of everyone from George Washington to Natalie Portman. See Chapter 11.

✔ A visit to **Concord** is a trip back in time — not just to the dawn of the Revolutionary War, but also to the heyday of 19th-century Transcendentalism and *Little Women* author Louisa May Alcott. This one-time country village, now a lovely suburb, celebrates its past all over town. See Chapter 14.

The Best Experiences for Kids

What can the kids do in Boston? A better question might be "What *can't* the kids do in Boston?" Whether your goal is family togetherness or just getting everyone home in one piece, a visit to a fun attraction can help. Here are some of my favorite child-friendly excursions, all thoroughly road-tested by members of the "Are we there yet?" set.

✔ Little kids (under about 10 years old) can't get enough of the **Children's Museum.** The interactive exhibits encourage everything from climbing around to blowing soap bubbles. See Chapter 11.

✔ The **Museum of Science** appeals to a wider age range — even teenagers won't be *too* embarrassed to be seen with the 'rents. It offers hundreds of interactive displays and fun activities, as well as IMAX movies and a planetarium that schedules laser shows. See Chapter 11.

✔ Did you follow *Charlotte's Web* and *Stuart Little* with E. B. White's other children's classic, *The Trumpet of the Swan*? Then your family will definitely want to check out the **Swan Boats,** which ply the lagoon in the Public Garden from mid-April through mid-September. The employees pedal while you try to convince the kids that you see Louis the trumpeter swan. (The resident swans are actually named Romeo, Juliet, Castor, and Pollux.) See Chapter 11.

✔ Less tame, longer, and considerably more exciting is a **harbor cruise.** It doesn't have to be a full-length sightseeing excursion, either — a ferry ride between Long Wharf, on the downtown water-front, and the Charlestown Navy Yard is both fun and cheap ($1.50 one-way). See Chapters 8 and 11.

✔ Every day trip from Boston offers countless family-friendly activities and diversions. Ask your friends who grew up in the area — particularly popular school field trip destinations include **Concord, Salem,** and **Plymouth.** See Chapter 14.

The Best Walks

When I'm sprinting across an intersection where the traffic lights have a seven-second "walk" cycle, the nickname "America's Walking City" doesn't seem to suit Boston particularly well. At other times, when I'm contemplating a fine architectural detail, a tree in full bloom, or a particularly enticing window display, it makes perfect sense. Here are some excellent routes for pedestrians.

✔ Yes, it's obvious, but the **Freedom Trail** springs to mind because there's nothing else quite like it. Banish "should" and "must" from your vocabulary for a little while and consider the fact that you're walking in nearly four centuries' worth of other people's footsteps. For example, Ralph Waldo Emerson led his mother's cows to graze on Boston Common each day before he headed to school on School Street. See "The Best Ways to Explore History," earlier in this chapter, and Chapter 11.

✔ **Commonwealth Avenue** (Comm. Ave. to the locals) begins at the Public Garden, the loveliest park in downtown Boston. You can confine your walk to the Public Garden — make sure to swing by *Make Way for Ducklings* — or wander the Commonwealth Avenue Mall, which is basically a long, narrow park between lanes of the Parisian-style boulevard. Comm. Ave. begins across the street from the equestrian statue of George Washington in the Public Garden, and its 19th–century architecture is a welcome distraction from the random collection of statuary on the Mall. See Chapter 11.

✔ One block away, **Newbury Street** is a festival of retail and one of the city's best venues for people-watching. From the elegantly coiffed matrons wandering into the Ritz to the extravagantly pierced students exploring Urban Outfitters, it's a cross section of Boston. See Chapter 12.

✔ **Harvard Square** is both a pedestrian paradise and the intersection of several great walking routes. **John F. Kennedy Street** leads past John F. Kennedy Park to the banks of the Charles River, both lovely places to take a break. On **Brattle Street,** retail gives way to gorgeous residential architecture, which peaks at the exquisite Longfellow National Historic Site. See Chapter 11. Finally, on **Mass. Ave.,** Cambridge's main artery, the people-watching is as good as it is on Newbury Street. A stroll north to Porter Square or east to Central Square exposes you to some of the Boston area's best shopping. See Chapter 12.

✔ The path around Concord's **Walden Pond** has been a popular route for hundreds of years — and for good reason. Whether surrounded by winter snow, spring buds, summer sunbathers, or (best of all) fall foliage, the pond is a wonderful destination all year. See Chapter 14.

Chapter 2

Digging Deeper into Boston

● ●

In This Chapter

▶ Taking a quick look at Boston's fascinating history

▶ Investigating the city's architecture

▶ Savoring a taste of the local chow

▶ Talking the talk

▶ Gearing up for your trip with Boston books and movies

● ●

*I*f you're like most visitors, you won't get out of Boston without at least a brief, painless history lesson. You can immerse yourself in the past, visit innumerable colonial and Revolutionary landmarks, and stuff your head full of random facts. But you don't need to — merely walking around exposes you to the Boston of a bygone age.

In this chapter, I offer a brief overview of the city's fascinating history. I also tell you about local architecture, suggest where to sample regional culinary specialties, translate local accents and figures of speech, and recommend books and movies set in Boston.

History 101: The Main Events

When Europeans established their first permanent settlement in Boston, in 1630, the peninsula's landmass was about one-third the size of the modern city. The outline of part of the **original shoreline** appears around the base of the statue of Samuel Adams in front of **Faneuil Hall.** Thanks to its excellent location on the deep, sheltered harbor, Boston grew quickly, becoming a center of shipbuilding, fishing, and commerce.

The Puritans who founded Boston dominated the young society, creating a legacy that endures to this day. They founded **Harvard College** in 1636 to train young men for the ministry. Four years later, the town fathers across the river set aside the land that's now **Boston Common** as public land. Another survivor of colonial Boston is the **Paul Revere House,** erected around 1680 and still standing in the North End.

The alphabet song

The streets of the Back Bay go in alphabetical order, starting at the Public Garden with Arlington Street and continuing with Berkeley, Clarendon, Dartmouth, Exeter, Fairfield, Gloucester, and Hereford. Mass. Ave. then jumps in, but if you study a map of the Fenway, you can make out a few more letters (on streets that are off the neat grid): Ipswich, Jersey, and Kilmarnock.

In the 18th century, relations between the Massachusetts Bay Colony and the British Crown steadily worsened. The first armed conflict, in 1770, was a skirmish between occupying troops and civilians that's now known as the **Boston Massacre.** A marker on State Street commemorates the event, and the victims' graves are in the Old Granary Burying Ground. Both are stops on the **Freedom Trail** (as is the Paul Revere House; see Chapter 11). Boston, Cambridge, **Lexington,** and **Concord** (see Chapter 14) preserve a number of other sites that recall the area's prominent role in the American Revolution.

After the Revolution, Boston again developed into a center of business. The city trailed New York and Philadelphia in size and influence, but the "Athens of America" became known for fine art and architecture — including the luxurious Federal-style homes you can still see on **Beacon Hill** — and a flourishing intellectual community.

Henry Wadsworth Longfellow, Ralph Waldo Emerson, Nathaniel Hawthorne, and Henry David Thoreau were just a few of the big names on the local literary scene. **Homes** of the first three are now open to visitors. Longfellow's is in Cambridge, and Emerson's and Hawthorne's are in Concord (where you can also see the site of Thoreau's cabin at Walden Pond). William Lloyd Garrison established the weekly *Liberator* newspaper, a powerful voice in the antislavery and social-reform movements. Boston was an important stop on the Underground Railroad; walking the **Black Heritage Trail** on Beacon Hill can help you explore that history.

The landfill projects of the 19th century transformed Boston's coastline and skyline. All over the city, the tops of hills (including Beacon Hill) went into the water; Boston tripled in area. The largest project, executed from 1835 to 1882, was the filling of the **Back Bay,** the body of mud flats and marshes that gave its name to the present-day neighborhood. It's the only central Boston neighborhood laid out in a grid.

Also around the 19th century, waves of immigrants flooded Boston, changing the social landscape as dramatically and permanently as the physical one. The upper crust benefited the less fortunate with cultural

Boston Timeline: 1630–2004

✔ **1630** John Winthrop leads settlers to present-day Charlestown. Seeking better water, they push on to the Shawmut peninsula (on Beacon Hill), which they call Trimountain. On September 7, they name it Boston in honor of the English hometown of many Puritans. On October 19, 108 voters attend the first town meeting.

✔ **1632** Boston becomes the capital of Massachusetts.

✔ **1635** Boston Latin School, America's first public school, opens.

✔ **1636** Harvard College is founded.

✔ **1704** America's first regularly published newspaper, the *Boston News Letter,* is founded.

✔ **1770** On March 5, five colonists are killed outside what is now the Old State House, an incident soon known as the Boston Massacre.

✔ **1773** On December 16, during the Boston Tea Party, colonists dump 342 chests of tea into the harbor from three British ships.

✔ **1775** On April 18, Paul Revere and William Dawes spread the word that the British are marching toward Lexington and Concord. The next day, "the shot heard round the world" is fired. On June 17, the British win the Battle of Bunker Hill but suffer heavy casualties.

✔ **1776** On March 17, royal troops evacuate by ship. On July 18, the Declaration of Independence is read from the balcony of the Old State House.

✔ **1825** The first city census lists 58,277 people.

✔ **1831** William Lloyd Garrison publishes the first issue of the *Liberator,* a newspaper dedicated to emancipation.

✔ **1870** Museum of Fine Arts is founded.

✔ **1872** The Great Fire burns 65 acres and 800 buildings and kills 33 people.

✔ **1876** Boston University professor Alexander Graham Bell invents the telephone.

✔ **1881** Boston Symphony Orchestra is founded.

✔ **1897** The first Boston Marathon is run. The first subway in America opens in Boston.

✔ **1918** The Red Sox celebrates its World Series victory; an 86-year championship drought begins.

✔ **1930s** The Great Depression devastates what remains of New England's industrial base.

✔ **1940s** World War II and the accompanying industrial frenzy restore some vitality to the economy, particularly the shipyards.

✔ **1946** Boston's 1st Congressional District sends John F. Kennedy to Congress.

✔ **1957** The Boston Celtics win the first of its 16 NBA championships.

✔ **1958** The Freedom Trail is mapped out and painted.

✔ **1959** Construction of the Prudential Center begins — and with it, the transformation of the skyline.

✔ **1962** Scollay Square is razed to make room for Government Center.

✔ **1966** Massachusetts Attorney General Edward Brooke, a Republican, becomes the first black elected to the U.S. Senate in the 20th century.

✔ **1969** Students protesting the Vietnam War occupy University Hall at Harvard.

✔ **1974** In September, 20 years after the U.S. Supreme Court made school segregation illegal, school busing begins citywide, sparking riots in Roxbury and Charlestown.

✔ **1976** The restored Faneuil Hall Marketplace opens.

✔ **1988** The Central Artery/Third Harbor Tunnel Project ("Big Dig") is approved.

✔ **1995** The FleetCenter (renamed the TD Banknorth Garden in 2005) opens, replacing Boston Garden as the home of the Celtics (basketball) and the Bruins (hockey). The first complete piece of the Big Dig — the Ted Williams Tunnel — opens.

✔ **1999** Busing quietly ends, not with a riot but with a court order.

✔ **2001** The 2000 Census shows Boston with a population of 589,141, of which 49.5 percent is white. On September 11, both planes that hit the World Trade Center originate in Boston.

✔ **2002** The New England Patriots win the Super Bowl.

✔ **2003** The Leonard P. Zakim Bunker Hill Bridge — the signature of the Big Dig and 21st-century Boston — opens to traffic.

✔ **2004** The Patriots win another Super Bowl. The Liberty Tunnel — the final major piece of the Big Dig — opens to traffic. The elevated Expressway is demolished, opening the North End to the rest of the city for the first time in half a century. The Red Sox wins the World Series.

institutions: the **Boston Symphony,** the **Boston Public Library,** and the **Museum of Fine Arts** all opened between 1870 and 1895. Irish immigrants and their descendents broke the Brahmins' grip on the political establishment. Boston elected its first Irish mayor in 1885, and in 1910 John F. Fitzgerald assumed the office. "Honey Fitz" is best known today as the father of Rose Fitzgerald, a **North End** native whose second son was **John F. Kennedy.**

The next great upheaval came after the Second World War, when the local student population swelled dramatically, thanks in part to the G.I. Bill. That development led directly to the **high-tech boom** that continues to this day. Old-timers and newcomers alike bonded over **sports** — the Celtics from the '50s to the '80s, the Bruins in the '70s, and always the Red Sox.

At the close of the 20th century, the **Big Dig** dominated Boston. The gargantuan highway-construction project rerouted I-93 from an elevated expressway above downtown to a tunnel beneath it, all without closing the interstate. The 15-year undertaking cost $14.6 billion and reconfigured many of the city's main roads, extending I-90 to the airport in East Boston and spanning the Charles River with the gorgeous **Leonard P. Zakim Bunker Hill Memorial Bridge.** The Big Dig is technically complete, but it lingers like a bad dream. Construction on the parks and buildings intended to replace it has barely begun, and leaks are already plaguing the Liberty Tunnel.

The biggest news in recent Boston history doesn't concern construction, politics, or anything else serious — except to sports fans. On October 27, 2004, **the Red Sox won the World Series,** ending an 86-year drought. The cheers are probably still echoing as you read this.

Building Blocks: Local Architecture

Boston is downright beautiful. Red-brick buildings and cobblestone streets contrast delightfully with modern glass towers (and concrete boxes that seemed like a good idea at the time). The wide and wild variety of architecture makes the city a visual treat.

Built around 1680, the **Paul Revere House** on North Square is a reminder that for Boston's first two centuries, most buildings were wood, and huge portions of the town regularly burned to the ground. The house is colonial in age but Tudor, rather than typically "colonial," in style. The casement windows and overhanging second floor are medieval features, and when the Reveres moved in, in 1770, the house was no longer fashionable. The one next door would have been: the **Pierce/Hichborn House** (ca. 1711), a sturdy brick structure with the symmetrical design that typifies the Georgian architecture often seen in 18th-century Boston.

After the Revolution, the **Federal** style dominated; it was the rage from 1780 to 1820. Austere features characterize the style: Ionic and Corinthian detailing, frequently in white against red brick or clapboard; fanlights over doors; and an almost maniacal insistence on symmetry. In Boston, the new style was closely associated with architect Charles Bulfinch. His work is all over Boston, most conspicuously in the **Massachusetts State House** (1797) and in many Beacon Hill residences.

At **141 Cambridge St.** (1796), the first home Bulfinch designed for Harrison Gray Otis, the obsession with symmetry resulted in the inclusion of a room with one false door to balance the real one. Bulfinch designed **St. Stephen's Church** (1804) in the North End; Harvard's **University Hall** (1814); and the central part of Massachusetts General Hospital, now known as **Bulfinch Pavilion** (1818). Bulfinch also planned the 1805 enlargement of **Faneuil Hall,** which is now three times the size it was when it opened in 1742.

No other architect is as closely associated with Boston as Bulfinch, but in a brief visit, you're likely to see just as much of the work of several others. Alexander Parris designed **Quincy Market** (1826), the centerpiece of Faneuil Hall Marketplace. The columns and facade facing the original Faneuil Hall epitomize Greek Revival style, which was wildly popular at the time. Across State Street from the marketplace, the 1847 **Custom House Tower** has a Greek Revival base. (It gained its colorful tower in 1915.)

Across town in Copley Square, **Trinity Church** (1877) is H. H. Richardson's masterwork. The heavy stone structure, with its polychrome building materials and distinctive tower, is a Romanesque showpiece. Facing it is Charles Follen McKim's **Boston Public Library** (1885 to 1895), an imposing structure with columns and majestic staircases influenced by the Bibliothèque Nationale in Paris; it combines elements of the Beaux Arts and Renaissance Revival styles.

Fascinating architectural areas lie north and south of Copley Square. Heading north, you come to the **Back Bay.** The street grid was planned in the 1860s and '70s, mostly by Arthur Gilman, and the Parisian flavor of the boulevards reflects his interest in the French Second Empire style. It's also evident in Gilman's design (with Gridley J.F. Bryant) of **Old City Hall** (1862), downtown on School Street. Its mansard roof was an early example of a style duplicated by countless Back Bay townhouses. South of Copley Square is the **South End,** another trove of Victoriana, whose park-studded layout owes more to London than to Paris.

Elaborate early 20th-century buildings adorn the city. The **Cutler Majestic Theater** (1903), at 219 Tremont St. in the Theater District, fairly drips with the ornamentation that characterizes Beaux Arts style, from the intricate facade to the interior arches. Classic Art Deco structures, characterized by dramatic geometric forms and graceful curves, include the 1932 **Paramount Theatre,** on Washington Street near Downtown Crossing (look for the huge vertical sign), and the 1931 building, originally the post office that gave Post Office Square its name, that's now the **McCormack Federal Courthouse.**

The architecture of the building boom that started in the 1960s owes a great deal to the fertile mind of a former Harvard instructor, **I. M. Pei.** His firm's sleek designs use mirrored glass to good effect in the

A neat trick

Architecture buffs, try this: standing on the Cambridge Street side of City Hall Plaza or in front of Faneuil Hall, face City Hall and hold up the "tails" side of a nickel upside-down. The resemblance to Monticello (Thomas Jefferson's Virginia estate) is eerie.

Christian Science Center (1973), the **John F. Kennedy Library** (1979), and the **West Wing of the Museum of Fine Arts** (1981). The landmark **John Hancock Tower** (1974) is the most dramatic point in the Boston skyline but began its life by shedding panes of glass onto the street below. (The problem has been corrected.)

To see other noteworthy 20th- and 21st-century structures, cross the river to Cambridge. The only building in North America designed by the Swiss-French architect **Le Corbusier** is the **Carpenter Center for the Visual Arts** (1963), at 24 Quincy St. on the Harvard campus. The longtime dean of the university's architecture school, **José Luis Sert,** designed a number of other Harvard buildings, but the MIT campus is a better destination for visitors interested in contemporary architecture. Alvar Aalto conceived the sinuous **Baker House** (1949) on Memorial Drive; Eero Saarinen designed the **Kresge Auditorium** (1955), off Mass. Ave.; and I. M. Pei creations dot the campus. The public is so interested in **Frank O. Gehry** that the information desk on the ground floor of the 2004 **Stata Center,** on Vassar Street off Main Street, distributes a pamphlet describing a self-guided tour.

A considerably less successful modern building is **Boston City Hall,** a utilitarian concrete monstrosity designed in the aptly named Brutalist style and opened in 1968. A small park breaks up the vast brick wasteland of **City Hall Plaza,** but it's still basically an enormous windswept desert that's most useful for occasional concerts. The best thing about the plaza at the moment is its sweeping view of a big chunk of the post-Big Dig landscape. As the new downtown evolves, City Hall Plaza will be a good place for keeping track of its progress.

Taste of Boston: Local Cuisine

First, let me assure you that you're not going to get scurvy from eating *only* New England clam chowder, Boston baked beans, and Boston cream pie. Local menus offer a lot more than stereotypical New England food, though many still serve the renowned chowder, beans, and pie. The locals eat tons of seafood, appreciate chefs' increasing interest in local and organic produce, and demonstrate a willingness to try just about anything once.

Some pointers: **Scrod** or **schrod** is a generic term for fresh white-fleshed fish, usually served in filets. **Local shellfish** includes Ipswich and Essex clams, Atlantic lobsters, Wellfleet oysters, scallops, mussels, and shrimp.

Restaurants price **lobster** by the pound; they typically charge at least $15 to $20 for a "chicken" (1- to 1¼-pound) lobster and more for bigger portions. If you don't feel like wrestling with an ornery crustacean, let someone else do the work and order lobster in a "pie" (casserole), in a "roll" (sandwich), stuffed and baked or broiled, in or over pasta, in salad, or in bisque.

Well-made **New England clam chowder** is a white soup studded with fresh clams (but not tomatoes) and thickened with cream. If you want clams but not soup, many places serve **steamers,** or soft-shell clams cooked in the shell, as an appetizer or main dish. They come with a container of broth, for rinsing off any lingering grit, and a cup of drawn butter for dipping. More common are hard-shell clams — **littlenecks** (small) or **cherrystones** (medium-size) — served raw, like oysters.

Traditional **Boston baked beans** date from colonial days, when the Puritans' strict rules about not working on the Sabbath meant no cooking on Sunday. A pot of beans would go into the oven in a brick kitchen fireplace on Saturday and cook in the retained heat. House-made baked beans can be hard to find (Durgin-Park does an excellent rendition), but where you do, you'll probably also find good cornbread and **brown bread** — more like a steamed pudding of whole wheat and rye flour, cornmeal, molasses, buttermilk, and usually raisins.

Finally, **Boston cream pie** is golden layer cake sandwiched around custard and topped with chocolate glaze — no cream, no pie.

For restaurant listings, turn to Chapter 10.

Word to the Wise: The Local Lingo

How much time do you have?

Seriously, the hard-core, I-pahked-my-cah-in-Hahvud-Yahd Boston accent is not as prevalent as it once was. The occasional dropped "r" is more typical than the full-blown "youz guys" dialect. It's all about pronunciation, which walks the line between British and big-wad-of-gum-in-the-mouth: for example, *aunt* is "ahnt" (not "ant").

Mispronouncing a geographic term is the fastest way to expose yourself as an out-of-towner. **Copley** is *cop*-ly (not cope-ly); pronounce the "w" in **Charlestown** (not Charleston); **Peabody** is *pea*-b'dy (not pea-body); the "c" in **Quincy** makes a "z" sound (*quin*-zee); and **Tremont** has a short "e" (*treh*-mont, not tree-mont).

25

Putting words in your mouth

Familiarizing yourself with some common terms, phrases, and idioms can make navigating Boston a little easier. If you're curious (or can't figure out whether that remark was a compliment or an insult), a great site to explore is www.boston-online.com/glossary.html. Here are a few terms to get you started:

Comm. Ave.: Commonwealth Avenue

Faneuil: rhymes with "Daniel"

frappe: rhymes with "slap"; means "milkshake"

Mass. Ave.: Massachusetts Avenue

Mem. Drive: Memorial Drive

regular coffee: coffee with cream and sugar

So don't I: So do I

T: The MBTA subway; also used to refer to a particular station (for example, "Meet you near the Arlington T")

Background Check: Recommended Books and Movies

Children's books offer the easiest and perhaps the best introduction to Boston. Here are my favorites, among dozens of good choices.

- ✔ *Make Way for Ducklings* (Viking Press, 1941; Puffin Books, Reprint edition, 1999), by Robert McCloskey, presents Mrs. Mallard and her babies making their way around the Back Bay. They wind up in the Public Garden, where you and your babies can play on bronze statues of the beloved fowl.

- ✔ *The Trumpet of the Swan* (HarperCollins, Collector's edition, 2000), by E. B. White, tells the tale of a trumpeter swan with a real trumpet. He eventually visits the Public Garden, where you'll want to take a turn around the lagoon on a Swan Boat.

- ✔ *Johnny Tremain* (Houghton Mifflin, 1943; Yearling Newbery, 1987), by Esther Forbes, is a fictional account of the events leading to the Revolutionary War. I love it as much for its nuanced portrait of the title character as for its vivid descriptions of Colonial Boston.

For **adults,** the options are considerably more numerous and diverse. My top choices are a tiny fraction of the excellent titles available.

- ✔ *Paul Revere and the World He Lived In* (Mariner Books, 1999), a Pulitzer Prize–winner by Esther Forbes (author of *Johnny Tremain*) originally published in 1942, is a portrait of the city and the man at a crucial time — for both.

- ✔ *Common Ground: A Turbulent Decade in the Lives of Three American Families* (Vintage edition, 1986), by J. Anthony Lukas, uses small details to illustrate a sweeping story about the busing crisis of the 1970s. *Common Ground* won the 1986 Pulitzer Prize for nonfiction.

- ✔ *The Perfect Storm* (Perennial; Harper edition, 1999), by Sebastian Junger, is the story of a fishing boat trapped at sea by a devastating storm. It's a compelling portrait of Gloucester, as well as a gripping account of the perils of getting food onto your plate. You'll never take fresh fish for granted again.

- ✔ *Cityscapes of Boston* (Houghton Mifflin, 1992), by Robert Campbell and Peter Vanderwarker, uses before-and-after photos of locations all over town to demonstrate how the face of the city has (and hasn't) changed.

- ✔ *A.I.A. Guide to Boston* (Globe Pequot Press, 1984), by Susan and Michael Southworth, is a field guide to the area's architecture that incorporates walking tours of notable neighborhoods.

- ✔ **"Paul Revere's Ride,"** the classic Longfellow poem about April 18 and 19, 1775, is historically questionable, but it's just as stirring today as it was nearly 150 years ago. Check it out before following the Freedom Trail or touring Lexington and Concord. You can pick up a copy of this poem at many gift shops along the Freedom Trail — mine cost about $3 at the Old North Church — or invest in a read-along version such as Puffin Books' 1996 edition, illustrated by Ted Rand.

For a list of suggested **guidebooks,** see the "Where to Get More Information" section of the Appendix.

Many **movies** are interesting solely for their scenery and others simply because you can hear them — and their dreadful renditions of the iconic Boston accent. But only a few films manage to combine a good story, not-too-embarrassing accents, and the thrill of recognizable locations.

- ✔ *Good Will Hunting* is my favorite Boston movie. Coauthors and costars Matt Damon (a Harvard dropout) and Ben Affleck grew up in Cambridge, and their authentic accents almost make up for Robin Williams's brogue.

- ✔ *Mystic River* features locations that will never make it onto the back of a postcard — in other words, actual blue-collar neighborhoods — and a compelling, if disturbing, plot.

✔ ***Next Stop Wonderland*** is a sort of valentine to the subway, of all things, with many great shots of the New England Aquarium. It's also an enchanting story of fate and coincidence.

✔ ***The Verdict*** is a memorable portrait of the local legal establishment, from ambulance chasing to blueblood snobbery.

✔ ***Love Story*** is as sappy as they come, with gorgeous montages of the Harvard campus. Keep an eye out for a cameo by the young Tommy Lee Jones, class of '68.

Chapter 3

Deciding When to Go

In This Chapter

▶ Figuring out the best time to visit

▶ Understanding Boston's climate

▶ Reviewing a calendar of special events

*E*very season is a good time to visit Boston. The climate is relatively temperate — with some exceptions, which I cover in this chapter. Citywide events are generally entertaining but not overwhelming — with some exceptions, which I also cover. The people are typically friendly and welcoming — with some exceptions, which you can (but hopefully won't) discover on your own.

Revealing the Secrets of the Seasons

For those of you lucky enough to have the luxury of traveling whenever you want to, this section presents the highlights and drawbacks of the four seasons.

Between April and November, Boston typically experiences few slow periods. Conventions take place all year, clustering in the spring and fall. The Convention and Visitors Bureau (see the Appendix for contact information) can tip you off to especially large gatherings.

Lots of places claim to be the inspiration for the weather cliché "If you don't like it, wait ten minutes," but a few days in Boston may persuade you that New England's climate gave birth to the expression. Table 3-1 gives you an idea of the conditions you can expect.

Table 3-1 Boston's Average Temperatures and Precipitation

	Jan	Feb	Mar	Apr	May	June	July	Aug	Sept	Oct	Nov	Dec
High (°F/°C)	36/ 2	38/ 3	46/ 8	56/ 13	67/ 19	76/ 24	82/ 28	80/ 27	73/ 23	63/ 17	52/ 11	40/ 4
A=Low (°F/°C)	22/ −5	23/ −5	31/ −1	40/ 4	50/ 10	59/ 15	65/ 18	64/ 18	57/ 14	47/ 8	38/ 3	27/ −3
Rainfall (in./cm.)	3.6/ 9.1	3.6/ 9.2	3.7/ 9.4	3.6/ 9.1	3.3/ 8.3	3.1/ 7.9	2.8/ 7.2	3.2/ 8.2	3.1/ 7.8	3.3/ 8.4	4.2/ 10.7	4.1/ 10.2

Springtime in Boston

The tenacious New England winter makes spring in Boston short —
really just April and May. Here are the best reasons to take advantage
of Boston during these two months:

- ✔ As it awakens from its long winter's nap, the city is both good-
  looking and good-natured. Spring flowers abound, and happy
  locals flock outdoors to enjoy moderating temperatures.

- ✔ Patriots' Day activities and Boston Marathon spectating are two
  of the most authentic and popular local experiences — because
  they're so much fun.

But keep in mind the following springtime pitfalls:

- ✔ Snow can linger into April. Snow or not, early spring is the height
  of mud season.

- ✔ Booking a hotel room for Marathon weekend can be tough, and
  Patriots' Day marks the start of a school vacation week — not
  exactly a restful time to visit.

- ✔ College graduation season begins in May. As a result, hotels fill in
  somewhat random patterns as confused out-of-state drivers flood
  the area.

Summer in Boston

June, July, and August are madly popular months to visit Boston. Here
are some of the high points:

- ✔ The weather turns reliably pleasant, and the long hours of sunlight
  mean that you can pack a lot of outdoor fun into a single day.

- ✔ Harborfest, which includes Boston's over-the-top Independence
  Day celebrations, is one of the most fun events in the country.

But summer isn't perfect, and here's why:

- ✔ Graduation pandemonium lingers into June, translating into a jump in hotel occupancy rates and room rates.

- ✔ In July and August, vacationing families flock to Boston, creating long lines and lots of tantrums.

- ✔ Summer is about the only time of year when you may encounter consecutive days of 90-plus temperatures, usually accompanied by debilitating humidity and abysmal air quality. Be ready to concentrate on indoor activities or willing to take it slow outside.

Fall in Boston

Autumn is the most popular — and expensive — time to visit Boston. Here's a look at the pluses of visiting in September, October, and November:

- ✔ After Labor Day, the weather turns cooler, and humidity drops. September and October are the months most likely to include a run of exhilarating weather, with comfortably warm days and cool to chilly nights.

- ✔ During foliage season, from late September to mid-November, the Boston area makes an excellent jumping-off point or base for "leaf-peeping."

- ✔ The Head of the Charles Regatta, on the third weekend of October, is a quintessential New England event that attracts hundreds of thousands of people. Crew racing is both fun to watch and a great excuse for a huge outdoor party.

And the minuses:

- ✔ Foliage season is the toughest time of year to book a room — tougher than summer, even. The tour buses causing gridlock in the streets are full of travelers who drive up hotel room rates.

- ✔ College starts in earnest, and post-adolescents crowd the streets; watch out for moving vans, especially on September 1.

- ✔ In November, the days shorten, and the weather may turn cold and raw. Many outdoor activities (such as walking tours and sightseeing cruises) shut down for the winter.

Winter in Boston

December through March is the slowest travel season of the year. Visiting at this time comes with the following advantages:

A weather report, for better or verse

This poem is the second-best rhyme about Boston to know (after "Paul Revere's Ride").
The description applies to the short column of lights on top of the old John Hancock building in the Back Bay:

Steady blue, clear view;
flashing blue, clouds due;
steady red, rain ahead;
flashing red, snow instead.

(In the summer, flashing red means bad weather has postponed the Red Sox game.)

✔ Many hotels offer great deals, especially on weekends. Hard-up hoteliers offer holiday shopping specials in December and deep discounts in the New Year.

✔ The original family-oriented, no-alcohol New Year's Eve celebration, Boston's renowned First Night, incorporates more activities and performances than you can possibly fit into one day.

But there are some disadvantages:

✔ The default weather condition is bitter cold with biting winds. You'll probably have to concentrate on indoor activities. In addition, a big storm can disrupt your travel schedule.

✔ On New Year's Eve, rooms fill with suburbanites who don't want to deal with driving home after midnight; book far in advance. During the February school vacation week (starting with Presidents' Day), kid-oriented places and activities fill up fast.

✔ Some suburban attractions close in the winter.

Perusing a Calendar of Events

Crowds flood Boston for many of these popular events. Expect full hotels and overbooked restaurants. To avoid disappointment, double-check before scheduling a trip to coincide with an event.

Spontaneous travelers and others who haven't planned ahead can pick up suggestions from the event hotline of the **Greater Boston Convention and Visitors Bureau** (☎ 800-SEE-BOSTON or 617-536-4100; www.bostonusa.com), the "Calendar" section of the Thursday *The Boston Globe* (www.boston.com/globe), and the "Edge" section of the Friday *Boston Herald* (www.bostonherald.com).

January/February

✔ **Mid-January:** Events surrounding **Martin Luther King, Jr., Day** (third Monday of January) include gospel celebrations and other musical happenings, lectures, and panel discussions at various venues. Check special listings in the Thursday *Globe* "Calendar" section for specifics.

✔ **Late January or early February:** For **Chinese New Year,** the dragon parade draws a crowd to Chinatown no matter how cold it is, and the **Children's Museum** (☎ 617-426-8855; www.bostonkids.org) puts on special programs. The date depends on the Chinese lunar calendar: In 2006, it's January 29; in 2007, it's February 18. The parade usually occurs on the weekend closest to the holiday. Call the city **Office of Special Events and Tourism** (☎ 617-635-3911) for information.

✔ **February:** Special museum exhibits and children's programs highlight **Black History Month.** Many institutions schedule concerts, films, and other activities. **National Park Service** rangers (☎ 617-742-5415; www.nps.gov/boaf) lead tours of the Black Heritage Trail.

✔ **Mid-February:** During **School Vacation Week,** which starts on President's Day, most elementary and high schools close. Special cultural activities include kid-oriented exhibitions, plays, concerts, and tours. Contact attractions for information on special offerings and extended hours.

March/April

✔ **Mid-March:** The **New England Spring Flower Show** is a perfect antidote to cabin fever. At the end of an especially snowy winter, expect huge crowds. Plan to use public transit. The **Massachusetts Horticultural Society** (☎ 617-536-9280; www.masshort.org) presents the show during the middle of March at the Bayside Expo Center in Dorchester.

✔ **Late March through early April:** The **Big Apple Circus** performs in a heated tent near the South Boston waterfront for about one month every spring. Proceeds support the Children's Museum. Visit the museum box office or contact **Ticketmaster** (☎ 617-931-ARTS; www.ticketmaster.com).

✔ **Late April:** On **Patriots' Day,** the third Monday of April, New England marks the unofficial end of winter. The state holiday commemorates the events of April 18 and 19, 1775, when the Revolutionary War began. Lanterns (as in "two if by sea") hang in the steeple of the **Old North Church** (☎ 617-523-6676; www.oldnorth.com), and riders dressed as Paul Revere and William Dawes travel from Boston's North End to Lexington and Concord.

"Minutemen" and "redcoats" reenact the battles on the town green in Lexington and at the Old North Bridge in Concord. See Chapter 14 for information on visiting Lexington and Concord.

✔ **Late April:** The legendary Boston Marathon starts at noon on Patriots' Day, the third Monday of April. The leaders cross the finish line, on Boylston Street in front of the Boston Public Library, beginning a little after 2 p.m. Good vantage points include Commonwealth Avenue and Kenmore Square. For information, call ☎ 617-236-1652 or visit www.bostonmarathon.org.

May/June

✔ **Mid-May: Lilac Sunday** is the only day of the year when the Arnold Arboretum permits picnicking. The gorgeous botanical garden, in Boston's Jamaica Plain neighborhood, boasts sensational spring flowers, including more than 400 varieties of lilacs. Call ☎ 617-524-1717 or visit www.arnold.harvard.edu. Second or third weekend of May.

✔ **Late May:** When the **Street Performers Festival** takes over Faneuil Hall Marketplace, musicians, magicians, jugglers, sword-swallowers, and artists strut their stuff. Call ☎ 617-338-2323 or check www.faneuilhallmarketplace.com for more information.

✔ **Mid-June:** The region's largest gay-pride parade is the **Boston Pride March.** The procession on the second Sunday of June from the Back Bay to Beacon Hill caps off a week of celebrating diversity in New England. Call ☎ 617-262-9405 or visit www.bostonpride.org.

July/August

✔ **July 4:** The Fourth of July is the high point of **Boston Harborfest** and a guaranteed blast. Events include fireworks, concerts, guided tours, cruises, the Boston Chowderfest, and the USS *Constitution*'s annual turnaround. Call ☎ 617-227-1528 or visit www.bostonharborfest.com for more information.

✔ **July 4:** The centerpiece of Fourth of July festivities is the **Boston Pops Concert and Fireworks Display,** at the Hatch Shell amphitheater on the Esplanade. Live music begins in the evening, but this event is an all-day affair — fans arrive at dawn to stake out pieces of the lawn in front of the stage. The program includes the "1812 Overture," with actual cannon fire, and amazing fireworks at about 10 p.m. (If you're not keen on roasting in the sun, wait until dark, ride the Red Line to Kendall/MIT, and watch the pyrotechnics from the Cambridge side of the river.) Visit www.july4th.org for more details.

✔ **August:** The North End is always fun to visit, and during the **Italian-American feasts** on summer weekends, it rocks. The street fairs begin in July and include food, games, live and recorded music, and dancing in the streets. The Fishermen's Feast in the middle of August and the Feast of St. Anthony at the end of August are the biggest. Check their Web sites, www.fishermansfeast.com and www.saintanthonysfeast.com, for highlights.

September/October

✔ **Mid-September:** Reports of celebrity sightings jump during the **Boston Film Festival.** Stars and directors turn up to promote and discuss their latest independent films; the public is welcome at most screenings. Check the newspapers for schedules; for information, call ☎ **781-925-1373** or visit www.bostonfilmfestival.org.

✔ **Mid-October:** It's not your imagination — elephants really are having lunch in the North End. It must be time for the **Ringling Brothers and Barnum & Bailey Circus'** annual two-week visit to the **TD Banknorth Garden** (formerly called the FleetCenter) (☎ **617-624-1000;** www.tdbanknorthgarden.com).

✔ **Late October:** Thousands of rowers plus hundreds of thousands of spectators flood Boston and Cambridge for the **Head of the Charles Regatta.** A huge party (without alcohol) rages on the banks of the Charles River and its bridges on Saturday afternoon and all day Sunday. Call ☎ **617-864-8415** or visit www.hocr.org. Third or fourth weekend of October.

✔ **October:** The Witch City observes its biggest holiday with **Salem Haunted Happenings.** Special offerings include parades, parties, fortune-telling, cruises, and tours. Visit www.salemhaunted happenings.com for the scoop on the activities.

November/December

✔ **Late November:** The spirit of the original **Thanksgiving Celebration** endures in Plymouth. The "stroll through the ages" showcases 17th- and 19th-century Thanksgiving preparations in historic homes. **Plimoth Plantation** (☎ **800-262-9356** or 508-746-1622; www.plimoth.org), which recreates the colony's first years, offers a reservation-only Victorian Thanksgiving feast. (Trust me, you're not sorry to miss out on Pilgrim food.) Call ☎ **800-USA-1620** or check out www.visit-plymouth.com. Fourth Thursday of November.

✔ **November through December:** Boston Ballet's *Nutcracker,* one of the country's biggest and best, starts its annual run the day after Thanksgiving. The spectacular sets help make the ballet an enticing way to introduce children to theatergoing. Contact **Tele-charge** (☎ **800-447-7400;** www.telecharge.com) as soon as you plan your trip, ask whether your hotel offers a *Nutcracker* package, or check for returned tickets in person at the Opera House box office at 539 Washington St.

✔ **Late December:** The year ends with **First Night,** an arts-oriented New Year's Eve blowout all over town from early afternoon to midnight. The parade is in the late afternoon; ice sculptures and art exhibitions dot the city; and theatrical performances and other entertainment run all day. The midnight fireworks display explodes over the harbor. For most activities, you need a First Night button, available for about $15 at visitor centers and stores around the city. Call ☎ 617-542-1399 or visit www.firstnight.org. December 31.

Part II
Planning Your Trip to Boston

The 5th Wave   By Rich Tennant

"What flavor would you like, Baked Bean,
Haddock, or Cod?"

In this part . . .

Careful travel planning can feel like ditch digging, but can pay off like gold mining. This part puts you (figuratively and perhaps literally) on the road to Boston. I explain the nitty-gritty of budgeting, give you the information you need to book your trip, and discuss the pros and cons of package deals and escorted tours. Travelers with special needs and interests can find out about resources tailored just for them. Finally, I double-knot the loose ends — including buying travel insurance (or not) and renting a car (or not) — and send you on your way.

Chapter 4

Managing Your Money

. . . .

In This Chapter

▶ Finding strategies for every budget

▶ Deciding how to spend: credit cards, traveler's checks, ATMs, and cash

▶ Stretching your money (but not by writing rubber checks)

. . . .

*B*oston has all the elements of an outrageously expensive destination, starting with a shortage of moderately priced downtown
hotels. Factor in a pricey meal, some unexpected incidentals, and the
siren song of low (or no) sales tax on clothes, and watch your carefully
calculated budget implode.

You can take a lesson from the Boston area's ever-present students.
They occupy a parallel universe where food is plentiful and reasonably
priced, entertainment is cheap or free, and the whole point of shopping
is getting the most out of your (and your parents') hard-earned money.

Of course, if you imitate the students too slavishly, you can wind up
sleeping in a stranger's bathtub and eating mystery meat. You get the
idea, though: Know what's important to you and try not to overpay
for it.

Planning Your Budget

A well-constructed budget is like a tricky jigsaw puzzle. Making it work
can be as satisfying as dropping that 1,000th puzzle piece into place.
Think hard (and ask your companions to do the same) about what's
important to you and consider the pointers in this chapter.

Table 4-1 offers some average costs for you to get started.

Table 4-1	What Things Cost in Boston
Item	*Cost*
Taxi from airport to downtown or Back Bay	$22–$30
Water taxi from airport to downtown	$10
Private van from airport to downtown or Back Bay	$10 and up
Subway token	$1.25
Local bus fare	90¢
Pay phone call	35¢
Double at Hotel Commonwealth	$249–$369
Double at Onyx Hotel	$209–$329
Double at Newbury Guest House	$140–$195
Double at Longwood Inn	$89–$109
Lunch for one at Ye Olde Union Oyster House	$11–$24
Lunch for one at Durgin-Park	$7–$21
Lunch for one at Bartley's Burger Cottage	$4.50–$11
Dinner for one, without wine, at Rialto	$23–$55
Dinner for one, without wine, at Legal Sea Foods	$14–$32
Dinner for one, without wine, at the Elephant Walk	$13–$24
Glass of beer	$3–$6
Can of soda	75¢–$1.50
Cup of coffee	$1 and up
Roll of ASA 100 Kodacolor film, 36 exposures	$7–$9
Adult admission to the Museum of Fine Arts	$15
Child (under 18) admission to the Museum of Fine Arts	Free weekdays after 3 p.m. and weekends
Movie ticket	$6–$10
Theater ticket	$30–$90

Transportation

Airfare (or the cost of another mode of transportation) is your first big fixed cost. If you travel during foliage season or at the height of summer, you can expect to pay peak prices. Visit at a slower time, and you may land a great promotional rate. Turn to Chapter 5 for more information.

Driving to Boston can appear to be a budget-conscious option, if you resign yourself to parking the car when you arrive and not retrieving it until you leave. But before you shout "road trip," compare the cost of tolls, gas, parking, and incidentals to the best airfare you can find — you may discover that driving isn't such a great deal after all.

Fortunately, once you arrive in Boston, the price of transportation is quite budget-friendly — in fact, it can be free. In this compact city, many popular destinations are easiest to reach on foot. (If you want to prorate the wear on your walking shoes, be my guest.)

I plan to harp on this point until out-of-state drivers are as rare as mastodons: You do not need a car to get around Boston and Cambridge. The things you think you get — flexibility and convenience — are exactly the things you sacrifice. Boston in particular is as nightmarish for drivers as New York or San Francisco, and that's before you consider the construction that continues on many downtown streets even though the Big Dig is substantially complete. If you decide to rent a car — say, for a day trip — make sure that the price the company quotes includes all taxes and fees.

Taxis are expensive and can be hard to find, but you can track one down eventually. The car-rental money you save can pay for several days' worth of cab rides. (See Chapter 8 for information on taxis.)

The Massachusetts Bay Transportation Authority (MBTA), known locally as the T, provides cheap transportation ($1.25 for a subway token, 90¢ for the local bus) in and around the city. Visitor passes good for unlimited local rides, and sold for one-, three-, and seven-day periods (costing $7.50, $18, and $35, respectively), can make public transit a better deal — but only if you plan to use it enough. Note that service shuts down by 1 a.m. during the week and 2:30 a.m. on weekends and doesn't go everywhere — that means more cabs. (For the lowdown on public transit, see Chapter 8.)

Lodging

Boston is a relatively small city with relatively expensive hotels. Although some new properties have opened in the past few years, demand still outstrips supply at busy times. Fixed costs are high, and even with a big discount, an outrageous rate drops to merely pricey. The average double-room rate is less than the $180 of the dot-com glory days, but it still flirts with $160. A great package or online deal can seriously undercut the average price, but at busy times, you're more likely to hear "take it or leave it" than "let's make a deal." See Chapter 9 for the lowdown on hotels.

If you can't book a relatively inexpensive B&B and prefer something nicer than a hostel, expect to spend at least $130 a night. That figure doesn't include a 12.45 percent hotel tax. The price of a centrally located chain hotel may seem high (and, except in the dead of winter, probably will be closer to $160 than to $110). Just remember that the lower cost of many suburban establishments doesn't include the time and expense of commuting to downtown attractions and businesses — or the psychic damage Boston-area traffic inflicts.

Dining

Thank the students: You can find tasty, inexpensive food all over the place. But don't get carried away. If you've been waiting for years to try fresh lobster, this is not the time to cut corners.

Serious penny-pinchers can enjoy a decent breakfast for $5 or less, lunch for $6 or so, and a more-than-adequate dinner for as little as $15. If your budget, appetite, or both are small, a good strategy is making lunch the big meal of the day. Or start with a bagel and coffee or juice ($2 to $3), lunch on a sandwich or salad ($5), and go wild at dinner.

Wolves in cheap clothing: Bargains that aren't

Looking back on other trips you've taken, you tend to focus on obvious missteps — the hotel renovation special, the discount tour with a guide your uncle saw on *America's Most Wanted,* and the time you said, "If it were that terrible, would it be a 'featured destination'?"

The cost-cutting steps to worry about are the ones that sound so good that you may forget they could be mistakes. Here are two biggies:

✔ **Sacrificing convenience for price.** Sometimes the deal is so good that you can't ignore it. (I've flown out of Providence instead of Boston to save $600, and I'd do it again.) But before you decide to save $50 by leaving at 6 a.m. and returning at 1 a.m. — a mere seven hours before your workday starts — think hard about just how good a deal that is.

✔ **Paying for things you don't need.** The three-day transit pass saves tons of money, but only when you use it enough. If you don't eat breakfast, the room rate that includes a big buffet is subsidizing someone else's meal. The weekend special at a hotel with a great spa is no deal for someone who just wants a lap pool. A bargain is a bargain only if you get something you wanted anyway.

Sightseeing

I would be remiss if I didn't tell you that plenty of people visit Boston just to shop, eat, and watch sports (namely the Red Sox and Patriots, plus the Celtics, Bruins, and local college teams). If you want to soak up some more culture, turn to Part V, make a list, and start adding those admission costs. First, check out potential deals. The Boston CityPass and Go Boston card offer good deals on attractions (see Chapter 11 for details), and many institutions, such as the Children's Museum, schedule hours when admission is cheap, by donation, or free.

Shopping

Budget what you like, not forgetting souvenirs — and not forgetting that a great deal from Filene's Basement makes a better keepsake than another T-shirt or refrigerator magnet ever could. Shopping-wise, Boston is celebrated for high-end arts and crafts, merchandise from its dozens of colleges, and deals on clothing. That doesn't mean that prices are especially good (unless, of course, you're at Filene's Basement) — it means the sales tax (5 percent) doesn't apply to clothing priced below $175. For more information on Boston's shopping scene, check out Chapter 12.

Nightlife

If culture is your main motivation, start with, say, the Boston Symphony Orchestra (known as the BSO) and build the rest of your budget around that. Good seats for the BSO, the Boston Pops, Boston Ballet, or a Broadway-bound show likely will set you back at least $50 a head. Less expensive but equally enjoyable options include numerous local performing-arts companies and superb jazz clubs (see Chapters 15 and 16 for details).

Even if a splashy night out isn't your thing, consider reserving time, money, and energy for an after-dark excursion. Boston offers lots of relatively inexpensive cultural opportunities, such as half-price theater tickets and cheap or free student performances in every artistic field. Or warm yourself at a congenial pub; a couple of hours and a couple of pints with the locals can often tell you more about the city than an army of tour guides. (For information on the city's nightlife, see Part V.)

Cutting Costs — But Not the Fun

You may hear that Boston is a great bargain because it's a college town. True, but a typical college kid isn't buying meals, snacks, subway tokens, and souvenirs for a family of four. Here are some tips to help you trim your travel costs:

✔ **Go off-season.** If you can visit Boston during nonpeak times (November through mid-April, and especially January through March), you may find hotel prices discounted as much as 50 percent from their high-season rates.

✔ **Travel midweek.** If you can travel on Tuesday, Wednesday, or Thursday, you may lock in a cheaper airfare. When you inquire about airfares, ask whether flying on a different day reduces the rate. See Chapter 5 for more tips on getting the best airfare.

✔ **Reserve your flight well in advance.** A ticket purchased 14 to 21 days in advance can save you more than $500 on a full fare. See Chapter 5 for details.

✔ **Reserve your flight only a couple of days in advance.** Last-minute Internet fares (released Wednesday for the weekend that starts two days later) aren't a sure thing, because you never know what destinations they'll include, but they sure are a bargain. Check out Chapter 5 for more information.

✔ **Don't fly to Boston.** You'll get to Boston eventually. Flying to Warwick, Rhode Island, or Manchester, New Hampshire, can be *much* cheaper than flying to Boston's Logan International Airport. If you have more time than money, these alternate cities are worth checking out. See Chapter 5 for details.

✔ **Try a package tour.** An arrangement that includes airfare, lodging, airport transfers, and perhaps some extras (such as a trolley tour) can save money and time. Turn to Chapter 5 for more details.

✔ **Bring only as much luggage as you can carry easily.** A pile of heavy bags weighs you down so much that jumping on the T isn't a reasonable option. So you'll wind up hailing a cab, which costs an awful lot more than a $1.25 subway token, and possibly tipping sky-caps and bellmen. Plan to handle your own lightly packed luggage, and don't forget to leave room for souvenirs you may carry home.

✔ **Reserve a room with a refrigerator and coffeemaker.** It may not feel like as much of a vacation if you do your own cooking and dishes, but eating in restaurants three times a day can be pricey. Even if you only make your own breakfast and take an occasional bag lunch, you'll still save money — and maybe calories, too.

✔ **Always ask for discount rates.** All that money you pay to belong to the auto club, AARP, a trade union, or another organization with group bargaining power can pay off — but only if you remember to ask about deals. When you book transportation and accommodations, have your membership cards handy.

✔ **Water is free.** It is at the hotel and at water fountains in attractions and visitor centers anyway. Bring a bottle from home, and fill it before you go sightseeing. If that seems a bit maniacal, consider picking up a six-pack at a drugstore or supermarket and stowing bottles in your room. It may sound silly, but buying individual bottles (for as much as $3) throughout the day can really add up.

✔ **Ask whether your kids can stay in the room with you.** A room with two double beds usually doesn't cost any more than one with a queen-size bed. And many hotels won't charge you the additional-person rate if the additional person is pint-size and related to you. Even if you have to pay $10 or $15 extra for a rollaway bed, you'll save hundreds by not taking two rooms.

✔ **Don't rent a car while in Boston and Cambridge.** If you're planning an out-of-town day trip, go wild. Otherwise, save the expense of renting and parking.

✔ **Keep a lid on incidentals.** In a day of spending $1 here and $5 there — on postcards, stamps, maps, snacks, sunscreen, and other random items — you can easily spend $20 or $30 and barely notice it.

✔ **Buy the MBTA's visitor pass.** But only if you plan to use it. The pass can be a great deal if you use it enough (see Chapter 8 for details).

✔ **Buy a Boston CityPass or Go Boston card.** The CityPass covers just six attractions (including the Museum of Fine Arts) but represents a 50 percent discount if you visit all of them. The Go Boston card covers a broader range of businesses, for a correspondingly higher price — which is also a good deal if you use it enough. See Chapter 11 for details.

✔ **Take advantage of free or cheap museum admission.** The USS *Constitution* Museum is free; the Children's Museum costs $1 after 5 p.m. on Friday; the Institute of Contemporary Art is free after 5 p.m. Wednesday; the Harvard art museums are free before noon Saturday; and the Harvard natural history museums are free on Sunday morning year-round and from 3 to 5 p.m. Wednesday during the academic year. The Museum of Fine Arts is pay-what-you-wish — but "suggests" a whopping $14 — after 4 p.m. Wednesday.

✔ **Try expensive restaurants at lunch instead of dinner.** Your lunch tab can be a fraction of the dinner bill at the same establishment, and the menu often includes many of the same specialties.

✔ **Pass on the souvenirs.** Your photographs and your memories should be the best mementos of your trip. If you're worried about money, you can do without the T-shirts and trinkets.

✔ **Let the kids do some planning.** You may be pleasantly surprised to discover that they consider a ride on a Swan Boat and a session of duck feeding at the Public Garden a full and fulfilling morning.

Handling Money

You're the best judge of how much cash you feel comfortable carrying and of your favorite alternate form of currency. That's not going to change much on your vacation. True, you'll probably be moving around more and incurring more expenses than you generally do (unless you happen to eat out every meal when you're at home), and you may let your mind slip into vacation gear and not be as vigilant about your safety as when you're in work mode. But those factors aside, the only type of payment that won't be quite as available to you away from home is your personal checkbook.

Using ATMs and carrying cash

The easiest and best way to get cash away from home is from an ATM (automated teller machine). The **Cirrus** (☎ 800-424-7787; www.mastercard.com) and **PLUS** (☎ 800-843-7587; www.visa.com) networks span the globe; the **NYCE** network (www.nycenet.com) operates in the eastern United States. Look at the back of your bank card to see which network you're on and then call or check online for ATM locations at your destination.

Be sure you know your personal identification number (PIN) before you leave home, and be sure to find out your daily withdrawal limit before you depart. Also, keep in mind that many banks impose a fee (rarely more than $1.50 for domestic transactions) every time you use your card at a different bank's ATM. On top of this charge, the bank from which you withdraw cash may charge its own fee. To compare banks' ATM fees within the United States, use www.bankrate.com.

If your ATM card is also a debit card, consider carrying at least one conventional credit card. When using a debit card, you're spending the equivalent of cash — and depleting your checking account. Some banks "freeze" part of the money in your account when you use a debit card for a transaction without a set amount (like a car rental or a tank of gas).

The largest banks in Massachusetts are **Bank of America** (☎ 800-841-4000) and **Citizens** (☎ 800-852-5577); their ATMs accept most networks' cards, subject to a service fee. State law says banks must warn you before imposing a fee for using a "foreign" bank card and offer you the chance to cancel the transaction.

The **SUM** network (www.sum-atm.com) gives customers of smaller banks and credit unions free access to other members' ATMs. Check to see whether your bank belongs to the SUM network or has another arrangement that can help you avoid fees.

Charging ahead with credit cards

Credit cards are a safe way to carry money. They also provide a convenient record of all your expenses. You can withdraw cash advances from your credit cards at banks or ATMs, provided you know your PIN. If you've forgotten yours or didn't even know you had one, call the number on the back of your credit card, and ask the bank to send it to you. It usually takes five to seven business days, though some banks will provide the number over the phone if you tell them your mother's maiden name or some other personal information.

Toting traveler's checks

These days, traveler's checks are less necessary because most cities (including Boston) have 24-hour ATMs that allow you to withdraw small amounts of cash as needed. However, keep in mind that you will likely be charged an ATM withdrawal fee if the bank is not your own, so if you're withdrawing money every day, you may be better off with traveler's checks — provided that you don't mind showing identification every time you want to cash one.

You can get traveler's checks at almost any bank. **American Express** offers denominations of $20, $50, $100, $500, and (for cardholders only) $1,000. You pay a service charge ranging from 1 to 4 percent. You can also get American Express traveler's checks over the phone by calling ☎ **800-221-7282;** Amex gold and platinum cardholders who use this number are exempt from the 1 percent fee.

Visa offers traveler's checks at Citibank locations nationwide, as well as at several other banks. The service charge ranges between 1.5 and 2 percent; checks come in denominations of $20, $50, $100, $500, and $1,000. Call ☎ **800-732-1322** for information. AAA members can obtain Visa checks without a fee at most AAA offices or by calling ☎ **866-339-3378. MasterCard** also offers traveler's checks. Call ☎ **800-223-9920** for a location near you.

 If you choose to carry traveler's checks, be sure to keep a record of their serial numbers separate from your checks in the event that they are stolen or lost. You'll get a refund faster if you know the numbers.

Dealing with a Lost or Stolen Wallet

Be sure to contact all of your credit-card companies the minute you discover your wallet has been lost or stolen and file a report at the nearest police precinct. Your credit-card company or insurer may require a police report number or record of the loss. Most credit-card companies have an emergency toll-free number to call if your card is lost or stolen; they may be able to wire you a cash advance immediately or deliver an emergency credit card in a day or two. Call the following emergency numbers in the United States:

- ✔ **American Express** ☎ **800-221-7282** (for cardholders and traveler's check holders)
- ✔ **MasterCard** ☎ **800-307-7309** or 636-722-7111
- ✔ **Visa** ☎ **800-847-2911** or 410-581-9994

For other credit cards, call the toll-free-number directory at ☎ **800-555-1212.**

If you need emergency cash over the weekend when all banks and American Express offices are closed, you can have money wired to you via **Western Union** (☎ **800-325-6000;** www.westernunion.com).

Identity theft and fraud are potential complications of losing your wallet, especially if you lose your driver's license along with your cash and credit cards. Notify the major credit-reporting bureaus immediately; placing a fraud alert on your records may protect you against liability for criminal activity. The three major U.S. credit-reporting agencies are **Equifax** (☎ **800-766-0008;** www.equifax.com), **Experian** (☎ **888-397-3742;** www.experian.com), and **TransUnion** (☎ **800-680-7289;** www.transunion.com). Finally, if you lose all forms of photo ID, call your airline and explain the situation; they may allow you to board the plane if you have a copy of your passport or birth certificate and a copy of the police report you've filed.

Chapter 5

Getting to Boston

. . . .

In This Chapter

▶ Traveling to Boston by airplane, car, or train

▶ Considering the pluses and minuses of package and escorted tours

. . . .

*I*f the details of trip planning start to bog you down, you may begin to suspect that the *longest* distance between two points is a straight line. You don't have to feel that way. In this chapter, I give you all the information you need to make the decisions that are right for you.

Flying to Boston

Logan International Airport (☎ **800-23-LOGAN;** www.massport.com/logan; airport code: BOS) serves Boston and is the primary air gateway to New England. In the popular "hub-and-spoke" airline model, Boston is typically a spoke — a destination, not a transfer point. No major airlines make their headquarters here.

Finding out which airlines fly there

The major domestic airlines that serve Logan are **AirTran** (☎ 800-247-8726; www.airtran.com), **American** (☎ 800-433-7300; www.aa.com), **America West** (☎ 800-235-9292; www.americawest.com), **ATA** (☎ 800-225-2995; www.ata.com), **Continental** (☎ 800-525-0280; www.continental.com), **Delta** (☎ 800-221-1212; www.delta.com), **JetBlue** (☎ 800-538-2583; www.jetblue.com), **Midwest** (☎ 800-452-2022; www.midwestexpress.com), **Northwest** (☎ 800-225-2525; www.nwa.com), **United** (☎ 800-241-6522; www.ual.com), and **US Airways** (☎ 800-428-4322; www.usairways.com).

International carriers include **American** (☎ 800-433-7300 in the U.S., 0345-789-789 in the U.K.; www.aa.com), **British Airways** (☎ 800-247-9297 in the U.S., 0345-222-111 or 0845-77-333-77 in the U.K.; www.british-airways.com), **Delta** (☎ 800-241-4141 in the U.S., 0800-414-767 in the U.K.; www.delta.com), **United** (☎ 800-538-2929 in the U.S., 0845-844-4777 in the U.K.; www.ual.com), and **Virgin Atlantic** (☎ 800-862-8621 in the U.S., 01293-747-747 in the U.K.; www.virgin-atlantic.com) from

England; **Aer Lingus** (☎ 800-474-7424 in the U.S., 01-886-8888 in Ireland; www.aerlingus.ie), American Airlines, and US Airways from Ireland; and **Air Canada** (☎ 888-247-2262; www.aircanada.ca) from Canada. **Qantas** (☎ 800-227-4500 in the U.S., 13-13-13 in Australia; www.qantas.com.au) flies to the West Coast of the United States and can provide connecting service to Boston.

Looking at attractive airport alternatives

If you have lots of time but not lots of money, booking a flight into Warwick, Rhode Island (outside Providence), or Manchester, New Hampshire, can be a great deal. **Southwest** (☎ 800-435-9792; www.iflyswa.com) broke these markets open, and many other carriers now serve both cities. Getting to Boston can be a hassle — the trip from either of these airports takes about 1½ hours — but the money you save on airfare may be worth it.

T. F. Green Airport (☎ **888-268-7222;** www.pvdairport.com; airport code: PVD) is in Warwick, Rhode Island, about 60 miles south of Boston. **Bonanza** (☎ **800-556-3815;** www.bonanzabus.com) offers bus service ($19 one-way; $34 round-trip) between the airport and Boston's South Station.

Manchester International Airport (☎ **603-624-6556;** www.flymanchester.com; airport code: MHT) is about 51 miles north of Boston. **Vermont Transit** (☎ **800-552-8737;** www.vermonttransit.com) operates bus service to and from South Station and Logan Airport ($12 one-way; $23 round-trip).

Getting the best deal on your airfare

Competition among the major U.S. airlines is unlike that of any other industry. Every airline offers virtually the same product (basically, a coach seat is a coach seat is a . . .), yet prices can vary by hundreds of dollars.

Business travelers who need the flexibility to buy their tickets at the last minute and change their itineraries at a moment's notice — and who want to get home before the weekend — pay (or at least their companies pay) the premium rate, known as the *full fare*. But if you can book your ticket far in advance, stay over Saturday night, and are willing to travel mid-week (Tuesday, Wednesday, or Thursday), you can qualify for the least expensive price — usually a fraction of the full fare. On most flights, even the shortest hops within the United States, the full fare is close to $1,000 or more, but a 7- or 14-day advance purchase ticket may cost less than half of that amount. Obviously, planning ahead pays.

The airlines also periodically hold sales, in which they lower the prices on their most popular routes. These fares have advance purchase requirements and date-of-travel restrictions, but you can't beat the prices. As you plan your vacation, keep your eyes open for these sales, which tend to take place in seasons of low travel volume — November to mid-April, with the best deals from January through March. You almost never see a sale around the peak summer vacation months of July and August, during the fall foliage season, or around Thanksgiving or Christmas.

Consolidators, also known as bucket shops, are great sources for international tickets, although they usually can't beat the Internet on fares within North America. Start by looking in Sunday newspaper travel sections; U.S. travelers should focus on *The New York Times, Los Angeles Times,* and *The Miami Herald.* For less developed destinations, small travel agents who cater to immigrant communities in large cities often have the best deals.

Bucket shop tickets are usually nonrefundable or rigged with stiff cancellation penalties, often as high as 50 to 75 percent of the ticket price, and some put you on charter airlines with questionable safety records.

Several reliable consolidators are worldwide and available on the Net. **STA Travel** (☎ **800-781-4040**; www.statravel.com) caters to young travelers, but offers good fares to people of all ages. **Flights.com** (☎ 800-TRAV-800; www.flights.com) has excellent fares worldwide and "local" Web sites in 12 countries.

Booking your flight online

The "big three" online travel agencies, **Expedia** (www.expedia.com), **Travelocity** (www.travelocity.com), and **Orbitz** (www.orbitz.com), sell most of the air tickets bought on the Internet. (Canadian travelers should try www.expedia.ca and www.travelocity.ca; U.K. residents can go for expedia.co.uk and opodo.co.uk.) Each has different deals with the airlines and may offer different fares on the same flights, so shopping around is wise. Expedia and Travelocity will also send you an **e-mail notification** when a cheap fare becomes available to your favorite destination. Of the smaller travel agency Web sites, **SideStep** (www.sidestep.com) receives good reviews from users. It's a browser add-on that purports to "search 140 sites at once," but in reality only beats competitors' fares as often as other sites do.

Great **last-minute deals** are available through free weekly e-mail services provided directly by the airlines. Most of these deals are announced on Tuesday or Wednesday and must be purchased online. Most are valid for travel that weekend only, but some (such as Southwest's) can be booked weeks or months in advance. Sign up for weekly e-mail alerts at airline Web sites or check megasites that compile comprehensive lists of last-minute specials, such as **Smarter Living** (www.smartertravel.com). Individual airline sites also offer schedules, flight booking, and information on late-breaking bargains. For last-minute trips, **Site59.com** (www.site59.com) in the United States often has better deals than the major-label sites.

Avoiding cabin fever

Whether you think of flying as an adventure or an ordeal, you're probably not thrilled by the prospect of a bone-dry cabin and a ration of personal space that would make a sardine claustrophobic. (Imagine how I'd sound if I didn't love flying.) Here are some strategies that may make your trip more tolerable:

- **Try to get a bulkhead seat, located in the front row of each cabin.** These seats usually offer the most legroom. Don't storm forward just yet. Without a seat in front of you, you must fit your carry-on bag into the overhead bin. The front row may not be the best place to see the in-flight movie, and many airlines save these seats for full-fare frequent fliers.

- **Try to get a seat in the emergency-exit row.** Like bulkhead seats, seats in the emergency-exit rows also offer extra legroom. Ask when you check in whether you can be seated in one of these rows; assignment is usually first come, first served. You must be at least 15 years old and able to open the emergency exit door and help direct traffic, if necessary.

- **Wear comfortable clothes and dress in layers.** The supposedly controlled cabin climate can leave you sweltering or shivering. You'll be glad to have a sweater or jacket.

- **Drink a lot of water.** This task won't make you any friends if you're in a window seat, but aisle-huggers won't be sorry. Not only does your body stay hydrated, but walking back and forth to the lavatory also helps keep your legs from cramping.

- **Bring some toiletries on long flights.** Take a travel-size bottle of moisturizer or lotion to refresh your face and hands at the end of the flight. On an overnight flight, always pack a toothbrush. You'll probably also want some petroleum jelly to keep your lips from cracking while you sleep in the dry cabin. If you wear contact lenses, take them out before you board or at least bring eye drops.

- **Order a special meal if you have special dietary needs, or pack your own — a good idea even before cutbacks made the in-flight meal an endangered species.** Most airlines can accommodate dietary restrictions, and nobody has to know that your restriction is that you're a picky eater. The airlines make special meals (vegetarian, kosher, and so on) to order, unlike the mass-produced chow they feed the other passengers.

- **If you're flying with kids, pack chewing gum to help with ear-pressure problems.** Don't forget diapers, toys, and a brand-new distraction (however small) — if a meltdown's looming, you want the element of surprise on your side.

If you're willing to give up some control over your flight details, use an *opaque fare service* like **Priceline** (www.priceline.com) or **Hotwire** (www.hotwire.com). Both offer rock-bottom prices in exchange for travel on a "mystery airline" at a mysterious time of day, often with a mysterious change of planes en route. The mystery airlines are all major, well-known carriers, and the possibility of being sent from Philadelphia to Chicago via Tampa is remote. But your chances of getting a 6 a.m. or 11 p.m. flight are pretty high. Hotwire tells you flight prices before you buy; Priceline usually has better deals than Hotwire, but you have to play its "name our price" game. *Note:* In 2004, Priceline added nonopaque service to its roster. You now have the option to pick exact flights, times, and airlines from a list of offers — or opt to bid on opaque fares as before.

Driving to Boston

The roads into Boston look perfectly manageable — on paper. But even with the new roads created by the $14.6 billion Big Dig, navigating downtown Boston is no picnic. Highway access *to* the Boston area is good, however. If you avoid rush hour and don't venture all the way into town, your trip probably won't be too awful.

The Massachusetts Turnpike (I-90), or Mass. Pike, is an east–west toll road that runs from the New York border to downtown Boston. The next-to-last exit serves Cambridge. The main north–south route through Boston is I-93, which extends north into New Hampshire. The main north–south route on the East Coast is I-95, which detours around Boston as a sort of beltway about 11 miles from downtown, where it's better known as Massachusetts Route 128.

 Try not to approach downtown Boston from 7 to 9 a.m. and 3:30 to 6:30 p.m. weekdays. Friday afternoon is especially problematic — make sure that the car has plenty of gas and coolant. Here are some basic directions for driving into Boston:

- ✓ **From New York City, points south, and southwestern Connecticut,** you have several options. My favorite is to take the Hutchinson River Parkway into Connecticut, where it becomes the Merritt/Wilbur Cross Parkway. Note that you can't use these roads if your car has commercial plates. About 20 miles south of Hartford, follow signs to I-91 north and take it to I-84 east. At Sturbridge, Massachusetts, pick up I-90, the Mass. Pike. (I-95 from New York, a busy truck route, is sometimes a bit faster.)

- ✓ **From Vermont and western New Hampshire,** take I-89 to Concord, New Hampshire, and then I-93 south.

- ✓ **From Maine and southeastern New Hampshire,** take I-95 south to Route 1 or I-93 south.

- ✓ **From Rhode Island and eastern Connecticut,** you're stuck with I-95. Where it intersects with I-93/Massachusetts 128, follow signs to Braintree and Boston.

Taking the Train to Boston

Amtrak (☎ **800-USA-RAIL** or 617-482-3660; www.amtrak.com) runs to Back Bay Station and South Station from the south and to North Station from the north (Portland, Maine). Use Back Bay Station, on Dartmouth Street across from the Copley Place mall, if you're staying in the Back Bay or the South End. Back Bay is also an Orange Line stop. Go to South Station, on Atlantic Avenue near the waterfront, if you're staying downtown or in Cambridge. (South Station is also a Red Line subway stop.)

 Airline-style booking strategies increasingly apply to train travel. Booking far ahead usually lands you a discounted excursion fare. Discounts don't apply during high-volume times such as Friday afternoon, Sunday afternoon, and periods around holidays.

Amtrak also operates **Acela** (www.acela.com) high-speed service on its Northeast Corridor route, between Boston and Washington, D.C. Trip time on the Washington–Boston route is just under six hours. Delays and equipment problems have plagued Acela almost since its inception, though; always call ahead to check the schedule before you run to catch this train. Call Amtrak or check its Web site for more details, schedules, and fares.

Choosing a Package Tour

For lots of destinations, package tours can be a smart way to go. In many cases, a package tour that includes airfare, hotel, and transportation to and from the airport costs less than the hotel alone on a tour you book yourself. That's because tour operators buy packages in bulk and resell them to the public. It's kind of like buying your vacation at a warehouse club — except that the tour operator is the one who buys the 1,000-count box of garbage bags and resells them 10 at a time at a cost that undercuts the local supermarket.

Package tours can vary as much as those garbage bags, too. Some offer a better class of hotels than others; others provide the same hotels for lower prices. Some book flights on scheduled airlines; others sell charters. In some packages, your choice of accommodations and travel days may be limited. Some let you choose between escorted vacations and independent vacations; others allow you to add just a few excursions or escorted day trips (also at discounted prices) without booking an entirely escorted tour.

Details of packages to Boston don't vary much, which makes comparison shopping relatively easy. Lodging options aren't extensive, simply because there aren't that many places to stay. The sightseeing component, if there is one, usually is a free or discounted one-day trolley tour rather than a customized offering.

Don't automatically add a rental car to your package. If you use the car every day and have access to free parking, it can be a good deal. If the car sits in the hotel garage racking up parking fees, you're wasting money.

On the other hand, an excursion to a suburb can be a worthwhile addition to your vacation. If time is short and you just can't leave town without seeing Plymouth (or Gloucester or another destination), paying someone to handle the logistics of a half- or full-day trip may be worth the money.

To find package tours, check out the travel section of your local Sunday newspaper or the ads in the back of national travel magazines such as _Travel & Leisure, National Geographic Traveler,_ and _Condé Nast Traveler._ **Liberty Travel** (call ☎ **888-271-1584** to find the store nearest you; www. libertytravel.com) is one of the biggest packagers in the Northeast and usually boasts a full-page ad in Sunday papers. Another travel behemoth, **Gray Line** (☎ **800-472-9546;** www.grayline.com), offers packages that include a choice of a huge variety of full- and half-day escorted tours to destinations throughout New England.

Another good source of package deals is the airlines themselves. Most major airlines offer air-land packages, including **American Airlines Vacations** (☎ 800-321-2121; www.aa.com), **Delta Vacations** (☎ 800-221-6666; www.deltavacations.com), **Midwest Airlines Vacations** (☎ 800-444-4479; www.midwestairlinesvacations.com), **United Vacations** (☎ 888-854-3899; www.unitedvacations.com), and **US Airways Vacations** (☎ 888-422-3861; www.usairwaysvacations.com).

Several big **online travel agencies** — Expedia, Travelocity, Orbitz, Site59, and Lastminute.com — also do a brisk business in packages. If you're unsure about the pedigree of a smaller packager, check with the Better Business Bureau in the city where the company is based or go online at www.bbb.org. If a packager won't tell you where it's based, don't fly with it.

Yankee Magazine Vacations (☎ 877-481-5986; www.yankeevacations. com) is a more local option. The basic package is a three-night stay with a one-day tour; add-ons include an impressive variety of excursions to other New England destinations.

If you live close enough to take advantage of **Amtrak Vacations** (☎ 800-805-9114; www.amtrakvacations.com), you may find taking a train a reasonable option. But don't book a train trip without at least checking your air options. Also, don't assume this choice is more reliable during bad weather. Snow falls on train tracks, too.

Joining an Escorted Tour

You may be one of the many people who love escorted tours. The tour company takes care of all the details and tells you what to expect during

A new leaf

Every fall, New England's colorful trees exert a magnetic pull over millions of people. Travelers sign up for bus tours that start and end in Boston and return home with the false impression that they've seen the city. I'm not telling you to skip these tours, but do consider this: Foliage season offers no guarantees. "Peak color" may not start or end when you think it will, and insane traffic and gloomy weather may keep you from making the best of your visit. If you're lucky enough to get a flight to Boston in October, consider making the city your base and scheduling a day trip or two (after you've seen the forecast) that includes some leaf-peeping.

each leg of your journey. You know your costs up front, and in the case of the tame ones, you don't get many surprises. Escorted tours can take you to the maximum number of sights in the minimum amount of time with the least amount of hassle.

The typical escorted tour that includes Boston bundles it with destinations as close as the suburbs and as far away as coastal Maine. Whether it's the "autumn color extravaganza," the "American history fiesta," or some other wacky theme, the usual tour seldom includes more than a day and a half in Boston. If you hope to get to know the city more than superficially, you're probably better off with a package deal (see the previous section).

If you decide to go with an escorted tour, I strongly recommend purchasing travel insurance, especially if the tour operator asks you to pay up front. But don't buy insurance from the tour operator! If the tour operator doesn't fulfill its obligation to provide you with the vacation you paid for, there's no reason to think it will fulfill its insurance obligations, either. Get travel insurance through an independent agency. (I tell you more about the ins and outs of travel insurance in Chapter 7.)

When choosing an escorted tour, along with finding out whether you have to put down a deposit and when final payment is due, ask a few simple questions before you buy:

✔ **What is the cancellation policy?** Can the company cancel the trip if it doesn't get enough people? How late can you cancel if you're unable to go? Do you get a refund if you cancel? If the company cancels?

✔ **How jam-packed is the schedule?** Does the tour schedule try to fit 25 hours into a 24-hour day, or does it give you ample time to relax by the pool or shop? If getting up at 7 a.m. every day and not returning to your hotel until 6 or 7 p.m. sounds like a grind, certain escorted tours may not be for you.

✔ **How large is the group?** The smaller the group, the less time you spend waiting for people to get on and off the bus. Tour operators may be evasive about this information, because they may not know the exact size of the group until everybody has made reservations, but they should be able to give you a rough estimate.

✔ **Is there a minimum group size?** Some tours have a minimum, and the operator may cancel the tour if it doesn't book enough people. If a quota exists, find out what it is and how close the company is to reaching it. Again, tour operators may be evasive in their answers, but the information may help you select a tour that's sure to happen.

✔ **What exactly is included?** Don't assume anything. You may have to pay to get yourself to and from the airport. An excursion may include a box lunch, but drinks may be extra. Beer may be included but not wine. How much flexibility do you have? Can you opt out of certain activities, or does the bus leave once a day, with no exceptions? Are all your meals planned in advance? Can you choose your entree at dinner, or does everybody get the same chicken cutlet?

Literally hundreds of tour operators offer itineraries that include Boston. On a busy fall weekend, out-of-state plates on lumbering buses are the rule rather than the exception all over town. And every single bus seems to wind up double-parked near the North End while the passengers sprint across a crowded street under the direction of a guide who's fretting because she's already half an hour behind schedule.

Chapter 6

Catering to Special Travel Needs or Interests

. . . .

In This Chapter

▶ Setting up a smooth family trip
▶ Traveling senior style
▶ Getting around with disabilities
▶ Finding tips for gay and lesbian travelers

. . . .

*O*ne-size-fits-all travel is a myth; travelers, especially those with particular needs, want their plans custom tailored. This chapter offers pointers for people in four categories: families, senior citizens, travelers with disabilities, and gay and lesbian travelers.

Traveling with the Brood: Advice for Families

If you have enough trouble getting your kids out of the house in the morning, dragging them thousands of miles away may seem like an insurmountable challenge. But family travel can be immensely rewarding, giving you new ways of seeing the world through smaller pairs of eyes.

Families from around the world flock to Boston because many, if not most, Boston-area activities appeal to children, and nearly every hotel and restaurant caters to kids. Just getting around becomes a family activity, because you're bound to do a fair amount of hand-in-hand strolling — a positive if walking tires the kids enough to make for an early bedtime, but a negative if it does the same to you.

 Some simple advice for family travelers: Give your kids a voice in the planning process. Also, make sure that everyone knows what to expect. (This suggestion is all too easy to forget even when you're traveling only with adults!) A huge part of Boston's appeal is that it's a working city, not a theme park, but that's no consolation to a child who thinks that *vacation* always means roller coasters and cotton candy.

Boston on the children's bookshelf

Your kids may know more about these tiny slices of Boston than you do (or more than you remember). Literally hundreds of children's books about Boston are available. Here are three of my favorites:

✔ *Make Way for Ducklings,* **by Robert McCloskey.** You may have lost count of how many times you've read this one to your preschoolers. Adorable bronze renderings in their own corner of the Public Garden illustrate the delightful story of the Mallard family.

✔ *The Trumpet of the Swan,* **by E. B. White.** He's not as famous as Charlotte the spider, but Louis the trumpeter swan has delightful adventures in Boston. Like the Mallard family, Louis frequents the Public Garden.

✔ *Johnny Tremain,* **by Esther Forbes.** This book offers a boy's-eye view (with several strong female characters) of the events that took place in Boston before the Revolutionary War. Johnny's interesting escapades make this book a painless introduction to the people and history of the period — and a cracking-good story.

So give your children some time with this book and a not-too-overwhelming assortment of other planning materials. (For a lesson in life skills, you can even ask your kids to lend a hand with the vacation budgeting.) After everyone contributes suggestions, all of you will have a better sense of what the other family members have in mind for your Boston vacation.

 Look for the Kid Friendly icon throughout this book for family-oriented tips and activities.

Family-friendly flying

To make traveling more manageable, book a nonstop flight. If you can't book a nonstop flight, try to fly early in the day. If you can't fly early in the day, try to at least avoid booking the last flight of the day. A canceled connecting flight may leave you stranded, especially in the winter, when weather delays plague the entire East Coast.

 If you fly, remember to pack chewing gum to help with ear-pressure problems.

Keeping the kids entertained

Flying or not, pack diversionary materials and toys — crayons or markers, a deck of cards, computer game, personal stereo or portable radio with headphones, or a favorite book. Keep a surprise diversion in reserve. These items are handy on the road and can buy weary parents some TV-free downtime in the middle of a busy day in Boston.

Relying on babysitting services

Don't put off thinking about child care. I *strongly* recommend that you book a sitter in advance — if possible, when you reserve your room. Most hotels in the Boston area can recommend reliable baby sitters. If you choose to use a child-care referral service, keep in mind that referral fees are steep. If you're in town on business, ask whether your host company has a corporate membership in a child-care referral service. If the company does, you may be able to save some serious money. See "Fast Facts," in the Appendix, for details about the local agency Parents in a Pinch.

Exploring Boston together

Be realistic. You may need to adjust your expectations to accommodate your traveling companions' short legs and shorter attention spans. Here are three important reminders: Don't try to do too much; don't forget to schedule some playtime; and don't assume that more expensive is better.

- ✔ *Prioritize.* You probably have a sense of your sightseeing timetable from the groundwork you laid at home. If your schedule isn't set, try this: Ask each child for a short list of top activity picks (no more than three, and no make-or-break choices). Then ask each child to select one activity from someone else's list. This process cuts down on the cries of "this wasn't my idea."

- ✔ *Split up.* Larger groups may consider splitting up for a while and reuniting to swap notes over a family dinner. This idea works especially well if the children are far apart in age. For example, the teenagers can explore the New England Aquarium while the younger kids check out the Children's Museum. This approach can help keep the peace and keep everyone satisfied.

- ✔ *Plan ahead.* For more Boston-specific advice and listings, visit the Web site of the *Boston Parents Paper* (http://boston.parenthood. com). You can also find good family-oriented vacation advice on the Internet from sites like the **Family Travel Forum** (www.family travelforum.com/ftf.html), a comprehensive site that offers customized trip planning; **Family Travel Network** (www.family travelnetwork.com), an award-winning site that offers travel features, deals, and tips; **Traveling Internationally with Your Kids** (www.travelwithyourkids.com), a comprehensive site that offers customized trip planning; and **Family Travel Files** (www. thefamilytravelfiles.com), which offers an online magazine and a directory of off-the-beaten-path tours and tour operators for families. **Familyhostel** (☎ 800-733-9753; www.learn.unh.edu/ familyhostel) takes the whole family, including kids ages 8 to 15, on moderately priced domestic and international learning vacations. A team of academics guides lectures, field trips, and sightseeing.

Making Age Work for You: Tips for Seniors

Many Boston-area businesses — including hotels, restaurants, museums, and movie theaters — offer discounts to seniors who present valid identification. The cutoff age usually is 65 or (less often) 62.

 To get around Boston, seniors 65 and over can buy passes that allow them to ride the MBTA (Massachusetts Bay Transportation Authority) subways for 35¢ (90¢ less than the regular fare) and local buses for 25¢ (65¢ less than the regular fare). On zoned and express buses and the commuter rail, the senior fare is half the regular fare. The Senior Pass is available for a nominal fee (currently, 50¢) from 8:30 a.m. to 5 p.m. weekdays at the Office for Transportation Access, Back Bay Station, 105 Dartmouth St. Or write to the **Office for Transportation Access,** 145 Dartmouth St., Boston, MA 02116 (☎ **617-222-5438** or 617-222-5854 [TTY]; www.mbta.com). Enclose a 1- by 1-inch photo and a check or money order for 50¢.

Mention the fact that you're a senior citizen when you make your travel reservations. Although all the major U.S. airlines except America West have cancelled their senior discount and coupon book programs, many hotels still offer discounts for seniors.

 Always ask whether a business offers a senior discount. Restaurants and theaters that extend discounts usually do so only during off-peak hours, but museums and other attractions may charge reduced rates at all times. Carry your driver's license or other document that shows your date of birth.

Members of **AARP** (formerly known as the American Association of Retired Persons), 601 E St. NW, Washington, DC 20049 (☎ **888-687-2277** or 202-434-2277; www.aarp.org), get discounts on hotels, airfares, and car rentals. AARP offers members a wide range of benefits, including *AARP: The Magazine* and a monthly newsletter. Anyone over 50 can join.

 A **Golden Age Passport** from the **National Park Service** is one of the best deals around. For $10, it gives you and immediate family members traveling with you free admission to all properties administered by the National Park Service, including parks, monuments, historic sites, recreation areas, and wildlife refuges. The passport, which is good for your lifetime, can pay for itself in one visit to the Boston area. For example, it covers the Longfellow House in Cambridge and the Maritime National Historic Site in Salem, among many other destinations. It's available to citizens and permanent residents 62 and older at any Park Service site that charges an entrance fee. Besides free entry, a Golden Age Passport also offers a 50 percent discount on fees for such activities as camping, swimming, parking, boat launching, and tours. For more information, go to www.nps.gov/fees_passes.htm or call ☎ **888-467-2757.**

Many reliable agencies and organizations target the 50-plus market. **Elderhostel** (☎ 877-426-8056; www.elderhostel.org) arranges study programs for those aged 55 and over (and a spouse or companion of any age) in the United States and in more than 80 countries around the world. Most courses last five to seven days in the United States (two to four weeks abroad), and many include airfare, accommodations in university dormitories or modest inns, meals, and tuition. **INTRAV** (☎ 800-456-8100; www.intrav.com) is a high-end tour operator that caters to the mature, discerning traveler, not specifically seniors, with trips around the world that include guided safaris, polar expeditions, private-jet adventures, and small-boat cruises down jungle rivers.

The following recommended publications offer travel resources and discounts for seniors:

- ✔ *Travel 50 & Beyond*, a quarterly magazine (www.travel50and beyond.com)

- ✔ *Travel Unlimited: Uncommon Adventures for the Mature Traveler* by Alison Gardner (Avalon)

- ✔ *101 Tips for Mature Travelers*, available from Grand Circle Travel (☎ 800-221-2610 or 617-350-7500; www.gct.com)

- ✔ *The 50+ Traveler's Guidebook* by Anita Williams and Merrimac Dillon (St. Martin's Press)

- ✔ *Unbelievably Good Deals and Great Adventures That You Absolutely Can't Get Unless You're Over 50* by Joann Rattner Heilman (McGraw-Hill)

 If you experience mobility difficulties, see the next section for information about getting around Boston.

Accessing Boston: Advice for Travelers with Disabilities

Boston is a generally accessible city, with some problematic exceptions. Widespread construction and uneven walking surfaces can keep you from getting around as quickly as you may like. I recommend that you allow plenty of time to reach your destinations, especially near the construction area that has replaced the Big Dig, which dominates downtown between North Station and South Station.

The narrow streets, cobbled thoroughfares, and brick sidewalks that make older neighborhoods like Beacon Hill and the North End so picturesque can make navigation difficult. Fortunately, after you reach the areas, almost all attractions are accessible. However, the upper levels of some historic buildings — for example, the second floor of the Paul Revere

House — can't accommodate wheelchairs. If you have severe mobility issues, contact attractions in advance for accessibility information.

 Many North End and Beacon Hill streets don't allow buses and trolleys. Motor tours touch on the edges of these neighborhoods, but the tours don't get up close. If you want to experience these areas, you must disembark from public transit and venture out on your own. (Beware of salespeople who try to tell you otherwise.) For example, the Paul Revere House is four blocks from the closest trolley stop.

 VSA Arts Massachusetts (formerly Very Special Arts), 2 Boylston St., Boston, MA 02116 (☎ **617-350-7713;** TTY 617-350-6836; www.vsamass. org), is an excellent source of information. The comprehensive Web site includes a searchable database of general access information and specifics about more than 200 arts and entertainment facilities in the state.

Most Boston-area lodgings comply with the Americans with Disabilities Act (ADA), but the true level of accessibility can be harder to gauge without asking some pointed questions. Be explicit about your needs when you make your reservations. If you have a specific concern that a certain hotel can't address, the staff should be able to direct you to a more appropriate establishment.

The **Royal Sonesta Hotel** in Cambridge (☎ **800-SONESTA**) trains its staff in disability awareness; at the **Westin Copley Place Boston** (☎ **800-WESTIN-1**), 48 accessible rooms adjoin standard units.

Under the ADA, all forms of public transit must provide special services to patrons with disabilities. Newer stations on the Red, Blue, and Orange lines are wheelchair accessible, and the MBTA is in the process of converting Green Line trolleys. Call ☎ **800-392-6100** (outside Massachusetts) or 617-222-3200 to see whether the stations you need are accessible. Make sure that you speak to a live person and that the information — especially about functioning elevators — is current.

 Don't rely on system maps to tell you which subway stations are accessible; they tend to be sorely out of date.

All **MBTA buses** are equipped with lifts or kneelers; call ☎ **800-LIFT-BUS** for more information. Some bus routes are wheelchair accessible at all times, but you may need to make a reservation as much as a day in advance for others. **Boston Cab** (☎ **617-536-5010**) is one taxicab company with wheelchair-accessible vehicles; advance notice is recommended. In addition, the **Airport Accessible Van** (☎ **617-561-1769**) offers wheelchair-accessible service within Logan Airport.

For discounted public-transit fares, persons with disabilities can apply for a $3 **Transportation Access Pass.** The process takes six to eight weeks and may not be worth the trouble for a short visit. Contact the

Office for Transportation Access, 145 Dartmouth St., Boston, MA 02116 (☎ **617-222-5438** or 617-222-5854 [TTY]; www.mbta.com).

If you need to rent a car, **Avis Rent a Car** has an "Avis Access" program that offers such services as a dedicated 24-hour toll-free number (☎ **888-879-4273**) for customers with special needs; car features such as swivel seats, spinner knobs, and hand controls; and accessible bus service.

The U.S. National Park Service offers a **Golden Access Passport** that gives free lifetime entrance to all properties administered by the National Park Service — national parks, monuments, historic sites, recreation areas, and national wildlife refuges — for persons who are visually impaired or permanently disabled, regardless of age. You may pick up a Golden Access Passport at any NPS entrance fee area by showing proof of medically determined disability and eligibility for receiving benefits under federal law. Besides free entry, the Golden Access Passport offers a 50 percent discount on fees charged for such activities as camping, swimming, parking, boat launching, and tours. For more information, visit www.nps.gov/fees_passes.htm or call ☎ **888-467-2757.**

Many travel agencies offer customized tours and itineraries for travelers with disabilities:

- ✔ **Flying Wheels Travel** (☎ **507-451-5005**; www.flyingwheels travel.com) offers escorted tours and cruises that emphasize sports and private tours in minivans with lifts.

- ✔ **Access-Able Travel Source** (☎ **303-232-2979**; www.access-able.com) offers extensive access information and advice for traveling around the world with disabilities.

- ✔ **Accessible Journeys** (☎ **800-846-4537** or 610-521-0339; www.disabilitytravel.com) caters to slow walkers and wheelchair travelers and their families and friends.

Organizations that offer assistance to travelers with disabilities include

- ✔ **MossRehab ResourceNet** (www.mossresourcenet.org), which provides a library of accessible-travel resources online

- ✔ **SATH,** or Society for Accessible Travel and Hospitality (☎ **212-447-7284**; www.sath.org; annual membership fees: $45 adults, $30 seniors and students), which offers a wealth of travel resources for all types of disabilities and informed recommendations on destinations, access guides, travel agents, tour operators, vehicle rentals, and companion services

- ✔ **American Foundation for the Blind** (☎ **800-232-5463**; www.afb.org), which is a referral resource for the blind or visually impaired that includes information on traveling with Seeing Eye dogs

For more information specifically targeted to travelers with disabilities, check out

- ✔ **iCan** (www.icanonline.net/channels/travel/index.cfm), a community Web site that has destination guides and several regular columns on accessible travel

- ✔ *Emerging Horizons,* a quarterly magazine ($14.95 per year, $19.95 outside the U.S.; www.emerginghorizons.com)

- ✔ *Open World Magazine,* published by SATH (subscription: $13 per year, $21 outside the U.S.)

- ✔ **Twin Peaks Press,** offering travel-related books for travelers with special needs (☎ **360-694-2462;** http://disabilitybookshop. virtualave.net/blist84.htm)

Following the Rainbow: Resources for Gay and Lesbian Travelers

Same-sex marriage has been legal in Massachusetts since 2004. The state capital, Boston, is one of the most gay- and lesbian-friendly year-round destinations in New England. (In summer, Provincetown holds the title.)

Boston's South End and Jamaica Plain and Cambridge's Porter Square are home to many gay men and lesbians. A number of nightclubs cater to a gay clientele at least one night a week. The Boston Pride March, on the second Sunday in June, is the largest gay-pride parade in New England.

For the most up-to-date information about events and entertainment, try the following gay-friendly publications:

- ✔ *Bay Windows* (☎ **617-266-6670;** www.baywindows.com) is a weekly newspaper that covers New England and offers extensive cultural listings.

- ✔ The arts-oriented weekly *Boston Phoenix* has a gay-interest Internet area at www.bostonphoenix.com.

- ✔ The *Pink Pages,* 66 Charles St. #283, Boston, MA 02114 (☎ **800-338-6550**), is a guide to gay- and lesbian-owned and gay-friendly businesses. Check the wide-ranging Web site at www.pinkweb.com/ boston.index.html. You can order a copy of the annual directory for $11, including shipping.

Other information sources include the **Gay, Lesbian, Bisexual and Transgender Helpline** (☎ 888-340-4528 or 617-267-9001), which offers information from 6 to 11 p.m. Monday through Friday and from 5 to 10 p.m. on weekends; the **Boston Alliance of Gay and Lesbian Youth**

(☎ 617-227-4314; www.bagly.org); and the **Bisexual Resource Center** (☎ 617-424-9595; www.biresource.org).

The International Gay and Lesbian Travel Association (☎ 800-448-8550 or 954-776-2626; www.iglta.org) is the trade association for the gay and lesbian travel industry and offers an online directory of gay- and lesbian-friendly travel businesses; go to the Web site and click Members.

The following agencies offer tours and travel itineraries specifically for gay and lesbian travelers:

- ✔ **Above and Beyond Tours** (☎ 800-397-2681; www.abovebeyond tours.com) is the exclusive gay and lesbian tour operator for United Airlines.

- ✔ **Now, Voyager** (☎ 800-255-6951; www.nowvoyager.com) is a well-known San Francisco–based gay-owned and operated travel service.

- ✔ **Olivia Cruises & Resorts** (☎ 800-631-6277 or 510-655-0364; www.olivia.com) charters entire resorts and ships for exclusive lesbian vacations and offers smaller group experiences for both gay and lesbian travelers.

The following travel guides are available at most travel bookstores and gay and lesbian bookstores, or you can order them from **Giovanni's Room** bookstore, 1145 Pine St., Philadelphia, PA 19107 (☎ 215-923-2960; www.giovannisroom.com):

- ✔ *Out and About* (☎ 800-929-2268 or 415-644-8044; www.outand about.com) offers guidebooks and a newsletter ($20 per year; 10 issues) packed with solid information on the global gay and lesbian scene.

- ✔ *Spartacus International Gay Guide* (Bruno Gmünder Verlag; www.spartacusworld.com/gayguide/) and *Odysseus* are both annual English-language guidebooks focused on gay men.

- ✔ The *Damron* guides (www.damron.com) include annual books for gay men and lesbians.

- ✔ *Gay Travel A to Z: The World of Gay & Lesbian Travel Options at Your Fingertips,* by Marianne Ferrari (Ferrari International; Box 35575, Phoenix, AZ 85069), is a very good gay and lesbian guide-book series.

Chapter 7

Taking Care of the Remaining Details

. . . .

In This Chapter

▶ Renting a car (and why you don't need to)
▶ Buying travel and medical insurance
▶ Dealing with illness away from home
▶ Keeping in touch while you're on the road
▶ Making your way through airport security

. . . .

*W*hat's worse than the nagging feeling that you forgot something, but you're not sure what it is? Probably the sensation of remembering what it was just as your plane leaves the ground.

This chapter attempts to relieve that sense of impending doom (or at least inconvenience) with a roundup of topics that can simplify your final planning.

For more information about money, budgeting, and cutting costs, turn to Chapter 4.

Renting a Car — Or Not

If you visit Boston and Cambridge, you won't have any problem getting around without a car. Public transportation and your feet are reliable, safe, and cheap. Parking is scarce and expensive — in both categories, among the worst in the country. Traffic is dreadful, worsening the closer you get to downtown, where a traffic jam can spring up at any hour of the day or night. Boston drivers in particular are hostile and unpredictable.

If you drive to the Boston area, park at the hotel and save the car for day trips. You can even arrange for the car to come to you: Some companies, including **Enterprise** (☎ 800-736-8222), offer pickup and drop-off service. If you decide to rent for a day or two, here's the scoop:

Car-rental rates vary even more than airline fares. The price depends on the size of the car, the rental period, where and when you pick up and drop off the car, where you drive, and a host of other factors. Asking a few key questions may save you hundreds of dollars.

- ✔ **Weekend rates may be lower than weekday rates.** If you keep the car five or more days, a weekly rate may be cheaper than the daily rate. Ask whether the rate is the same for pickup Friday morning as Thursday night and whether you incur a penalty for early drop-off of a weekly rental.

- ✔ **Some companies may assess a drop-off charge.** You may incur this fee if you don't return the car to the pickup location. National is one of the few companies that doesn't charge this fee.

- ✔ **Find out whether age is an issue.** Many car-rental companies add a fee for drivers under 25 — or don't rent to those drivers at all.

- ✔ **If you see an advertised price in your local newspaper, be sure to ask for that specific rate.** If not, you may be charged the standard (higher) rate. Don't forget to mention membership in AAA, AARP, and trade unions. These memberships usually entitle you to upgrades or to discounts ranging from 5 to 30 percent.

- ✔ **Check your frequent-flier accounts.** Not only are your favorite (or most used) airlines likely to send you discount coupons, but most car rentals add at least 500 miles to your account as well.

- ✔ **Use the Internet to comparison-shop for a car rental.** You can check rates at most of the major agencies' Web sites. All the major booking sites — **Travelocity** (www.travelocity.com), **Expedia** (www.expedia.com), **Yahoo! Travel** (www.travel.yahoo.com), and **Cheap Tickets** (www.cheaptickets.com), for example — utilize search engines that can dig up discounted car-rental rates. Once you enter the size of the car you want, the pickup and return dates, and the location, the site returns a price. You can even make the reservation through any of these sites.

In addition to the standard rental prices, optional charges apply to most car rentals (as do some not-so-optional charges, such as taxes). Many credit-card companies cover the **Collision Damage Waiver (CDW),** which requires you to pay for damage to the car in a collision. Check with your credit-card company before you go so that you can avoid paying this hefty fee (as much as $20 a day).

The car-rental companies also offer additional **liability insurance** (if you harm others in an accident), **personal accident insurance** (if you harm yourself or your passengers), and **personal effects insurance** (if your luggage is stolen from your car). Your insurance policy on your car at home probably covers most of these unlikely occurrences. However, if your own insurance doesn't cover you for rentals or if you don't have auto insurance, definitely consider the additional coverage. (Ask your car-rental agent for more information.) Unless you're toting around the Hope diamond — and you don't want to leave that in your car trunk anyway — you can probably skip the personal-effects insurance. However, driving around without liability or personal-accident coverage is never a good idea; even if you're a good driver, other people may not be, and liability claims can be complicated.

Some companies also offer **refueling packages,** in which you pay for your initial full tank of gas up front and return the car with an empty gas tank. The prices can be competitive with local gas prices, but you don't get credit for any gas remaining in the tank. If you reject this option, you pay only for the gas you use, but you need to return your rental car with a full tank or face charges of $3 to $4 a gallon for any shortfall. In my experience, gas prices in the refueling packages are at the high end. I usually forgo the refueling package and allow plenty of time for refueling en route to the car-rental return. However, if you usually run late and a refueling stop may make you miss your plane, you're a perfect candidate for the fuel-purchase option.

Playing It Safe with Travel and Medical Insurance

Three kinds of travel insurance are available: trip-cancellation insurance, medical insurance, and lost-luggage insurance. The cost of travel insurance varies widely, depending on the cost and length of your trip, your age and health, and the type of trip you're taking, but expect to pay between 5 to 8 percent of the vacation itself. Here is my advice on all three.

- ✔ **Trip-cancellation insurance** helps you get your money back if you have to back out of a trip, if you have to go home early, or if your travel supplier goes bankrupt. Allowed reasons for cancellation can range from sickness to natural disasters to the State Department's declaring your destination unsafe for travel.

  A good resource is **"Travel Guard Alerts,"** a list of companies considered high-risk by Travel Guard International (www.travel insured.com). Protect yourself further by paying for the insurance with a credit card — by law, consumers can get their money back on goods and services not received if they report the loss within 60 days after the charge is listed on their credit-card statement.

  Note: Many tour operators, particularly those offering trips to remote or high-risk areas, include insurance in the cost of the trip or can arrange insurance policies through a partnering provider, a convenient and often cost-effective way for the traveler to obtain insurance. Make sure that the tour company is a reputable one, however: Some experts suggest you avoid buying insurance from the tour or cruise company you're traveling with, saying it's better to buy from a "third-party" insurer than to put all your money in one place.

✔ For domestic travel, buying **medical insurance** for your trip doesn't make sense for most travelers. Most existing health policies cover you if you get sick away from home — but check before you go, particularly if you belong to an HMO.

✔ **Lost-luggage insurance** isn't necessary for most travelers. On domestic flights, checked baggage is covered up to $2,500 per ticketed passenger. On international flights (including U.S. portions of international trips), baggage coverage is limited to approximately $9.07 per pound, up to approximately $635 per checked bag. If you plan to check items more valuable than the standard liability, see whether your homeowner's policy covers your valuables, get baggage insurance as part of your comprehensive travel-insurance package, or buy Travel Guard's "BagTrak" product. Don't buy insurance at the airport, where it's usually overpriced. Be sure to take any valuables or irreplaceable items with you in your carry-on luggage — airline policies don't cover many valuables (including books, money, and electronics).

If your luggage is lost, immediately file a lost-luggage claim at the airport, detailing the luggage contents. For most airlines, you must report delayed, damaged, or lost baggage within four hours of arrival. The airlines are required to deliver luggage, once found, directly to your house or destination free of charge.

For more information, contact one of the following recommended insurers: **Access America** (☎ 866-807-3982; www.accessamerica. com); **Travel Guard International** (☎ 800-826-4919; www.travel guard.com); **Travel Insured International** (☎ 800-243-3174; www. travelinsured.com); and **Travelex Insurance Services** (☎ 888-457-4602; www.travelex-insurance.com).

Staying Healthy When You Travel

Getting sick will ruin your vacation, so I *strongly* advise against it. (Of course, last time I checked, the bugs weren't listening to me any more than they probably listen to you.)

For domestic trips, most reliable healthcare plans provide coverage if you get sick away from home. See the Appendix for listings of local hospitals. For information on purchasing additional medical insurance for your trip, see the previous section of this chapter.

Avoiding "economy-class syndrome"

Deep vein thrombosis, or as it's known in the world of flying, "economy-class syndrome," is a blood clot that develops in a deep vein. It's a potentially deadly condition that can be caused by sitting in cramped conditions — such as an airplane cabin — for too long. During a flight (especially a long-haul flight), get up, walk around, and stretch your legs every 60 to 90 minutes to keep your blood flowing. Other preventive measures include frequent flexing of the legs while sitting, drinking lots of water, and avoiding alcohol and sleeping pills. If you have a history of deep vein thrombosis, heart disease, or another condition that puts you at high risk, some experts recommend wearing compression stockings or taking anticoagulants when you fly; always ask your physician about the best course for you. Symptoms of deep vein thrombosis include leg pain or swelling, or even shortness of breath.

Talk to your doctor before leaving on a trip if you have a serious or chronic illness. For conditions such as epilepsy, diabetes, or heart problems, wear a **MedicAlert identification tag** (☎ 888-633-4298; www.medicalert.org), which immediately alerts doctors to your condition and gives them access to your records through MedicAlert's 24-hour hotline.

Staying Connected by Cellphone or E-Mail

Staying in touch with the folks at home (or with each other) is much easier these days thanks to the rapidly expanding cellphone networks and various plans that give you plenty of unlimited minutes. Access to the Internet from your phone or at hotel or public terminals (or from your own laptop, via Wi-Fi, or via a handy modem cord and plug) also makes communicating while traveling much less complicated.

Using a cellphone across the United States

Just because your cellphone works at home doesn't mean it works elsewhere in the country (thanks to our nation's fragmented cellphone system). But it's a good bet that your phone works in major cities. To be sure, look at your wireless company's coverage map on its Web site before heading out. The Boston area, including popular day-trip destinations, is well wired; the only places you're likely to encounter dead spots are in the countryside.

If you're not from the United States, you may be appalled at the poor reach of our **GSM (Global System for Mobiles) wireless network,** which is used by much of the rest of the world. (To see where GSM phones

work in the United States, check out www.t-mobile.com/coverage/
national_popup.asp). Your phone probably works in most U.S. cities,
but you may not be able to send SMS (text messages) home. Assume
nothing — call your wireless provider, and get the full scoop. In a worst-
case scenario, you can always rent a phone; **InTouch USA** (☎ 800-872-
7626; www.intouchglobal.com) delivers to hotels, but be aware that
you'll pay $1 a minute or more for airtime.

Accessing the Internet away from home

Travelers have any number of ways to check their e-mail and access the
Internet on the road. Of course, using your own laptop, PDA, or modem-
equipped electronic organizer gives you the most flexibility. But even if
you don't have a computer, you can still gain access to your e-mail and
even your office computer from cybercafes.

It's hard nowadays to find a city that *doesn't* have a few cybercafes.
Although there's no definitive directory for cybercafes — these are independent businesses, after all — two places to start looking are www.
cybercaptive.com and www.cybercafe.com.

Boston is one of the most wired cities in the country, which makes cybercafes less vital (and less numerous) than they are in less-plugged-in areas.
Why pay for access when it's free at work, school, and any number of
other places? **Tech Superpowers,** 252 Newbury St., third floor (☎ 617-
267-9716; www.newburyopen.net), is both a cybercafe and the hub of
the free-wireless paradise that is upper Newbury Street (the Mass. Ave.
end). **Trident Booksellers & Café,** 338 Newbury St. (☎ 617-267-8688;
www.tridentbookscafe.com), is part of Tech Superpowers' upper
Newbury Street free-wireless network.

Aside from formal cybercafes, most **youth hostels** have at least one computer you can use. And most **public libraries** across the world offer
Internet access free or for a small charge. The Boston Public Library
offers free wireless access, but only to people with BPL library cards.
Though it's hardly a hangout, **Kinko's** (see the Appendix for addresses)
is an option in many neighborhoods. Avoid **hotel business centers**
unless you're willing to pay exorbitant rates.

Most major airports now have **Internet kiosks** scattered throughout
their concourses. These kiosks, which you also see in shopping malls,
hotel lobbies, and tourist information offices around the world, give you
basic Web access for a per-minute fee that's usually higher than cybercafe prices. The kiosks' clunkiness and high price mean that they should
be avoided whenever possible.

To retrieve your e-mail, ask your **Internet Service Provider (ISP)** if it
has a Web-based interface tied to your existing e-mail account. If your
ISP doesn't have such an interface, you can use the free **mail2web** service (www.mail2web.com) to view and reply to your home e-mail. For

more flexibility, you may want to open a free, Web-based e-mail account with **Yahoo! Mail** (http://mail.yahoo.com) or **MSN Hotmail** (www.hotmail.com). Your home ISP may be able to forward your e-mail to the Web-based account automatically.

If you need to access files on your office computer, look into a service called **GoToMyPC** (www.gotomypc.com). The service provides a Web-based interface for you to manipulate a distant PC from anywhere — even a cybercafe — provided your "target" PC is on and has an always-on connection to the Internet (such as with Road Runner cable). The service offers top-quality security, but if you're worried about hackers, use your own laptop rather than a cybercafe computer to use the GoToMyPC system.

If you're bringing your own computer, **Wi-Fi** (wireless fidelity) access is available at more and more hotels, cafes, and retailers. Wi-Fi "hotspots" allow high-speed connection without cable wires, networking hardware, or a phone line. You can connect in several ways. Many laptops have built-in wireless capability (an 802.11b wireless Ethernet connection). Mac owners have their own networking technology, Apple AirPort. If you have an older computer, you can plug an 802.11b/**Wi-Fi card** (around $50) into your laptop.

You sign up for paid wireless access much as you do for cellphone service, through a plan offered by one of several commercial companies that have made service available in airports, hotel lobbies, and coffee shops. **T-Mobile Hotspot** (www.t-mobile.com/hotspot) serves up wireless connections at more than 1,000 Starbucks coffee shops nationwide. **Boingo** (www.boingo.com) and **Wayport** (www.wayport.com) have networks in airports and high-class hotel lobbies. **iPass** (www.ipass.com) providers also give you access to a few hundred wireless hotel lobby setups. Best of all, you don't need to be a guest to use a hotel's network; just set yourself up on a nice couch in the lobby. The companies' pricing policies can be byzantine, with a variety of monthly, per-connection, and per-minute plans, but in general you pay around $30 a month for unlimited access — and as companies jump on the wireless bandwagon, prices are likely to get more competitive.

If Wi-Fi is not available at your destination, most hotels throughout the world offer dataports for laptop modems. Many hotels offer high-speed Internet access using an Ethernet network cable; it's free at some properties but costs as much as $11 per 24-hour period at others. You can bring your own cables, but most hotels rent them for around $10. **Call your hotel in advance** to find out your options.

In addition, major Internet Service Providers (ISP) have **local access numbers** around the world, allowing you to go online by simply placing a local call. Check your ISP's Web site or call its toll-free number and ask how you can use your current account away from home, and how much it will cost. If you're traveling outside the reach of your ISP, the **iPass**

Online traveler's toolbox

Veteran travelers usually carry some essential items to make their trips easier. Following is a selection of handy online tools to bookmark and use.

- ✔ **Airplane seating and food.** Find out which seats to reserve and which to avoid (and more) on all major domestic airlines at www.seatguru.com. And check out the type of meal (with photos) you'll likely be served on airlines around the world at www.airlinemeals.net.

- ✔ **Foreign Languages for Travelers** (www.travlang.com). Learn basic terms in more than 70 languages and click any underlined phrase to hear what it sounds like.

- ✔ **Intellicast** (www.intellicast.com) and **Weather.com** (www.weather.com). Gives weather forecasts for all 50 states and for cities around the world.

- ✔ **Mapquest** (www.mapquest.com). This best of the mapping sites lets you choose a specific address or destination, and in seconds, it returns a map and detailed directions.

- ✔ **Subway Navigator** (www.subwaynavigator.com). Download subway maps and get savvy advice on using subway systems in dozens of major cities around the world.

- ✔ **Time and Date** (www.timeanddate.com). See what time (and day) it is anywhere in the world.

- ✔ **Visa ATM Locator** (www.visa.com), for locations of PLUS ATMs worldwide, or **MasterCard ATM Locator** (www.mastercard.com), for locations of Cirrus ATMs worldwide.

network has dial-up numbers in most of the world's countries. You have to sign up with an iPass provider, which then tells you how to set up your computer for your destination(s). For a list of iPass providers, go to www.ipass.com and click Reseller Locator and then Individual. One solid provider is **i2roam** (www.i2roam.com; ☎ **866-811-6209** or 920-235-0475).

Wherever you go, bring a **connection kit** of the right power and phone adapters, a spare phone cord, and a spare Ethernet network cable — or find out whether your hotel supplies them to guests.

Keeping Up with Airline Security Measures

With the federalization of airport security, security procedures at U.S. airports are more stable and consistent than ever. Generally, you're fine if you arrive at the airport **1 hour** before a domestic flight and **2 hours** before an international flight; if you show up late, tell an airline employee, and she'll probably whisk you to the front of the line.

Bring a **current, government-issued photo ID** such as a driver's license or passport. Keep your ID at the ready to show at check-in, the security checkpoint, and sometimes even the gate. (Children under 18 don't need government-issued photo IDs for domestic flights, but they do for international flights to most countries.)

In 2003, the TSA phased out **gate check-in** at all U.S. airports. And **e-tickets** have made paper tickets nearly obsolete. With an e-ticket, you can beat the ticket-counter lines by using airport **electronic kiosks** or even **online check-in** from your home computer. Online check-in involves logging on to your airline's Web site, plugging in your reservation number, and printing your boarding pass — and the airline may even offer you bonus miles to do so! If you're using a kiosk at the airport, bring the credit card you used to book the ticket or your frequent-flier card. Print your boarding pass from the kiosk and simply proceed to the security checkpoint with your pass and a photo ID. If you're checking bags or looking to snag an exit-row seat, you're able to do so using most airline kiosks. Even the smaller airlines are employing the kiosk system, but always call your airline to make sure that these alternatives are available. **Curbside check-in** is also a good way to avoid lines, although a few airlines still ban it; call before you go.

Security checkpoint lines are getting shorter, but some doozies remain. If you have trouble standing for long periods, tell an airline employee; the airline will provide a wheelchair. Speed up security by **not wearing metal objects** such as big belt buckles. If you have metallic body parts, a note from your doctor can prevent a long chat with the security screeners. Keep in mind that only **ticketed passengers** are allowed past security, except for folks escorting disabled passengers or children.

Federalization has stabilized **what you can carry on** and **what you can't.** The general rule is that sharp things are out, nail clippers are okay, and food and beverages must be passed through the X-ray machine — but that security screeners can't make you drink from your coffee cup. Bring food in your carry-on bag rather than checking it, because explosive-detection machines used on checked luggage have been known to mistake food (especially chocolate, for some reason) for bombs. Travelers in the United States are allowed one carry-on bag, plus a "personal item" such as a purse, briefcase, or laptop bag. Carry-on hoarders can stuff all sorts of things into a laptop bag; as long as it has a laptop in it, it's still considered a personal item. The Transportation Security Administration (TSA) has issued a list of restricted items; check its Web site (`www.tsa.gov/public/index.jsp`) for details.

Airport screeners may decide that your checked luggage needs to be searched by hand. You can now purchase luggage locks that allow screeners to open and re-lock a checked bag if hand-searching is necessary. Look

Frommers.com: The Complete Travel Resource

Frommers.com (www.frommers.com), voted Best Travel Site by *PC Magazine*, offers indispensable travel tips, reviews, monthly vacation giveaways, bookstore, and online-booking capabilities. (Of course, I'm a bit biased, considering that I write online updates about Boston for Frommers.com, too!) Among the special features are the popular **Destinations** section, where you can receive expert travel tips, hotel and dining recommendations, and advice on the sights to see for more than 3,500 destinations around the globe; the **Frommers.com Newsletter,** with the latest deals, travel trends, and money-saving secrets; the **Community** area, featuring **Message Boards,** where Frommer's readers post queries and share advice (sometimes, even the authors show up to answer questions); and the **Photo Center,** where you can post and share vacation tips. When your research is done, the **Online Reservations System** (www.frommers.com/book_a_trip) takes you to Frommer's preferred online partners for booking your vacation at affordable prices.

for Travel Sentry certified locks at luggage or travel shops and Brookstone stores (you can buy them online at www.brookstone.com). Luggage inspectors can open the TSA-approved locks with a special code or key. For more information on the locks, visit www.travelsentry.org. If you use something other than TSA-approved locks, your lock will be cut off your suitcase if a TSA agent needs to hand-search your luggage.

Part III
Settling Into Boston

The 5th Wave   By Rich Tennant

"The closest hotel room I could get you to Copley Square for that amount of money is in Cleveland."

In this part . . .

1 n this part, I help you get oriented in Boston with a look at
the airport, the neighborhoods, and the public-transit
system. After you know where you're going and how to get
there, I try to make sure that you get enough sleep and some
good food. I explain the city's lodging options and various
ways of booking a room so that you can choose a hotel that's
right for you. You also get the lowdown on one of the liveliest
restaurant markets in the country.

Chapter 8

Arriving and Getting Oriented

In This Chapter

▶ Getting in from the airport
▶ Figuring out new neighborhoods
▶ Finding information once you arrive
▶ Getting around Boston

*B*oston's streets appear to have minds of their own. They head off in random directions, they change names at the drop of a Red Sox cap, and an awful lot of them aren't wearing signs. How can you find your way around? Ask directions, for one thing. And remember: You can't get *that* lost.

Making Your Way to Your Hotel

This orientation to Boston begins at your arrival point. Whether you arrive by plane, train, or car, I tell you how to get to your next destination — your hotel.

If you arrive by plane

Logan International Airport suffers from insufficient capacity and ongoing construction. Good administration means that neither situation typically causes much trouble, but you should be ready for air and ground delays all the same.

 Logan is one of the most security-conscious airports in the country — both planes that hit the World Trade Center on September 11, 2001, originated in Boston. Expect long check-in lines and don't expect any sympathy if you decide to joke about having a bomb in your luggage. Airport security officers can, literally, make a federal case out of it.

Logan has five terminals, A through E. A brand-new Terminal A was under construction at press time and should open sometime in 2005. Good signage and small terminals make getting lost difficult, except in construction areas, where employees usually can point the way.

Gates are on the upper level, and baggage claim and ground transportation are on the first level. Terminal C has a shopping concourse and children's play space. Each terminal has an ATM, Internet kiosks, a fax machine, and an information booth (near baggage claim). The booth in Terminal C is a Visitor Service Center, where staffers can arrange hotel and restaurant reservations, theater and sports tickets, and tours.

The airport is in East Boston, 3 miles across the harbor from downtown. Signs in the terminals indicate the curbside stops for each mode of transportation (shuttle bus, taxi, and so on). Nearby tunnels connect "Eastie" to downtown. Sound simple? As I write this book, one entire lane of the tunnel that runs from East Boston to downtown is closed until further notice for post–Big Dig fine-tuning.

When traffic is heavy — rush hours, Sunday evening, any holiday period — or the weather is bad, public transportation is the fastest way to reach downtown. If you have another destination, crossing the harbor by boat or train and grabbing a cab can still be faster than driving.

The **Massachusetts Port Authority** (☎ 800-23-LOGAN; www.massport. com/logan) coordinates airport transportation. The phone line has information about getting to the city and suburbs. The line is open 24 hours a day, with live operators weekdays from 8 a.m. to 7 p.m.

Taking public transportation to your hotel

Free airport shuttle buses run in a loop from 5:30 a.m. to 1 a.m. daily. Number 11 runs terminal to terminal; numbers 22, 33, 55, and 66 connect to public transit.

The quickest way to downtown is by water; crossing the harbor takes just seven minutes and costs $10. The Number 66 bus serves the airport dock. Since the dedicated water shuttle ceased operation, one commuter ferry and two on-call taxi services have taken up the slack. The ferry company, **Harbor Express** (☎ 617-376-8417; www.harborexpress. com), serves Long Wharf, off Atlantic Avenue near the New England Aquarium. The **City Water Taxi** (☎ 617-422-0392; www.citywatertaxi. com) connects over a dozen stops on the harbor, including Long Wharf and the federal courthouse at Fan Pier. The **Rowes Wharf Water Taxi** (☎ 617-406-8584; www.roweswharfwatertaxi.com) serves Rowes Wharf, off Atlantic Avenue behind the Boston Harbor Hotel. Months and days of operation for water taxis are subject to change; at the moment, only the Rowes Wharf taxi operates year-round. You must call ahead from the dock for water-taxi service.

The subway is almost as fast and can be more convenient. Shuttle numbers 22 and 33 run to the Blue Line's Airport station. Before 7 a.m. and after 10 p.m., Number 55 covers both. At the station, buy a $1.25 token or visitor pass. The line can be long but moves quickly.

State (for the Orange Line) and Government Center (for the Green Line) are transfer points from the Blue Line. Transfers are free. Trips to Government Center take ten minutes. To reach Cambridge, switch to the Green Line at Government Center, go one stop, and transfer at Park Street to the Red Line.

Taking private transportation to your hotel

Taxis queue up at every terminal. The trip takes 10 to 45 minutes, depending on traffic and time of day. The fare to downtown or the Back Bay should be about $22 to $30.

Cab companies pass along government charges to customers. At press time, these charges included $6.50 in airport and tunnel fees. The meter starts at $1.75, which means you're out $8.25 before you even fasten your seatbelt (which you should always do). The surcharges seem to jump every year or so — the staff at the information desk inside the terminal can give you the total.

The Ted Williams Tunnel connects the airport to South Boston. On a map, this path looks like a pricey detour, but it's the fastest route to the Back Bay and Cambridge. When traffic is bad, the tunnel is the best way to parts of downtown, too.

Back Bay Coach (☎ **888-BACK-BAY,** 888-222-5229, or 617-746-9909; www. backbay-coach.com) operates vans from the airport to Boston proper and many suburbs. Prices start at $10 per person. Call or surf ahead for reservations and exact fares.

To arrange limousine service, you must call ahead — drivers can't cruise for fares. Ask whether your hotel recommends a company or try **Carey Limousine Boston** (☎ **800-336-4646** or 617-623-8700) or **Commonwealth Limousine Service** (☎ **800-558-LIMO** outside Massachusetts, or 617-787-5575).

The major car-rental companies operate shuttles. If you must pick up a car immediately, ask the staff to map a route with the latest traffic patterns and construction sites. Make sure that you obtain directions for returning, too, but don't worry if you go astray — the main airport road is a loop.

If you arrive by car

If you're staying downtown, call your hotel the day before you plan to arrive to ask for directions and the latest traffic patterns. For the Back

Bay hotels, take the Mass. Pike to the Copley exit. For Cambridge hotels, take the Mass. Pike to the Allston/Cambridge exit and follow Storrow Drive to the Harvard Square exit.

If you arrive by train

South Station is a train and commuter rail terminal, bus station, and subway stop at Atlantic Avenue and Summer Street. Cabs line up on Atlantic Avenue.

Back Bay Station is on Dartmouth Street between Huntington and Columbus avenues. This station is the next-to-last Amtrak stop and serves the Orange Line and commuter rail. Cabs line up on Dartmouth Street.

North Station is on Causeway Street in the same building as the TD Banknorth Garden (formerly called the FleetCenter). Amtrak trains from Portland, Maine, arrive at this station, which also serves the commuter rail. Also here are the North Station stops on the Green and Orange lines of the T.

Figuring Out the Neighborhoods

The following neighborhoods contain the city's main attractions. Most are small and walkable, with loose boundaries and (except in the Back Bay) confusing street patterns. Try to familiarize yourself with the city's layout by taking a look at the "Boston Neighborhoods" map in this chapter. Then start wandering.

Considering Boston's well-founded reputation as a city of neighborhoods, the question of location is surprisingly easy to answer. The central city is so tiny, and the neighborhoods so small, that the most popular parts of Boston break neatly into two main sections. Spread out the map in this section and find Boston Common. For your purposes, downtown is north and east of this area, and the Back Bay is west and south. Cambridge and slightly less central areas such as Brookline, which I describe as "in the vicinity," are the other major options.

The neighborhood descriptions in this section correspond to those in the rest of the book, including hotel listings (see Chapter 9). Here's a rundown of the high and low points of each area, including reasons you might want to stay there.

Downtown

I define *downtown* as the Waterfront, North End, Faneuil Hall Marketplace, Government Center, Beacon Hill, Downtown Crossing, the Financial District, and Charlestown. Here are descriptions of each:

✔ **The Waterfront:** Located along Commercial Street and Atlantic Avenue, the Waterfront faces the Inner Harbor. Here, you find the New England Aquarium and the wharves that handle tour boats and ferries.

✔ **North End:** The Freedom Trail runs through the North End, which lies east of I-93. No longer separated from the rest of downtown by an elevated highway (thanks to the Big Dig), the North End is easy to reach. The longtime immigrant enclave maintains a reputation as the city's Italian neighborhood (*never* called "Little Italy"), though, through commerce rather than population — newcomers outnumber Italian-American residents. The Paul Revere House and the Old North Church are here.

✔ **Faneuil Hall Marketplace:** Where the North End meets the Waterfront, cross Atlantic Avenue to find Faneuil Hall Marketplace (also called Quincy Market, the name of the central building). This tourist magnet abounds with shops, restaurants, and bars.

✔ **Government Center:** This cluster of ugly city, state, and federal office buildings is across Congress Street from Faneuil Hall.

✔ **Beacon Hill:** Rest your eyes with a stroll around Beacon Hill, the architectural treasure between Government Center, Boston Common, and the river. If you conjure a mental picture of Boston, it probably includes Beacon Hill's Federal-style homes and red-brick sidewalks.

✔ **Downtown Crossing:** This shopping and business district is across Boston Common from Beacon Hill, adjacent to Chinatown. Most of the Freedom Trail is in this area.

✔ **Financial District:** The Financial District lies east of Downtown Crossing and west of the Waterfront. The area's giant office towers loom over the landmark Custom House and the colorful clock tower.

✔ **Charlestown:** Home to the last two stops on the Freedom Trail, Charlestown lies across the Inner Harbor from the North End.

Advantages to staying downtown include

✔ Easy access to many popular attractions and business destinations.

✔ Convenient public transportation.

✔ The lively atmosphere, especially during the day and around Faneuil Hall Marketplace.

Drawbacks include

✔ The distance from the Back Bay and Cambridge. Factor in the time and cost of getting back and forth.

Boston Neighborhoods

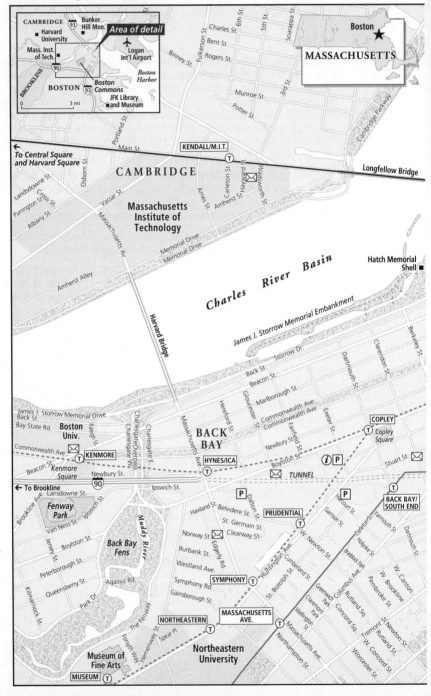

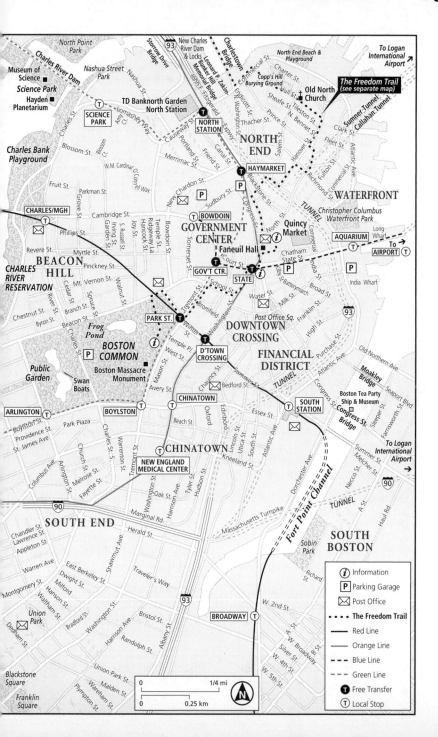

✔ The less-than-lively atmosphere at night, particularly in areas that aren't near Faneuil Hall.

✔ The Big Dig. Gone but hardly forgotten, the Big Dig has given way to a sizable construction area as buildings and parks spring up to replace the ugly elevated Expressway that came down in 2004.

The Back Bay

For my purposes, "the Back Bay" covers hotels in the centrally located neighborhoods outside downtown, including the Back Bay proper. The other neighborhoods I lump in are (working east to west) Chinatown, the Theater District, the South End, and Kenmore Square. This area is a safe one, with the exception of the parks and a small part of the Theater District, where you should be cautious at night. Incidentally, Boston has no "midtown" or "uptown."

The neighborhood Bostonians know as the Back Bay starts at the Public Garden and the river and extends, approximately, to Massachusetts Avenue (or Mass. Ave.) — though some say Kenmore Square — and Huntington Avenue. One of New England's prime shopping destinations, particularly on Newbury and Boylston streets, this area has a posh air but also abounds with budget-conscious students. Trinity Church, the Boston Public Library, the Hancock Tower, Copley Place, the Prudential Center, and the Hynes Convention Center also are in this area.

Remember "two if by sea"? Incredibly, the Back Bay was the "sea." (In the Longfellow poem, Paul Revere watched the steeple of the Old North Church for a signal telling him whether to alert the Minutemen to watch for British troops approaching over land — one lantern — or by water.) In 1775, when British troops set out for Lexington and Concord, present-day Charles Street (between Boston Common and the Public Garden) was the shoreline. This neighborhood was a marshy body of water until 1835, when development began pushing west from downtown. The Back Bay attained its current contours by 1882.

Chinatown is a congested area where you find an enormous assortment of Asian restaurants and shops. This neighborhood lies south of Downtown Crossing and west of I-93. The **Theater District,** a small area around the intersection of Tremont and Stuart streets, holds the largest professional Boston theaters. Widespread sprucing-up notwithstanding, it's not a great area to wander around late at night.

Victorian brownstones distinguish the **South End,** which lies south of the Back Bay proper. The landmark district underwent extensive gentrification beginning in the 1970s. The South End has a large gay community and some of the best restaurants in the city.

At Beacon Street and Commonwealth Avenue, **Kenmore Square** spreads out below an enormous white-and-red Citgo sign, one of the city skyline's most famous features. Fenway Park lies 3 blocks away.

Here are some of the perks of staying in this area:

- ✔ The abundance of hotel rooms and the range of prices.
- ✔ Decent public transportation. The creaky Green Line is no prize, but the Orange Line is reasonably close. The bus to Cambridge runs along Massachusetts Avenue, better known as Mass. Ave.
- ✔ Everything you need to shop till you drop.

Here are some of the drawbacks:

- ✔ The need to commute to the downtown attractions.
- ✔ The inconvenience of getting to Cambridge (the bus can be slow).
- ✔ Everything you need to shop till you drop.

Cambridge

The Red Line of the subway cuts through the city known (but only to the tourist office) as Boston's "Left Bank." **Harvard Square** — where you find upscale shops, historic landmarks, and, oh yeah, a big university — is the most popular destination. The city's other world-famous institution is Massachusetts Institute of Technology (MIT), in and around Kendall Square. **Central Square,** a rapidly gentrifying area that abounds with ethnic restaurants and clubs, lies between the two. **Porter Square,** where you find quirky shops like those that once characterized Harvard Square, is one stop past Harvard.

Harvard Square offers a good mix of transit access, sightseeing, and shopping. This isn't a typical bohemian college town but a generally expensive area that centers on the Harvard T stop. The train station sits beneath the intersection of John F. Kennedy Street, Brattle Street, and Mass. Ave. Moving away from the train station, things grow quieter; the peaceful Charles River is nearby. Downtown Boston is a 15- to 20-minute subway ride away, and the Back Bay is approximately 30 minutes away on the Mass. Ave. bus.

Pluses of staying in Cambridge include

- ✔ The energetic, student-oriented atmosphere.
- ✔ Good public transportation.
- ✔ Excellent shopping and sightseeing options.

Drawbacks include

- ✔ The price of lodging.
- ✔ Crowds of students, shoppers, and sightseers.
- ✔ The commute to Boston attractions.

In the vicinity

If busier, more centrally located areas aren't for you, consider staying a little farther out. The large town of Brookline begins just past Kenmore Square. Prices are generally lower, life is less rushed, and most of the popular attractions are less convenient. Without a car, you'll essentially be a commuter (it's 15 to 30 minutes to downtown), usually on the ancient Green Line. (One hotel in this area, the Doubletree Guest Suites, isn't on a public-transit line.) Check a map — only spoiled Bostonians would seriously think of this area as out of the way, but Brookline can feel inconvenient, especially at night and when you're spending a lot of time in Cambridge.

Good reasons to stay in the vicinity include

- ✔ Generally lower prices.
- ✔ A more residential, less frantic atmosphere.
- ✔ Easy access to the Back Bay and Fenway Park.

Drawbacks include

- ✔ The distance from most of the top attractions.
- ✔ The necessity of relying on the Green Line.
- ✔ The inconvenience of getting to Cambridge, unless you rent a car.

Finding Information After You Arrive

Make your first stop the concierge desk or front desk of your hotel. Many hotels have racks full of brochures and other information.

The **Boston National Historic Park Visitor Center,** 15 State St. (☎ 617-242-5642; www.nps.gov/bost), across the street from the Old State House and the State Street T station, is another good resource. The center is open 9 a.m. to 5 p.m. daily except January 1, Thanksgiving Day, and December 25. You can find other information centers at the following locations:

- ✔ The Freedom Trail begins at the **Boston Common Information Center,** 146 Tremont St., on the Common (open 8:30 a.m. to 5 p.m. Monday through Saturday, 9 a.m. to 5 p.m. Sunday).
- ✔ The **Prudential Information Center,** on the main level of the Prudential Center, is open 9 a.m. to 8 p.m. Monday through Saturday, 11 a.m. to 6 p.m. Sunday.
- ✔ The **Greater Boston Convention & Visitors Bureau** (☎ 888-SEE-BOSTON or 617-536-4100) operates both.

✔ At **Faneuil Hall Marketplace,** between Quincy Market and the South Market Building, a small booth is staffed in spring, summer, and fall 10 a.m. to 6 p.m. Monday through Saturday, noon to 6 p.m. Sunday.

✔ In the heart of **Harvard Square,** in Cambridge, a kiosk (☎ **617-497-1630**) near the T entrance at Mass. Ave. and John F. Kennedy Street is open 9 a.m. to 5 p.m. Monday through Saturday, 1 to 5 p.m. Sunday.

Getting Around Boston

Some people consider an African safari an adventure. Others say whitewater rafting in the Rockies is a daring experience. Still others, perhaps overdramatic but no less serious, call driving in downtown Boston the scariest thing they do.

Congestion, construction, unmarked streets — Boston has it all. My goal is to scare you into walking everywhere. (How am I doing so far?) But sometimes you can't — destinations are too far, or you're too late or tired. This chapter contains pointers for getting from place to place by foot and, because you may need to take another means of transportation, by subway, bus, boat, taxi, and car — all without steering you into adventure territory.

On foot

You packed your good walking shoes, right? The compact size and baffling layout of the central city make it a pedestrian's pleasure. Everywhere you turn, something picturesque catches your attention, and not being in a speeding vehicle means that you can check out sights for as long as you like.

Here are some trekking tips to keep in mind:

✔ The only steep areas are Beacon Hill and Copp's Hill, in the North End behind the Old North Church.

✔ All over town, brick and cobblestone sidewalks ripple gently, just waiting to trip you and mess up the heels of your good shoes. Step carefully.

✔ The Back Bay is the only neighborhood laid out in a grid. The cross streets begin at the Public Garden with Arlington Street and proceed alphabetically (until Mass. Ave. jumps in after Hereford).

✔ At many downtown intersections, the timing mechanism that controls the traffic light allows pedestrians just 7 seconds to walk (sprint, really) across. Ignore the locals, and stay put until the light changes.

✔ Always look both ways before crossing — careless drivers, bikers, and skaters blithely ignore one-way signs.

By public transit

The full name of the T is the **Massachusetts Bay Transportation Authority,** or MBTA (☎ **800-392-6100** outside Massachusetts, or 617-222-3200; www.mbta.com). The system operates subway lines, surface transit, trains to the suburbs, and Inner Harbor ferries. Call the main information number for round-the-clock automated information and assistance from live operators 6:30 a.m. to 8 p.m. Monday through Friday, 7:30 a.m. to 6 p.m. weekends. Visit the Web site to view maps and schedules and to buy passes online (subject to a service charge).

You'll hear subway stops called "T stops," "T stations," and just "T," as in "I'll meet you near the Government Center T." If someone gives you directions that include a subway ride, be sure you know which exit to use (most stations have more than one).

On subways and buses, kids under age 5 accompanied by an adult ride free, and kids ages 5 to 11 get a 50 percent discount. The commuter rail family fare (equal to twice the adult fare) also applies to one adult traveling with as many as four kids under 18.

The **MBTA's visitor pass** (☎ **877-927-7277** or 617-222-5218; www.mbta.com) covers the subway, local buses, commuter rail zones 1A and 1B, and Inner Harbor ferries. The price is $7.50, $18, and $35, respectively, for one day, three consecutive days, or seven consecutive days — that's a lot of traveling. Estimate the number of trips you're likely to take, and figure out whether tokens are cheaper. Passes are available over the phone or on the Web (a shipping charge applies), and in person at the Airport, Government Center, and Harvard T stops, South Station, Back Bay Station, and North Station. The Boston Common, Prudential Center, and Faneuil Hall Marketplace information centers and some hotels sell passes, too.

The subway and trolley systems

Red, Orange, and Blue Line subways and **Green Line trolleys,** which cover most areas you're likely to visit, are the quickest nonpedestrian way to get around. The T is generally dependable and safe, with a couple of caveats: The Green Line is sometimes unreliable, and you should take the precautions (such as watching out for pickpockets) that you would on any big-city transit system.

The local fare is $1.25, and transfers are free. You need a token or visitor pass to enter subway stations; if you're boarding a Green Line trolley above ground (as you leave the Museum of Fine Arts, for instance), pay at the front of the first car. Tokens are for sale at booths in every station and at machines at many stops. Buy an extra token for your return trip.

In 2005, the T begins the two-year process of phasing in an automated fare-collection system. Check the Web site or peruse displays at the station for tips on buying and using the "Charlie Card."

Boston Transit

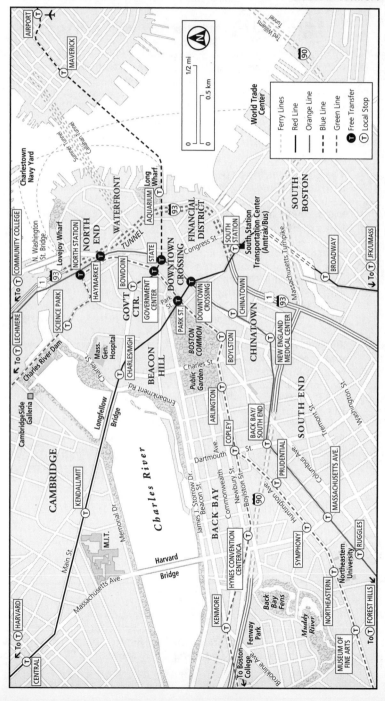

Late-night weekend bus service

The MBTA operates Night Owl bus service Friday and Saturday until 2:30 a.m. (In Boston, that's late.) Several popular routes continue after regular closing time, and additional bus routes parallel the subway lines above ground. The fare is $1.50 in coins. For information and to make sure that the service is still operating — budget considerations periodically threaten it — check with the T (☎ 800-392-6100 outside Massachusetts or 617-222-3200; www.mbta.com).

The T operates from about 5:15 a.m. until at least 12:30 a.m., but no later than 1 a.m., Sunday through Thursday. For information about bus service until 2:30 a.m. on Friday and Saturday, see the "Late-night weekend bus service" sidebar. On New Year's Eve, service is free after 8 p.m. and shuts down at 2 a.m.

The antiquated Green Line, which serves many areas of interest to visitors, is the most complicated. When riding the Green Line, make sure that you know which branch (B, C, D, or E) you need. Each starts and ends at a different station; all four serve every stop between Government Center and Copley. If you take the wrong westbound train, you may need to backtrack and switch lines; ask the conductor to leave you at the right stop.

System maps, available on request from most token-booth clerks, display the subway lines (in the designated colors) and the commuter rail (in purple). The maps in this book also show subway stops. To get route and fare information before your visit, check the Web site.

Renovations are under way to make the Green Line wheelchair-accessible. Updated system maps show accessible stations on other lines, but not all stations display up-to-date maps. (Check the date, if you can find one.) To find out more, call the main information number (☎ 800-392-6100 outside Massachusetts or 617-222-3200), or contact the **Office for Transportation Access** (☎ 617-222-5976 or 617-222-5854 [TTY]; www.mbta.com). Also see Chapter 6 for more information on getting around with disabilities.

Check a map that shows T stations superimposed on a street map before automatically hopping on the subway to get around downtown. South Station to Aquarium, for example, is a three-train trip but an easy ten-minute walk.

The bus system

T buses and trackless trolleys (electricity-powered buses) serve Boston, Cambridge, and other nearby suburbs. The local fare is 90¢. Fare boxes accept tokens but don't make change. Express-bus fares start at $2.20. Buses with wheelchair lifts cover many routes; call ☎ 800-LIFT-BUS for information.

Here are local routes you may find useful:

> ✔ **Number 1,** along Mass. Ave. from Dudley Station in Roxbury through the Back Bay and Cambridge to Harvard Square. During off-peak hours, this route is usually faster than the subway.
>
> ✔ **Numbers 92 and 93,** between Haymarket and Charlestown. Freedom Trail walkers may be too tired for anything except the bus, but the ferry (see the following section, "The ferry system") is more fun.
>
> ✔ **Number 77,** along Mass. Ave. north of Harvard Square to Porter Square, North Cambridge, and Arlington.

The ferry system

Water-transportation options change periodically, according to demand and other factors. Two popular routes cross the Inner Harbor. The first connects Long Wharf, on State Street near Atlantic Avenue, with the Charlestown Navy Yard; this is a good break from the Freedom Trail. The second runs from Lovejoy Wharf, near North Station and the TD Banknorth Garden (formerly known as the FleetCenter), off Causeway Street, to the World Trade Center, on Northern Avenue. The fare is $1.50; you can use your visitor pass on both routes. Call ☎ **617-227-4321** or visit www.mbta.com for more information.

By taxi

Taxis are pricey and can be tough to hail. At busy times such as rush hours and early morning (when bars and clubs are closing), you shouldn't have much trouble — the drivers go where the business is. Otherwise, find a cab stand or call a dispatcher.

Cabs line up near hotels and at designated stands. You'll find cabs queuing at Faneuil Hall Marketplace (on North Street and State Street), South Station, Back Bay Station, and on two stretches of Mass. Ave. in Harvard Square — near Brattle Street and near Dunster Street.

 If the hour is late and you're desperate, look in front of a 24-hour business such as Dunkin' Donuts.

To call ahead for a cab, try the **Independent Taxi Operators Association** (☎ 617-426-8700), **Boston Cab** (☎ 617-536-5010), **Town Taxi** (☎ 617-536-5000), or **Metro Cab** (☎ 617-242-8000. In Cambridge, call **Ambassador Brattle** (☎ 617-492-1100) or **Yellow Cab** (☎ 617-547-3000). Boston Cab can dispatch a wheelchair-accessible vehicle; advance notice of an hour or so is recommended.

The *drop rate* (the rate for the first ¼ mile) is $1.75. After that, the fare adds up at 30¢ per ⅛ mile. *Wait time* (the time the driver waits for you) is extra, and the passenger pays all tolls, as well as $6.50 in fees (which include the tunnel toll) on trips leaving Logan Airport. The law forbids charging a flat rate within Boston. If you need a cab to a suburb, the driver will charge you the price on the Police Department's list of flat rates (and show the list to you if you ask).

Cabs licensed in Boston are painted mostly white. Strenuously enforced regulations call for acceptable maintenance of vehicle and driver.

 Always, always ask for a receipt, which should state the name of the company. And always fasten your seatbelt. If you lose something or want to report a problem, call the **Police Department** (☎ 617-536-8294).

By car

Driving is not a good idea, but sometimes you have no choice. Start by buckling up, even if you never do at home. No kidding.

When you reach Boston or Cambridge, park the car and then walk or use public transportation. Do all you can to stay off the roads during rush hours and weekend afternoons. Make sure that you have a map and, if possible, a cool-headed navigator. Most streets are one-way, and your out-of-state plates make you more of a moving target than an object of sympathy.

 Be alert — no snacks or phone calls. (Those bumper stickers that say HANG UP AND DRIVE come from Cambridge.) Watch out for cars that change lanes or leave the curb without signaling. Look both ways at intersections, even on one-way streets. Also keep an eye out for wrong-way bicyclists.

You may turn right at a red light after stopping when traffic permits, unless a sign says otherwise. Seatbelts are mandatory for adults and children, children under 12 must ride in the back seat, and infants and children under 5 must be strapped into car seats.

Under state law, pedestrians in the crosswalk have the right of way, and vehicles already in a *rotary* (traffic circle or roundabout) have the right of way. Most suburbs post and enforce the crosswalk law; signs state the right-of-way law in every rotary, with little discernible effect.

Had enough? It's time for the round-the-clock headache of parking. Meters regulate most street spaces, where nonresidents may park for no more than two hours (sometimes much less), and only between 8 a.m. and 6 p.m. The penalty is at least a $25 ticket, and parking-enforcement officers work long hours every day except Sunday. Most Boston and Cambridge meters take quarters only. In busy areas, that quarter buys you only 15 minutes — start hoarding now.

 To see whether your "missing" car is in the city tow lot, call ☎ 617-635-3900. Make sure that you have your wallet, because the fines and fees can easily top $100. Then take a taxi to 200 Frontage Rd., South Boston, or ride the Red Line to Andrew and flag a cab.

A parking lot or garage is easier but still no prize. The daily rate downtown, reputedly tops in the country, can be as much as $45; hourly rates (as much as $18) are outrageous, too. Weekends and evenings usually are cheaper. Many establishments discount weekday rates if you enter and exit before certain times. Some restaurants have deals with nearby garages; ask when you make your reservation.

Prices are slightly lower than public lots at the city-operated garage under Boston Common (☎ 617-954-2096). The entrance is on Charles Street between Boylston and Beacon streets. The Prudential Center garage (☎ 617-267-1002) offers a discount if you make a purchase at the Shops at Prudential Center and have your ticket validated. Enter from Boylston Street, Huntington Avenue, Exeter Street, or Dalton Street (at the Sheraton Boston Hotel). The Copley Place garage (☎ 617-375-4488) extends a discount to shoppers, too. The garage is off Huntington Avenue near Exeter Street. Many Faneuil Hall Marketplace shops and restaurants validate parking at the 75 State St. Garage (☎ 617-742-7275).

Other good-sized garages are at Government Center off Congress Street (☎ 617-227-0385), Sudbury Street off Congress Street (☎ 617-973-6954), the New England Aquarium (☎ 617-723-1731), Zero Post Office Square (☎ 617-423-1430), and near the Hynes Convention Center on Dalton Street (☎ 617-247-8006).

Harvard Square is even less hospitable to motorists than downtown Boston. The congested area has a few costly garages and parking lots, and many tow-away zones disguised as tempting university spaces. Be patient, and have a backup plan and budget in case you don't find a metered space (maximum stay, 30 minutes to 2 hours).

 Parking is free on North Harvard Street and Western Avenue, on the Boston side of the Charles River near Harvard Business School. Harvard Square is some distance away (use the bridge at Memorial Drive and John F. Kennedy Street), but it's not a bad walk, and the price is right.

Chapter 9

Checking In at Boston's Best Hotels

- -

In This Chapter

▶ Booking the right room at the right price

▶ Checking out the best hotels in the city

▶ Considering alternatives in case your top picks are full

- -

Some people book a room by calling a hotel, asking for a reservation, and agreeing to the price the clerk quotes. These people also pay sticker price for their cars. That person won't be you, though, because this chapter shows you how to find the best hotel rates.

The Boston area offers travelers many options. Although prices tend to be high, amenities and service are good, and just about every property is in excellent shape. The options that suit your wishes and wallet are out there. This chapter helps you find the landing pad that's right for you.

Getting to Know Your Options

The Boston area offers a full range of accommodations, but not in the same abundant numbers as other destinations. At busy times, you may find yourself on the business end of a tough lesson about the law of supply and demand. Here's a look at what to expect.

The Goldilocks factor: What hotel feels right?

Giant chain hotels tend to be well appointed, centrally located, and somewhat boring. But don't reflexively dismiss the chains — the benefits of size include a larger supply of rooms and a wider range of prices. The listings in this chapter include some agreeable choices, and the suburbs boast plenty of reliable options as well. (See the Appendix for a list of the major chains' toll-free numbers and Web sites.)

Independent hotels tend to compare favorably with the megachains, with less of a cookie-cutter feel and more personal service. These smaller establishments can't compete with chains in every area, though, so know which features are most important to you. (If you *must* swim a mile every morning, even remarkable service won't make an on-premises pool materialize.)

This chapter also lists some motels, inns, and guesthouses. These smaller properties tend to be less conveniently located, less luxurious, and less expensive than larger establishments. If all you want is a comfy place to rest your head, this choice can be just right.

The only truly underrepresented category of lodging in the immediate Boston area is moderately priced family-oriented chains; they gravitate toward suburbs with less expensive real estate. You won't even find the strip of cheap motels that's under the flight path of most other airports (in Boston, that's in the harbor).

See Chapter 8 for descriptions of the neighborhoods in these listings. Indexes of the properties by neighborhood and price appear at the end of this chapter.

The ABCs of B&Bs

A room at a bed-and-breakfast can be a viable alternative to a hotel room, especially if money is tight (though some properties are just as opulent and pricey as plush hotels). Your best bet is to use an agency that specializes in B&Bs. Here are some reliable choices:

- ✔ **Bed and Breakfast Agency of Boston** (☎ 800-248-9262 or 617-720-3540; ☎ 0800-89-5128 from the U.K.; www.boston-bnbagency.com)

- ✔ **Bed & Breakfast Reservations North Shore/Greater Boston/Cape Cod** (☎ 800-832-2632 outside Massachusetts, 617-964-1606, or 978-281-9505; www.bbreserve.com)

- ✔ **Bed and Breakfast Associates Bay Colony** (☎ 888-486-6018 or 617-720-0522; ☎ 0800-731-3553 from the U.K.; www.bnbboston.com).

Finding the Best Room at the Best Rate

The **rack rate** is the maximum rate a hotel charges for a room. It's the rate you get if you walk in off the street and ask for a room for the night. You sometimes see these rates printed on the fire/emergency exit diagrams posted on the back of your door.

Hotels are happy to charge you the rack rate, but you can almost always do better. Perhaps the best way to avoid paying the rack rate is surprisingly simple: Just ask for a cheaper or discounted rate. You may be pleasantly surprised.

Smart shopping

In all but the smallest accommodations, the rate you pay for a room depends on many factors — chief among them, how you make your reservation. A travel agent may be able to negotiate a better price with certain hotels than you can get by yourself. (That's because the hotel often gives the agent a discount in exchange for steering his or her business toward that hotel.) A package tour may include a cheaper room than you can book on your own. See Chapter 5 for information about package tours.

Reserving a room through the hotel's toll-free number may also result in a lower rate than calling the hotel directly. On the other hand, the central reservations number may not know about discount rates at specific locations. For example, local franchises may offer a special group rate for a wedding or family reunion, but they may neglect to tell the central booking line. Your best bet is to call both the local number and the toll-free number, and see which one gives you a better deal.

Room rates (even rack rates) change with the season, as occupancy rises and falls. See the calendar of events in Chapter 3 for information about citywide events that may drive up prices. And note that even within a given season, room prices are subject to change without notice, so the rates quoted in this book may be different from the rate you receive when you make your reservation.

The most expensive time to book a room in Boston is fall foliage season, followed closely by summer, which begins with college-graduation season in May. New England weather makes January through March the only truly slow season, especially if conditions are cold and snowy. (A mild winter can be surprisingly busy.) The hospitality industry aims its midwinter "Boston Overnight! Just for the Fun of It" campaign at suburban weekenders, but travelers from farther away can take advantage of discounts, too. Check the Greater Boston Convention & Visitors Bureau Web site (www.bostonusa.com) for information.

Be sure to mention membership in AAA, AARP, frequent-flier programs, or any other corporate rewards programs you can think of — or your honorary membership in Uncle Joe's Elks lodge, for that matter — when you call to book. You never know when the affiliation may be worth a few dollars off your room rate, especially if you try this approach: Ask for the price and then mention the status that qualifies you for a discount.

Boston and Cambridge levy a 12.45 percent room tax. When you make your reservation, be sure to ask whether the quoted rate includes taxes.

Package rates generally do. Brookline doesn't charge the 2.75 percent of the tax that goes for a new convention center, but don't choose a hotel based on that — the savings are negligible and probably don't offset the extra transportation costs.

Surfing the Web for hotel deals

Travelers generally shop online for hotels in one of two ways: through the hotel's or chain's own Web site or through an independent booking agency (or a fare-service agency like Priceline). Internet hotel agencies have multiplied in mind-boggling numbers of late, competing for the business of millions of consumers surfing for accommodations around the world. This competitiveness can be a boon to consumers who have the patience and time to shop and compare the online sites for good deals — but shop they must, because prices can vary considerably from site to site. And keep in mind that hotels at the top of a site's listing may be there for no other reason than that they paid money to get the placement.

Turn to Chapter 5 for a description of package tours, which can save you big bucks even at the busiest times. You'll want to compare aggressively — the prices for virtually identical packages can vary from operator to operator (or hotel chain, airline, or other packager) by hundreds of dollars.

Of the "big three" sites, **Expedia** offers a long list of special deals and "virtual tours" or photos of available rooms so that you can see what you're paying for (a feature that helps counter the claims that the best rooms are often held back from bargain booking Web sites). **Travelocity** posts unvarnished customer reviews and ranks its properties according to the AAA rating system. Also reliable are **Hotels.com** and **Quikbook.com**. An excellent free program, **TravelAxe** (www.travelaxe.net), can help you search multiple hotel sites at once, even ones you may never have heard of — and conveniently lists the total price of the room, including the taxes and service charges. Another booking site, **Travelweb** (www.travelweb.com), is partly owned by the hotels it represents (including the Hilton, Hyatt, and Starwood chains) and is therefore plugged directly into the hotels' reservations systems — unlike independent online agencies, which have to fax or e-mail the hotel their reservation requests, a good portion of which get misplaced in the shuffle. However, if you choose to book a room through any of these Web sites, consider calling the hotel to confirm your reservation. More than once, travelers who booked rooms online have arrived at the hotel only to be told that they have no reservation.

To be fair, many of the major sites are undergoing improvements in service and ease of use, and Expedia will soon be able to plug directly into the reservations systems of many hotel chains. In the meantime, it's a good idea to **get a confirmation number** and **print a copy** of any online booking transaction.

In the opaque Web site category, **Priceline** and **Hotwire** are even better for hotels than for airfares; with both, you pick the neighborhood and quality level of your hotel before offering up your money. Priceline's hotel product even covers Europe and Asia, though it's much better at getting five-star lodging for three-star prices than at finding anything at the bottom of the scale. On the down side, many hotels stick Priceline guests in their least desirable rooms. Be sure to go to the BiddingforTravel Web site (www.biddingfortravel.com) before bidding on a hotel room on Priceline; it features a fairly up-to-date list of hotels that Priceline uses in major cities. For both Priceline and Hotwire, you pay up front, and the fee is nonrefundable.

Note: Some hotels do not provide loyalty program credits or points or other frequent-stay amenities when you book a room through opaque online services.

The Web sites of the **Greater Boston Convention & Visitors Bureau** (www.bostonusa.com) and the **Massachusetts Office of Travel and Tourism** (www.mass-vacation.com) offer searchable databases and secure online reservations. But don't book through either site until you do enough shopping to know that you're getting a competitive price.

Reserving the best room

After you make your reservation, asking one or two pointed questions can go a long way toward making sure that you get the best room in the house.

- ✔ **Always ask for a corner room.** They're usually larger, quieter, and have more windows and light than standard rooms, and they don't always cost more.

- ✔ **Request a room on a high floor.** Upper floors often hold club- or concierge-level rooms; if you don't want to pay for extra features, ask for the highest standard floor.

- ✔ **Ask whether the hotel is renovating.** If it is, request a room away from the construction work.

- ✔ **Inquire, too, about the location of the restaurants, bars, and discos in the hotel.** All are sources of annoying noise.

If you need a room where you can smoke, be sure to request one when you reserve. If you can't bear the lingering smell of smoke, tell everyone who handles your reservation that you need a smoke-free room or floor. Smoking is illegal in just about every public place in Massachusetts, which means that smokers often retreat to their hotel rooms to light up.

Finally, if you aren't happy with your room when you arrive, return to the front desk right away. If another room is available, the staff should be able to accommodate you, within reason.

Arriving without a Reservation

You didn't make arrangements in advance? If it's foliage or graduation season, hang your head. Let it droop all the way down to the floor of the airport terminal, because that may be where you spend the night. Or stand up straight and try one or more of the following strategies:

- ✔ **Call the Hotel Hot Line (☎ 800-777-6001).** A service of the Greater Boston Convention & Visitors Bureau, it can help with reservations even during the busiest times. People, not recordings, handle calls until 8 p.m. weekdays, 4 p.m. weekends.

- ✔ **If you're at the airport, head to the Visitor Service Center in Terminal C.** Staff members with concierge training can lend a hand.

- ✔ **Phone hotels from the airport or train station.** Ask *everyone* you reach who doesn't have a room available to suggest another property.

- ✔ If you drive from the west, **stop at the Massachusetts Turnpike's Natick rest area,** and try the **reservation service** at the visitor information center.

- ✔ **Call a B&B referral agency and ask whether any properties have cancellations.** (See "The ABCs of B&Bs," earlier in this chapter, for details.)

- ✔ **Rent a car and head for the suburbs.** Although not being downtown is inconvenient, many lodgings lie within commuting distance. If you have a favorite chain, call the toll-free reservations number for information about Boston-area locations and tips for reaching the properties from the airport.

Boston's Best Hotels

Although I complain about Boston's limited lodging choices, keeping this list to a manageable size is difficult. The hotels in this chapter are my favorites, the ones I suggest when friends call to ask for recommendations. Although I list my top picks, these lodgings are by no means the only acceptable choices. Near the end of this chapter, I also include options that can be helpful if you find your favorites booked. I also include indexes that list hotels by neighborhood and price.

Each listing in this chapter includes a $ symbol that indicates the price range of the hotel's rack rates. Prices are for a standard double room for one night, not including taxes.

Table 9-1	Key to Hotel Dollar Signs	
Dollar Sign(s)	**Price Range**	**What to Expect**
$	Less than $125	Basic accommodations — essentially, comfortable spots to crash after a day of sightseeing. Don't expect lots of extras, such as room service or a health club. Some lodgings may have shared bathrooms. These establishments tend to be small and not all that convenient, but they're clean, safe, and well kept.
$$	$125–$225	These establishments generally don't offer room service, but the room rate may include continental breakfast. These places are more centrally located, and some offer access to pools or fitness rooms. (Ask whether an extra charge applies.) In a less competitive market, most would be inns and family-run motels. In Boston, many are part of moderately priced chains.
$$$	$226–$325	Now things get confusing. In this range, the repeat business customer is the gold standard, and these hotels cater to that market. Rooms tend to be decent-sized and well-appointed, with abundant business amenities. Each hotel offers a range of perks and facilities, but every property defines *essential* differently. For example, some don't provide minibars or swimming pools. Ask about features that matter to you.
$$$$	$326 and up	Here, you find tycoons, international travelers whose currency is strong against the dollar, and honeymooners. Expect everything you'd get at a $$$ hotel, delivered to your huge room by an employee who calls you by your name and can't do enough for you, plus such extras as courtesy cars and personal office equipment.

In Boston's tight market, a hotel that doesn't offer every imaginable perk can still get away with charging breathtaking prices. The feature that's most likely to be missing in the $$$ and $$$$ price ranges is an on-premises health club with a pool. They don't all offer 24-hour room service, and many of these costly properties either don't have wireless Internet access or charge extra (as much as $11 a day) for it. If a certain amenity is crucial to you, be sure to ask about it.

This icon indicates hotels that are especially family-friendly. Most of these accommodations have swimming pools, some offer family pack-ages (usually on weekends), and all supply their all-ages clientele with plenty of patience and good advice. Bear in mind that every hotel in town accommodates children's needs; a listing without this symbol doesn't mean "kid-unfriendly." Most properties allow kids to stay free with their parents, but the cutoff age varies. Always ask when you're booking.

Every hotel in this chapter is clean and safe. As I said, I'd send a friend to any one of these properties — but I wouldn't send every friend to every one. These hotels all offer TVs and air-conditioning; almost all rooms have phones and private bathrooms. And all are within walking distance of the T.

Anthony's Town House
$ In the Vicinity (Brookline)

The Green Line runs past Anthony's Town House, embodying the pluses and minuses of this well-kept, old-fashioned brownstone. The trolley is handy, but the street is busy and can be noisy. The price is great, but you don't get your own bathroom or phone. Each floor holds one bathroom and three good-sized rooms with high ceilings, TVs, and air-conditioning; units that face the street are larger but less quiet. The agreeable residen-tial neighborhood lies about a mile from Boston's Kenmore Square and 15 to 20 minutes from downtown.

See map p. 104. 1085 Beacon St. (near Hawes Street). ☎ *617-566-3972. Fax: 617-232-1085.* www.anthonystownhouse.com. *12 units. T: Hawes Street (Green Line C). Parking: Free. Rack rates: $68–$98. Ask about winter discounts. No credit cards.*

Boston Harbor Hotel
$$$–$$$$ Downtown (Waterfront)

This luxurious edifice overlooking the harbor and the Big Dig is the finest hotel downtown. The hotel offers every perk or appointment you may want or need — from easy access to the airport (the water taxi docks out back) to top-of-the-line business and fitness facilities, including a 60-foot lap pool. Guest rooms are spacious and plush, with traditional mahogany furniture and great views. The hotel has a wine-oriented restaurant and a lobby cafe, Intrigue, that offers seasonal outdoor dining.

See map p. 104. 70 Rowes Wharf (entrance on Atlantic Avenue at High Street, off Northern Avenue). ☎ *800-752-7077 or 617-439-7000. Fax: 617-330-9450.* www.bhh.com. *230 units. T: South Station (Red Line); walk 2½ blocks north. Or Aquarium (Blue Line); walk 2½ blocks south. Parking: Valet $34 per day, self $30 per day; weekend discounts. Rack rates: $295–$595 and up. Ask about weekend packages. AE, DC, DISC, MC, V.*

Chandler Inn Hotel
$$ Back Bay (South End)

You can't beat this location at this price. The rooms and bathrooms are comfortable but small — a real-estate ad might say "cozy," which is accurate in this case. The contemporary-style rooms contain queen-size or double beds or two twin beds, hair dryers, and climate control. Rates include continental breakfast, and the staff is accommodating and friendly. This property is the largest gay-owned hotel in town, and the inn is popular with bargain hunters of all persuasions. Fritz, the bar off the lobby, is a lively neighborhood hangout.

See map p. 104. 26 Chandler St. (at Berkeley Street). ☎ *800-842-3450 or 617-482-3450. Fax: 617-542-3428.* www.chandlerinn.com. *56 units. T: Back Bay (Orange Line); cross Columbus Avenue, turn left onto Chandler Street, and walk 2 blocks. Parking: Nearby public garages and lots ($20 and up). Rack rates: $139–$169. Ask about winter discounts. AE, DC, DISC, MC, V.*

The Charles Hotel
$$$–$$$$ Cambridge

The most prestigious short-term address in Cambridge, the Charles represents an appealing contrast of sleek, contemporary style and luxurious appointments. In a great location off Harvard Square, the hotel offers large rooms with Shaker-style furnishings and indulgent extras such as a Bose Wave radio in every room and a TV in each bathroom. Room rates include access to the pool and facilities at the adjacent WellBridge Health and Fitness Center. The pool sets aside time each afternoon for children under 16. The hotel complex also includes a posh day spa; two excellent restaurants; and the Regattabar, one of the best jazz clubs in the area (see Chapter 16).

See map p. 106. 1 Bennett St. (off Eliot Street, near Mount Auburn Street). ☎ *800-882-1818 outside Massachusetts, or 617-864-1200. Fax: 617-864-5715.* www.charleshotel.com. *293 units. T: Harvard (Red Line); follow Brattle Street 2 blocks, bear left onto Eliot Street, and go 2 blocks. Parking: Valet or self $28. Rack rates: $229–$599 and up. Ask about weekend, spa, and other packages. AE, DC, MC, V.*

Charlesmark Hotel
$–$$$ Back Bay (Copley Square)

A great location and reasonable prices make the Charlesmark a prime example of a lodging style I call "budget boutique." The hotel has a welcoming staff and a high comfort level without a lot of the extras that can drive up the bill at larger lodgings. Although the rooms in the renovated 1886 building are small, careful design and sleek custom furnishings — with pillow-top mattresses and tons of built-ins — make them feel bigger. Rates include breakfast, local phone calls, use of the computer and printer in the second-floor lobby, and light refreshments (such as bottled water and fruit) available at all hours.

See map p. 104. 655 Boylston St. (between Dartmouth and Exeter streets). ☎ *617-247-1212. Fax: 617-247-1224.* www.thecharlesmark.com. *33 units. T: Copley (Green Line); follow Boylston Street ½ block, past Old South Church. Parking: Self $32 in nearby garage. Rack rates: $99–$249. AE, DC, DISC, MC, V.*

The Fairmont Copley Plaza Hotel
$$$–$$$$ Back Bay

The Copley Plaza is classic Boston: a stately, old-fashioned luxury hotel that evokes an era of grand accommodations, excellent service, and ornate architecture. The Edwardian elegance of the 1912 building belies the up-to-date features of the large guest rooms, which contain every perk you can think of (and then some), including VCRs and oversized towels. The hotel, which completed a $29 million overhaul in 2004, has two restaurants, two bars, a business center, and a fitness center (but no pool).

See map p. 104. 138 St. James Ave. (at Dartmouth Street, facing Copley Square). ☎ *800-527-4727 or 617-267-5300. Fax: 617-247-6681.* www.fairmont.com. *379 units. T: Copley (Green Line); cross Copley Square. Or Back Bay (Orange Line); walk 1½ blocks on Dartmouth Street with Copley Place on your left. Parking: Valet $32. Rack rates: $249 and up. Ask about weekend packages. AE, DC, MC, V.*

 Four Seasons Hotel
$$$$ Back Bay

This hotel is the best in New England. You may stay here at the same time as a movie star, CEO, rock legend, or head of state, and (here's the key) the superior staff makes you feel as important as the celebrities. The accommodations, amenities, business center, health club, and restaurants are all top of the line. The bill is, too. The second-floor restaurant, Aujourd'hui, is one of Boston's best, and the Bristol, off the lobby, serves a celebrated afternoon tea (as well as lunch and dinner).

See map p. 104. 200 Boylston St. (at Arlington Street). ☎ *800-332-3442 or 617-338-4400. Fax: 617-423-0154.* www.fourseasons.com. *288 units. T: Arlington (Green Line); walk 1 block on Boylston Street, opposite the Public Garden. Parking: Valet $36. Rack rates: $425–$815 and up. Ask about weekend packages. AE, DC, DISC, MC, V.*

Boston Hotels

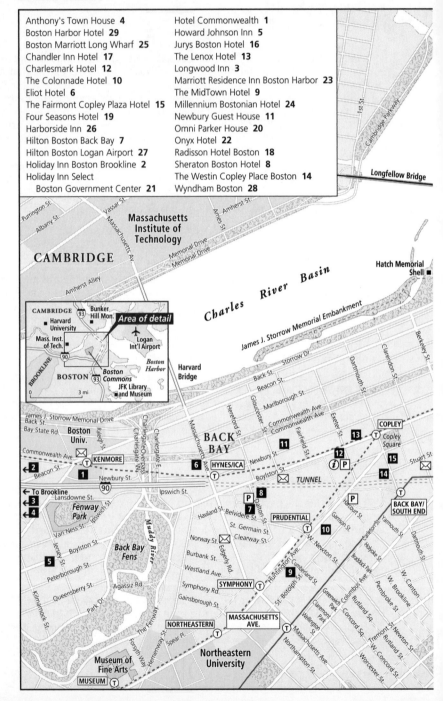

Anthony's Town House **4**
Boston Harbor Hotel **29**
Boston Marriott Long Wharf **25**
Chandler Inn Hotel **17**
Charlesmark Hotel **12**
The Colonnade Hotel **10**
Eliot Hotel **6**
The Fairmont Copley Plaza Hotel **15**
Four Seasons Hotel **19**
Harborside Inn **26**
Hilton Boston Back Bay **7**
Hilton Boston Logan Airport **27**
Holiday Inn Boston Brookline **2**
Holiday Inn Select
    Boston Government Center **21**

Hotel Commonwealth **1**
Howard Johnson Inn **5**
Jurys Boston Hotel **16**
The Lenox Hotel **13**
Longwood Inn **3**
Marriott Residence Inn Boston Harbor **23**
The MidTown Hotel **9**
Millennium Bostonian Hotel **24**
Newbury Guest House **11**
Omni Parker House **20**
Onyx Hotel **22**
Radisson Hotel Boston **18**
Sheraton Boston Hotel **8**
The Westin Copley Place Boston **14**
Wyndham Boston **28**

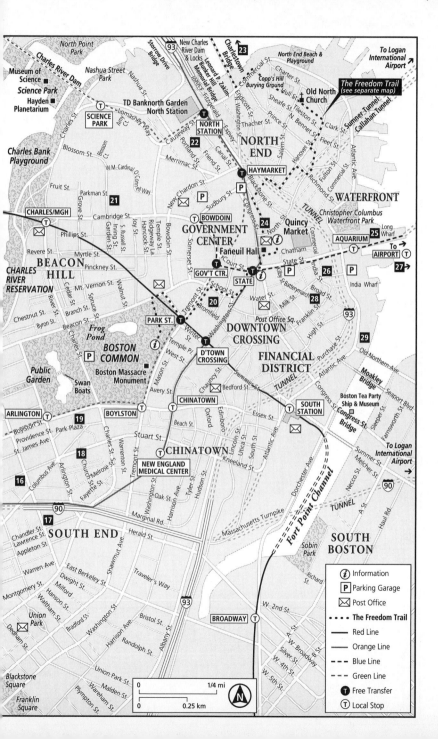

Cambridge Hotels

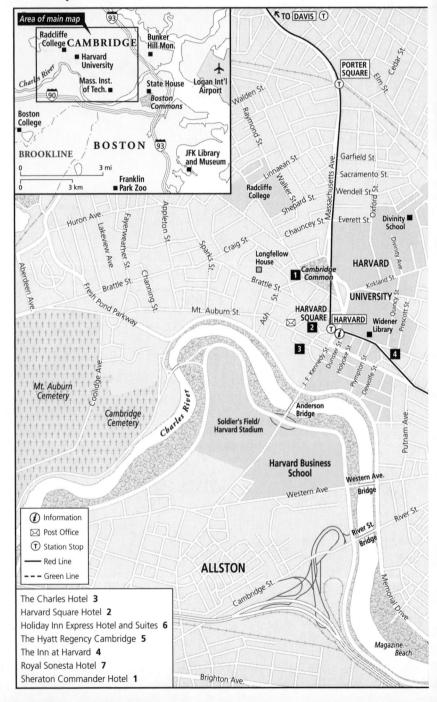

Area of main map

93

Radcliffe
College **CAMBRIDGE**

Bunker
Hill Mon.

■ Harvard
University

Charles River

90

Mass. Inst.
of Tech. ■

State House

Logan Int'l
Airport

Boston
Commons

Boston
College

BROOKLINE

BOSTON

93

JFK Library
and Museum

0 ——— 3 mi

0 ——— 3 km

Franklin
■ Park Zoo

TO DAVIS Ⓣ

PORTER
SQUARE
Ⓣ

Cedar St.

Elm St.

Walden St.

Raymond St.

Garfield St.

Sacramento St.

Linnaean St.

Walker St.

Shepard St.

Massachusetts Ave.

Wendell St.

Oxford St.

Everett St.

**Divinity
School** ■

Radcliffe
College

Chauncey St.

Divinity Ave.

Huron Ave.

Fayerweather St.

Appleton St.

Craig St.

Longfellow
House

HARVARD

Sparks St.

1 **Cambridge
Common**

Kirkland St.

UNIVERSITY

Quincy St.

Lakeview Ave.

Brattle St.

Channing St.

Brattle St.

St.

Prescott St.

Aberdeen Ave.

Fresh Pond Parkway

Mt. Auburn St.

Ash

**HARVARD
SQUARE**

⊠

2

HARVARD

Ⓣ ⓘ

Widener
Library

3

4

**Mt. Auburn
Cemetery**

Coolidge Ave.

**Cambridge
Cemetery**

Charles River

Soldier's Field/
Harvard Stadium

J. F. Kennedy St.

Dunster St.

Holyoke St.

Plympton St.

DeWolfe St.

Anderson
Bridge

Putnam Ave.

**Harvard Business
School**

Western Ave.

Bridge

Western Ave.

River St.

River St.
Bridge

ⓘ Information

⊠ Post Office

Ⓣ Station Stop

—— Red Line

--- Green Line

ALLSTON

Cambridge St.

Memorial Drive

*Magazine
Beach*

Brighton Ave.

The Charles Hotel **3**
Harvard Square Hotel **2**
Holiday Inn Express Hotel and Suites **6**
The Hyatt Regency Cambridge **5**
The Inn at Harvard **4**
Royal Sonesta Hotel **7**
Sheraton Commander Hotel **1**

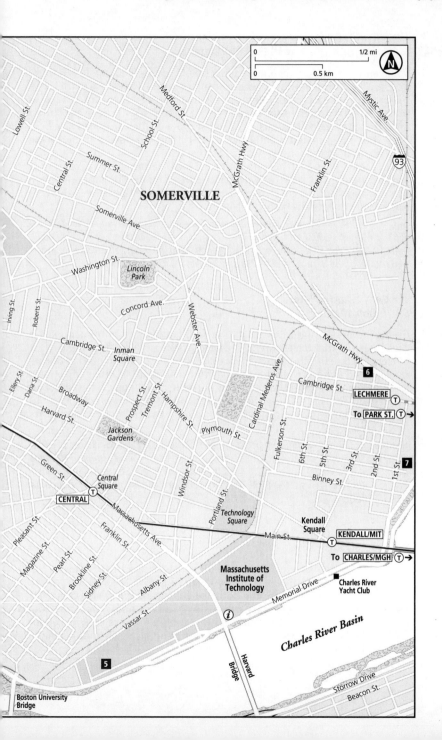

0   1/2 mi

0   0.5 km

Mystic Ave.

93

Medford St.

School St.

Summer St.

Central St.

Lowell St.

SOMERVILLE

McGrath Hwy.

Franklin St.

Somerville Ave.

Washington St.

Lincoln
Park

Concord Ave.

Irving St.

Roberts St.

Webster Ave.

McGrath Hwy.

Cambridge St.

Inman
Square

Cardinal Mederos Ave.

Cambridge St.

6

LECHMERE (T)

To **PARK ST.** (T) →

Ellery St.

Dana St.

Broadway

Harvard St.

Prospect St.

Tremont St.

Hampshire St.

Plymouth St.

Fulkerson St.

6th St.

5th St.

3rd St.

2nd St.

1st St.

7

Jackson
Gardens

Windsor St.

Binney St.

Green St.

Central
Square

CENTRAL (T)

Massachusetts Ave.

Portland St.

Technology
Square

Kendall
Square

KENDALL/MIT (T)

Pleasant St.

Franklin St.

Main St.

To **CHARLES/MGH** (T) →

Magazine St.

Pearl St.

Brookline St.

Sidney St.

Albany St.

**Massachusetts
Institute of
Technology**

Memorial Drive

■ **Charles River
Yacht Club**

Vassar St.

(i)

Charles River Basin

5

Harvard
Bridge

Storrow Drive

**Boston University
Bridge**

Beacon St.

Harborside Inn
$–$$ Downtown (Faneuil Hall Marketplace)

Value and location are the main selling points of this renovated 1858 warehouse. The Harborside Inn's features can't compete with those of the city's business-oriented pleasure domes — but neither can the price. The location, across the street from Faneuil Hall Marketplace, is an easy stroll from most downtown destinations. Each guest room contains a queen-size bed, hardwood floors, and Oriental rugs. The ceilings are lower in the rooms on the top floor, but the views are better; units that face the atrium are quieter than those that face the street. All local phone calls and voice mail are free, and room service is available until 10 p.m. The inn, under the same ownership as the Newbury Guest House (see listing later in this section), has a restaurant in the lobby.

See map p. 104. 185 State St. (between India Street and Atlantic Avenue). ☎ **800-437-7668** *or 617-723-7500. Fax: 617-670-2010.* www.harborsideinnboston.com. *54 units. T: Aquarium (Blue Line) or State (Orange Line). Parking: $20 off-site (reservation required). Rack rates: $120–$210 and up. AE, DC, DISC, MC, V.*

Harvard Square Hotel
$$ Cambridge

Comfortable and unpretentious, this well-maintained hotel occupies a great location that makes up for the lack of bells and whistles. In the heart of Harvard Square, the hotel is a good place to retreat after a day of running around (whether sightseeing, visiting a student, or doing business). Rooms aren't large, but they have comfortable furnishings, dataports, and voice mail. This hotel is not the place for coddled business travelers, but the low-key atmosphere makes it a good alternative to pricier competitors in the area.

See map p. 106. 110 Mount Auburn St. (at Eliot Street). ☎ **800-458-5886** *or 617-864-5200. Fax: 617-864-2409.* www.harvardsquarehotel.com. *73 units. T: Harvard (Red Line); follow Brattle Street 2 blocks, bear left onto Eliot Street, and go 1 block. Parking: $25. Rack rates: $129–$209. Ask about corporate, AAA, and AARP discounts. AE, DC, DISC, MC, V.*

Hilton Boston Back Bay
$$–$$$ Back Bay

A business hotel with terrific weekend packages, the Hilton offers a full range of chain amenities in a handy location across the street from the Prudential Center complex. The hotel is near the Back Bay action but not right at the center — which isn't necessarily a bad thing. The large, contemporary rooms are quite plush; units on higher floors offer excellent views. The hotel has a swimming pool and 24-hour health club, a restaurant, and a bar.

See map p. 104. 40 Dalton St. (off Boylston Street at Belvidere Street, opposite the Hynes Convention Center). ☎ ***800-874-0663,*** *800-HILTONS, or 617-236-1100. Fax: 617-867-6104. Internet:* www.hiltonbostonbackbay.com. *385 units. T: Hynes/ICA (Green Line B, C, or D); turn left onto Mass. Ave. and left onto Boylston Street, take the first right onto Dalton Street, and walk 2 blocks. Parking: Valet $26; self $17. Rack rates: $179–$295 and up. Ask about packages and AAA discounts. AE, DC, DISC, MC, V.*

Hilton Boston Logan Airport
$$–$$$ **In the Vicinity (Logan Airport)**

An airport hotel that courts a business clientele may not seem a logical choice for sightseers, but the airport Hilton is a sensible option for both types of travelers. It offers proximity to downtown, good access to public transit, and fine weekend packages. The newly constructed building (unusual in a market where renovations dominate) opened in 1999. The spacious, quiet guest rooms contain plentiful business perks. A health club with a lap pool is off the lobby; the hotel has a restaurant, a pub that serves lunch and dinner, and a coffee bar. The 24-hour shuttle bus serves all airport destinations, including car-rental offices and the ferry dock.

See map p. 104. 85 Terminal Rd., Logan International Airport (between Terminal A [a short walk] and Terminal E [a long walk]). ☎ ***800-HILTONS*** *or 617-568-6700. Fax: 617-568-6800. Internet:* www.hiltonbostonloganairport.com. *599 units. T: Airport (Blue Line); take shuttle bus. Parking: Valet $25; self $22. Rack rates: $169–$259 and up. Ask about weekend and other packages. AE, DC, DISC, MC, V.*

Holiday Inn Boston Brookline
$$–$$$ **In the Vicinity (Brookline)**

A pleasant residential setting and good access to downtown make this Holiday Inn a reasonable alternative to hotels that are more convenient but more expensive. The large, well-maintained guest rooms offer no surprises (pleasant or unpleasant) — basically, this is an agreeable chain hotel. The inn has a small indoor pool, whirlpool, and exercise room. The Green Line stops out front; downtown Boston is about 15 minutes away. Coolidge Corner, a nongeneric shopping destination, is a ten-minute walk away.

See map p. 104. 1200 Beacon St. (at St. Paul Street). ☎ ***800-HOLIDAY*** *or 617-277-1200. Fax: 617-734-6991.* www.holiday-inn.com. *225 units. T: St. Paul (Green Line C). Parking: Self $15. Rack rates: $139–$239 and up. Ask about AAA and AARP discounts. AE, DC, DISC, MC, V.*

Hotel Commonwealth
$$$–$$$$ **Back Bay (Kenmore Square)**

The Commonwealth's traditional facade belies its ultra-plush interior and great business features. Although it looks older, it opened in 2003, just a stone's throw from Boston University (a partner in the hotel) and Fenway

Park. It's more centrally located than the nearby all-suite Eliot Hotel, which is more romantic and generally more expensive. Units that overlook Commonwealth Avenue each have a heavy curtain that guests can pull across the center of the room, separating the bed from the "parlor." Smaller Fenway rooms face the Mass. Turnpike and the ballpark. The hotel has a seafood restaurant and an exercise room.

See map p. 104. 500 Commonwealth Ave. (at Kenmore Street). ☎ *866-784-4000 or 617-933-5000. Fax: 617-266-6888.* www.hotelcommonwealth.com. *150 units. T: Kenmore (Green Line B, C, D); left at turnstiles. Parking: Valet $32. Rack rates: $249–$369 and up. Ask about packages and AAA discount. AE, DC, DISC, MC, V.*

Howard Johnson Inn
$–$$ Back Bay

This motel sits on a busy street in a commercial–residential neighborhood a long fly ball from Fenway Park. T access is somewhat inconvenient, but the Back Bay colleges, the Museum of Fine Arts, and the Isabella Stewart Gardner Museum are nearby. Rooms are basic, decent-sized Howard Johnson's accommodations. The outdoor pool is open 9 a.m. to 7 p.m. in the summer.

See map p. 104. 1271 Boylston St. (at Jersey Street). ☎ *800-654-2000 or 617-267-8300. Fax: 617-267-2763.* www.hojo.com. *94 units. T: Fenway (Green Line D); follow Brookline Avenue ½ block, turn left (walking around the ballpark), follow Yawkey Way 2 blocks, and turn left. Or Kenmore (Green Line B, C, or D); go left at turnstiles, right at stairs, at first intersection (½ block up), turn left onto Brookline Avenue, cross bridge, pass ballpark, turn left onto Yawkey Way, and take second right onto Boylston Street (whew!). Total walking time: 10–15 minutes. Parking: $10. Rack rates: $125–$195. Ask about family packages and senior and AAA discounts. AE, DC, DISC, MC, V.*

Longwood Inn
$ In the Vicinity (Brookline)

This Victorian guesthouse in a quiet residential area projects a homey feel to go with affordable rates. Seventeen units include private bathrooms, and all rooms have air-conditioning and phones. Guests may use the fully equipped kitchen and common dining room, coin laundry, and TV lounge. An apartment, which sleeps four, has a private kitchen and balcony. The tennis courts, running track, and playground at the school next door are open to the public.

See map p. 104. 123 Longwood Ave. ☎ *617-566-8615. Fax: 617-738-1070.* www.longwood-inn.com. *22 units. T: Longwood (Green Line D); turn left, walk ½ block to Longwood Avenue, turn right, and walk 2½ blocks. Or Coolidge Corner (Green Line C); walk 1 block south on Harvard Street (past Trader Joe's), turn left, and go 2 blocks on Longwood Avenue. Parking: Free. Rack rates: $89–$109 ($89–$119 for 1-bedroom apartment). Ask about winter discounts. No credit cards.*

Marriott Residence Inn Boston Harbor
$$ Downtown (Charlestown)

Location, amenities, and value make the Residence Inn a real find, despite its somewhat generic vibe. On the Freedom Trail adjacent to the Charlestown Navy Yard, the hotel consists of studio and one- and two-bedroom suites with full kitchens; you may not even need to use your kitchen, because room rates include breakfast. Views are excellent all the way from the lobby, where you find the lap pool and fitness room, up to the eighth (top) floor. Patrons tend to be business travelers on weeknights and families on weekends. The location is even better from April to October, when the water taxi ($10 one-way) connects the dock off the lobby with more than a dozen stops around the harbor.

See map p. 104. 33–44 Charles River Ave. (off Chelsea Street, near Rutherford Avenue). ☎ *866-296-2297, 800-331-3131 (Marriott), or 617-242-9000. Fax: 617/242-5554.* www.marriottresidenceinnbostonharbor.com. *168 units. T: Blue Line to Aquarium and ferry from Long Wharf to Navy Yard; exit through main gate and walk 1 block. Or Green or Orange Line to North Station; follow Causeway Street 2 blocks south (with the TD Banknorth Garden on your left) to North Washington Street, turn left, and cross bridge; hotel is on the right. Total walking time: 10 minutes. Or Orange Line to Community College; cross Rutherford Avenue using pedestrian bridge, turn right, and go 2 long blocks (past City Square park). Total walking time: 10 minutes. Parking: Valet $25. Rack rates: $179–$209. Ask about packages and AAA, government, long-term, and winter discounts. AE, DC, DISC, MC, V.*

The MidTown Hotel
$–$$ Back Bay

This two-story establishment near the Prudential Center is the most centrally located Boston hotel with free parking. The rooms are large and attractively outfitted in contemporary style, but bathrooms are small. Business travelers can request units with two-line phones and high-speed Internet access; families can ask for adjoining rooms with connecting doors. The hotel's popularity with tour groups and convention-goers is a potential drawback, as is the busy street — rooms on the Huntington Avenue side of the low-rise building can be a little noisy. The heated outdoor pool is open from Memorial Day through Labor Day.

See map p. 104. 220 Huntington Ave. (at Cumberland Street, near Mass. Ave.). ☎ *800-343-1177 or 617-262-1000. Fax: 617-262-8739.* www.midtownhotel.com. *159 units. T: Symphony (Green Line E); from the corner diagonally across from Symphony Hall, walk 1 block on Huntington Avenue. Or Mass. Ave. (Orange Line); turn left, walk 2 blocks, turn right, and go 1 block on Huntington Avenue. Parking: Free (one car per room). Rack rates: $89–$219. Ask about AAA, AARP, and government-employee discounts. AE, DC, DISC, MC, V.*

Newbury Guest House
$$ Back Bay

Considering its location, the Newbury Guest House is a bargain. In a pair of renovated 19th-century town houses, it has a comfortable atmosphere and helpful staff. Rooms are modest in size but thoughtfully appointed and mercifully quiet. Rates include a buffet breakfast served in the ground-level dining room, which adjoins a brick patio. This B&B, which has the same owners as the Harborside Inn (see listing earlier in this section), operates near capacity all year; reserve early.

See map p. 104. 261 Newbury St. (between Fairfield and Gloucester streets). ☎ *617-437-7666. Fax: 617-262-4243.* www.newburyguesthouse.com. *32 units. T: Copley (Green Line); follow Dartmouth Street 1 block away from Copley Square (past Old South Church), turn left on Newbury Street, and go 2½ blocks. Or Hynes/ICA (Green Line B, C, or D); exit onto Newbury Street and walk away from Mass. Ave. for 2½ blocks. Parking: Self $15 (reservation required). Rack rates: $140–$195. Minimum 2 nights on weekends. Ask about winter discounts. AE, DC, DISC, MC, V.*

Onyx Hotel
$$–$$$ Downtown (North Station)

A drab side street near North Station is the unlikely location of this contemporary boutique hotel, part of the chic Kimpton group. The medium-sized rooms, decorated in rich jewel tones, feel bigger because they have high ceilings. Units on higher floors of the ten-story building have intriguing city views. The rapidly improving neighborhood sits within walking distance of downtown and Beacon Hill. The Onyx has a lobby lounge and a basement exercise room.

See map p. 104. 155 Portland St. (off Causeway Street). ☎ *866-660-6699, 800-KIMPTON, or 617-557-9955. Fax: 617-557-0005.* www.onyxhotel.com. *112 units. T: North Station (Green or Orange Line); with the TD Banknorth Garden on your right, follow Causeway Street to Portland Street, turn left, and go ½ block. Parking: Valet $28. Rack rates: $209–$329 double. Ask about packages and AARP and AAA discounts. AE, DC, DISC, MC, V.*

Radisson Hotel Boston
$$–$$$$ Back Bay (Theater District)

The central location, business features, and relatively reasonable rates make this Radisson popular with business and leisure travelers. The well-maintained guest rooms are among the largest in the city; each opens onto a private balcony, with terrific views from the higher floors. The hotel has an indoor pool and exercise room. The property also has a restaurant; cafe; and the Stuart Street Playhouse, a professional theater that usually presents one-person and cabaret-style shows.

See map p. 104. 200 Stuart St. (at Charles Street South). ☎ *800-333-3333 or 617-482-1800. Fax: 617-451-2750.* www.radisson.com. *356 units. T: Boylston (Green Line); follow Tremont Street away from Boston Common 1 block, turn right onto Stuart*

Street, and go 2 blocks. Or New England Medical Center (Orange Line); turn left, walk ½ block, turn left, and go 3 blocks. Parking: Valet $21; self $19. Rack rates: $160–$359. Ask about weekend and theater packages. AE, DC, DISC, MC, V.

Sheraton Boston Hotel
$$–$$$$ Back Bay

Although I'm usually not big on huge hotels, this Sheraton is an exception (the Westin, a little later in this chapter, is another). Direct access to the Prudential Center complex appeals to travelers of all stripes. The Sheraton courts three major markets with scads of meeting space and features for convention-goers, well-outfitted rooms for business travelers, and a gigantic indoor/outdoor pool with a retractable dome that's a magnet for vacationing families. Rooms are fairly large, with pillow-top beds; bathrooms are medium-sized but (unless you have a magazine named after you) better appointed than your bathroom at home. Units on upper floors afford excellent views. The hotel has a large, well-equipped health club, restaurant, and lounge.

See map p. 104. 39 Dalton St. (at Belvidere Street, between Huntington Avenue and Boylston Street). ☎ 800-325-3535 or 617-236-2000. Fax: 617-236-1702. www. sheraton.com. 1,181 units. T: Prudential (Green Line E); facing tower, bear left onto Belvidere Street and walk 1 block. Or Hynes/ICA (Green Line B, C, or D); turn left onto Mass. Ave. and left onto Boylston Street, take first right onto Dalton Street, and walk 2 blocks. Parking: Valet $35; self $33. Rack rates: $129–$409 and up. Ask about weekend packages and student, faculty, and senior discounts. AE, DC, DISC, MC, V.

Sheraton Commander Hotel
$$–$$$$ Cambridge

The Sheraton Commander's low-key atmosphere appeals to guests who find the Charles too trendy (and too pricey). The hotel's well-kept guest rooms are moderate in size and traditional in decor. A restaurant, cafe, and small fitness center are on the premises. Harvard Yard is four blocks away.

See map p. 106. 16 Garden St. (at Waterhouse Street, opposite Cambridge Common). ☎ 800-325-3535 or 617-547-4800. Fax: 617-868-8322. www.sheratoncommander. com. 175 units. T: Harvard (Red Line); with Harvard Yard on your right, follow Mass. Ave. north 1 or 2 blocks to Garden Street, turn left, and walk 4 blocks. Parking: Valet $18. Rack rates: $129–$385 and up. Ask about weekend packages and AAA and AARP discounts. AE, DC, DISC, MC, V.

The Westin Copley Place Boston
$$$–$$$$ Back Bay

A giant chain hotel that doesn't feel generic is a real find, and this is one (the Sheraton Boston, mentioned earlier in this chapter, is another). In a great location adjoining the Copley Place–Prudential Center complex, the hotel has the full range of business amenities, plus an excellent health club

Getting out of town: The suburban motel question

After you read the hotel listings in this chapter, you'll have an idea of what you can expect to pay for a stay at specific Boston properties. When your budget won't allow it, the notion of a moderately priced suburban chain hotel tends to arise. After all, staying outside the city is an excellent option in many other places. Whether it works for you depends on your answers to the following questions:

✔ **What season is it?** If you plan to visit Boston during the foliage and graduation seasons, just finding a place to stay somewhere in the state of Massachusetts can feel like a triumph.

✔ **Do you mind commuting?** You'll likely drive or take the commuter rail (or both) to downtown Boston. Before you reserve your room, nail down the specifics of the journey, including prices (for train tickets and parking at the station), whether the hotel operates a shuttle to the station, and how late and how often the train runs. If it sounds like a hassle, try another place.

✔ **How long will you be in the Boston area?** A few extra days of vacation may mean that you don't mind spending some time commuting. In addition, not being stuck downtown can make day-tripping easier.

✔ **Are you behind the wheel?** If you must drive, you may welcome the combination of a chain hotel's free parking (if offered) and driving yourself into the city.

✔ **Are the kids with you?** Their expectations may be entirely different from yours. (A swimming pool, vending machines, and a game room were usually enough to satisfy me and my siblings.) Talk to your kids before booking an expensive hotel with business features youngsters don't care about and easy access to activities that have little appeal to kids.

✔ **How deep are your pockets?** An out-of-the-way location doesn't necessarily mean a deal. Account for hidden costs before you book a room. For example, if you need to drive to Boston or Cambridge, parking fees can easily add $25 a day to your travel expenses. If the "bargain" room rate saves $30 a day, that's no deal.

If you opt for a suburban motel, check with your travel agent, pick one from a guidebook (AAA is my favorite for this sort of thing), or call your favorite chain and ask for a room in the Boston area. (You can find contact information for hotels in the Appendix.) Be sure you understand the definition of *Boston area* before you hang up the phone — Rhode Island and New Hampshire aren't in that area, but you'd never know that to judge from some motels' names.

with a pool. Guest rooms are large and well appointed, and the views (rooms are all above the seventh floor) are amazing. Two first-class restaurants, the Palm and Turner Fisheries, face the street at ground level; there's a lounge off the second-floor lobby.

See map p. 104. 10 Huntington Ave. (at Dartmouth Street, accessible through Copley Place). ☎ *800-WESTIN-1 or 617-262-9600. Fax: 617-424-7483.* www.westin.com. *800 units. T: Copley (Green Line); walk 1 block on Dartmouth Street past the Boston Public Library. Or Back Bay (Orange Line); walk 1½ blocks on Dartmouth Street past Copley Place. Parking: Valet $36. Rack rates: $239–$599 and up. Ask about weekend packages. AE, DC, DISC, MC, V.*

Wyndham Boston
$$–$$$$ Downtown (Financial District)

Three blocks from Faneuil Hall Marketplace and two blocks from the harbor, the Wyndham offers business and leisure travelers a handy location and excellent accommodations. The large, quiet guest rooms abound with amenities, including high-speed Internet access and high ceilings that make them feel even larger. The only potential minuses are the lack of a swimming pool and the (long by spoiled-Bostonian standards) walk to the T. The hotel has a restaurant off the lobby and a 24-hour fitness center.

See map p. 104. 89 Broad St. (at Franklin Street). ☎ *800-WYNDHAM or 617-556-0006. Fax: 617-556-0053.* www.wyndham.com. *362 units. T: State (Blue or Orange Line); follow State Street downhill 2 blocks, turn right, and go 3½ blocks on Broad Street. Parking: Valet $32. Rack rates: $129–$399 and up. Ask about weekend, holiday, and other packages. AE, DC, DISC, MC, V.*

Runner-Up Hotels

Here are some suggestions if your top choices are booked:

Boston Marriott Long Wharf
$$$–$$$$ Downtown   The great location, within shouting distance of the New England Aquarium and the Financial District, makes up for the generic atmosphere. *See map p. 104. 296 State St., at Atlantic Avenue.* ☎ *800-228-9290 or 617-227-0800. www.marriottlongwharf.com.*

The Colonnade Hotel
$$$$ Back Bay   The Colonnade is sleek and elegant, with large guest rooms and a seasonal rooftop pool that add to the Euro-chic atmosphere. *See map p. 104. 120 Huntington Ave., at West Newton Street (opposite the Prudential Center).* ☎ *800-962-3030 or 617-424-7000. www.colonnadehotel.com.*

Eliot Hotel
$$$$ Back Bay   A luxurious, romantic all-suite hotel, with superb business amenities; the residential feel and handy location add to the Eliot's considerable appeal. *See map p. 104. 370 Commonwealth Ave., at Mass. Ave.* ☎ *800-44-ELIOT or 617-267-1607. www.eliothotel.com.*

Holiday Inn Express Hotel and Suites

$$ Cambridge (East Cambridge)   This hotel is not exactly peaceful or plush, but the convenient location and reasonable prices make it popular with business and leisure travelers. *See map p. 104. 250 Msgr. O'Brien Hwy. (3 blocks from the Green Line Lechmere stop).* ☎ *888-887-7690 or 617-577-7600. www.holiday-inn.com.*

Holiday Inn Select Boston Government Center

$$ Downtown (Beacon Hill)   The Holiday Inn lies within easy walking distance of many downtown and Back Bay addresses and the Red Line to Cambridge. The decent-sized rooms include good business features, and many enjoy picture-window views. *See map p. 104. 5 Blossom St. (at Cambridge Street).* ☎ *800-HOLIDAY or 617-742-7630. www.holiday-inn.com.*

The Hyatt Regency Cambridge

$$$ Cambridge (Central Cambridge)   Business travelers enjoy tons of perks and proximity to MIT and some high-tech neighbors; fantastic weekend packages help vacationers overlook the scarcity of convenient public transit. *See map p. 106. 575 Memorial Dr. (near the BU Bridge).* ☎ *800-233-1234 or 617-492-1234. www.hyatt.com.*

The Inn at Harvard

$$$ Cambridge (Harvard Square)   The inn is elegant and traditional, with good business features and easy access to the university, right across the street. *See map p. 106. 1201 Massachusetts Ave. (at Quincy Street).* ☎ *800-458-5886 or 617-491-2222. www.theinnatharvard.com.*

Jurys Boston Hotel

$$$–$$$$ Back Bay   Plush accommodations, good-sized bathrooms, and terrific business amenities make it easy to forget that this thoroughly renovated building used to be police headquarters. *See map p. 104. 350 Stuart St. (at Berkeley Street).* ☎ *866-JD-HOTELS or 617-266-7200. www.jurysdoyle.com.*

The Lenox Hotel

$$$$ Back Bay   This is a boutique hotel in everything but size, with outstanding business amenities in the posh, high-ceilinged guest rooms, a dozen of which have working fireplaces. *See map p. 104. 710 Boylston St. (at Exeter Street).* ☎ *800-225-7676 or 617-536-5300. www.lenoxhotel.com.*

Millennium Bostonian Hotel

$$$ Downtown   Nonstop luxury comes with important extras: The location attracts business travelers and shoppers; romance-minded vacationers revel in the atmosphere of the renovated 19th-century warehouses. *See map p. 104. 40 North St. (opposite Faneuil Hall Marketplace).* ☎ *800-343-0922 or 617-523-3600. www.millenniumhotels.com.*

Omni Parker House

$$–$$$ Downtown (Government Center)   The oldest continuously operating hotel in the country (since 1855) offers a wide variety of rooms, from snug to spacious. *See map p. 104. 60 School St. (at Tremont Street).* ☎ *800-THE-OMNI or 617-227-8600. www.omnihotels.com.*

Royal Sonesta Hotel

$$$ Cambridge (East Cambridge)   Luxurious and contemporary, the Royal Sonesta draws high-tech businesspeople during the week and families (who love the large indoor/outdoor pool) on weekends. *See map p. 106. 5 Cambridge Pkwy. (around the corner from the Museum of Science).* ☎ *800-SON-ESTA or 617-806-4200. www.sonesta.com.*

Index of Accommodations by Neighborhood

Index of Accommodations by Price

$

Anthony's Town House (In the Vicinity)
Charlesmark Hotel (Back Bay)
Harborside Inn (Downtown)
Howard Johnson Inn (Back Bay)
Longwood Inn (In the Vicinity)
The MidTown Hotel (Back Bay)

$$

Chandler Inn Hotel (Back Bay)
Charlesmark Hotel (Back Bay)
Harborside Inn (Downtown)
Harvard Square Hotel (Cambridge)
Hilton Boston Back Bay (Back Bay)
Hilton Boston Logan Airport (In the Vicinity)
Holiday Inn Boston Brookline (In the Vicinity)
Holiday Inn Express Hotel and Suites (Cambridge)
Holiday Inn Select Boston Government Center (Downtown)
Howard Johnson Inn (Back Bay)
Marriott Residence Inn Boston Harbor (Downtown)
The MidTown Hotel (Back Bay)
Newbury Guest House (Back Bay)
Omni Parker House (Downtown)
Onyx Hotel (Downtown)
Radisson Hotel Boston (Back Bay)
Sheraton Boston Hotel (Back Bay)
Sheraton Commander Hotel (Cambridge)
Wyndham Boston (Downtown)

$$$

Boston Harbor Hotel (Downtown)
Boston Marriott Long Wharf (Downtown)
The Charles Hotel (Cambridge)
Charlesmark Hotel (Back Bay)
The Fairmont Copley Plaza Hotel (Back Bay)
Hilton Boston Back Bay (Back Bay)

Hilton Boston Logan Airport (In the Vicinity)
Holiday Inn Boston Brookline (In the Vicinity)
Hotel Commonwealth (Back Bay)
The Hyatt Regency Cambridge (Cambridge)
The Inn at Harvard (Cambridge)
Jurys Boston Hotel (Back Bay)
Millennium Bostonian Hotel (Downtown)
Omni Parker House (Downtown)
Onyx Hotel (Downtown)
Radisson Hotel Boston (Back Bay)
Royal Sonesta Hotel (Cambridge)
Sheraton Boston Hotel (Back Bay)
Sheraton Commander Hotel (Cambridge)
The Westin Copley Place Boston (Back Bay)
Wyndham Boston (Downtown)

$$$$

Boston Harbor Hotel (Downtown)
Boston Marriott Long Wharf (Downtown)
The Charles Hotel (Cambridge)
The Colonnade Hotel (Back Bay)
Doubletree Hotel Boston Downtown (Back Bay/Chinatown)
Eliot Hotel (Back Bay)
The Fairmont Copley Plaza Hotel (Back Bay)
Four Seasons Hotel (Back Bay)
Hotel Commonwealth (Back Bay)
Jurys Boston Hotel (Back Bay)
The Lenox Hotel (Back Bay)
Radisson Hotel Boston (Back Bay)
Sheraton Boston Hotel (Back Bay)
Sheraton Commander Hotel (Cambridge)
The Westin Copley Place Boston (Back Bay)
Wyndham Boston (Downtown)

Chapter 10

Dining and Snacking in Boston

. . . .

In This Chapter

▶ Discovering the best local places

▶ Exploring the ethnic scene

▶ Grabbing a quick bite on the go

▶ Dishing up options by price, location, and cuisine

. . . .

*O*ut-of-towners ask the same question everywhere: Where do people who live in Boston (or Paris or Seattle or Harrisburg) go to eat? This chapter offers an overview of the local dining scene. For more information about local cuisine, see Chapter 2.

Getting the Dish on the Local Scene

New England cuisine abounds with seafood and local produce, but there's no particular "Boston style." Thanks to constant turnover, though, every chef in town seems to have supervised or worked for nearly every other chef. Many kitchens show signs of similar influences, particularly in the mingling of ethnic elements and ingredients.

Boston has shaken a reputation for stodgy food and stodgier restaurants, even among hard-core snobs and wannabe New Yorkers. Pockets of Gotham-esque see-and-be-seen action enliven the market in various neighborhoods. The hottest places as I write (they could be different as you read) are **Union Bar and Grille,** 1357 Washington St., South End (☎ 617-423-0555; www.unionrestaurant.com); **Great Bay,** in the Hotel Commonwealth, 500 Commonwealth Ave., Kenmore Square (☎ 617-532-5300; www.hotelcommonwealth.com/dining); and **Excelsior,** 272 Boylston St., Back Bay (☎ 617-426-7878; www.excelsior restaurant.com).

Hot on the trail of celebrity chefs

So you've seen a certain Boston-area chef on TV, in a national magazine, or at a culinary expo. The thrill of dropping a big name may not compare with being the first to "discover" an emerging talent, but the big name usually is a reliable indicator of excellent dining. In cooking, unlike a lot of other reputation-driven fields, fame generally does correlate with talent.

Important note: If you're planning a special trip to sample a celebrity chef's culinary expertise, call ahead to make sure that the chef whose name you want to drop plans to be behind the stove — or is still in the kitchen.

Here's a selection of Boston's noted chefs and the restaurants where you're most likely to see them working (nearly all of them both own and run their restaurants):

✔ Todd English (www.toddenglish.com): **Olives** ($$$–$$$$), 10 City Sq., Charlestown (☎ 617-242-1999); **Bonfire** ($$$$), in the Boston Park Plaza Hotel, 50 Park Plaza, Back Bay (☎ 617-262-3473); and **Kingfish Hall** ($$$–$$$$), 1 Faneuil Hall Marketplace (☎ 617-523-8862).

✔ Gordon Hamersley: **Hamersley's Bistro** ($$$), 553 Tremont St., South End (☎ 617-423-2700; www.hamersleysbistro.com).

✔ Ken Oringer: **Clio** ($$$$), in the Eliot Hotel, 370 Commonwealth Ave., Back Bay (☎ 617-536-7200; www.cliorestaurant.com).

✔ Lydia Shire: **Locke-Ober** ($$$$), 3–4 Winter Place, Downtown Crossing (☎ 617-542-1340; www.lockeober.com), and **Excelsior** ($$$$), 272 Boylston St., Back Bay (☎ 617-426-7878; www.excelsiorrestaurant.com). At Locke-Ober, jackets are suggested for men; no shorts or sneakers allowed.

✔ Jasper White: **Summer Shack** ($$), 149 Alewife Brook Parkway, Cambridge (☎ 617-520-9500; www.summershackrestaurant.com), and 50 Dalton St., Back Bay (☎ 617-867-9955). Reservations aren't accepted.

As in any city of neighborhoods, the local standby occupies an honored place. Depending on the neighborhood, this dependable establishment may be a pocket-sized bistro, an ethnic counter, a diner, or an elegant dining room. I suggest a few here, but never dismiss a restaurant just because you can't find it in a guidebook. Your friends who can't shut up about the great place around the corner may be ahead of the curve.

You don't need to know much else to pass for a local. Here's a quick cheat sheet:

✔ Book ahead for **Friday or Saturday night** at any restaurant that takes reservations. If you know where you want to eat, try to call before you leave home. If the night you want is booked, call when you reach Boston and ask about cancellations. At lunch, a party of two usually shouldn't have trouble landing a table, but a reservation is a good idea for larger groups.

✔ Bostonians tend to **eat early,** even on weekends. Don't count on dropping in and getting a table at what seems to you to be an off-peak hour. "Early" is 5:30 or 6 p.m., and "too late" can be as early as 9:30 p.m., especially in the off season, when business is slow.

✔ The state **meal tax** (which also applies to takeout food) is 5 percent.

✔ A few restaurants ask that men wear jackets at dinner, but most restaurants have **no formal dress code.** At casual places near campuses and in tourist areas, just about anything goes, particularly at lunch. That includes shorts in the summer and jeans and sneakers all year. At more upscale places, if you take the time to look presentable, you'll fit in better, and the staff may even take you more seriously. Save your breath — I've heard all the arguments. In theory, yes, you should get the same treatment whether you're in footie pajamas or a tux. Get over it.

✔ Some places let you **eat at the bar** without a reservation. The location is not ideal, and the menu may have different choices from the menu in the dining room, but eating in the bar can be a great option if you're desperate to check out a particular restaurant. Make sure that the host or hostess knows you're willing to move to a table if a last-minute cancellation occurs.

✔ Finally, remember that **smoking is illegal** in all Massachusetts workplaces, including restaurants. Take your filter-tipped little friend outside — you won't be alone.

Trimming the Fat from Your Budget

Boston dining is terrific, but you're not here just to eat. You'll probably want some cash left over for other activities.

The best cost-cutting move is to eat your big meal at lunch. Many restaurants serve dinner only, but the ones that open at midday (or even for breakfast) offer great values at lunch.

Remember, many locals are students, who come from all over the world with lots of ambition and tuition, and often not much else. When going out to eat, they're willing to experiment but not to overpay. Seek out a busy place near a campus when you're looking for generous portions and reasonable prices.

Other strategies include the following:

  ✔ Split an appetizer or dessert.

  ✔ Skip the alcohol.

  ✔ If possible, skip beverages altogether — those $2 Diet Cokes can really add up.

  ✔ Order the fixed-price or *prix-fixe* menu (not available everywhere, but always a good deal).

  ✔ Walk or take the T; valet parking can cost as much as $20.

  ✔ Plan a picnic for lunch and run up the bill at dinner.

A server who rattles off daily specials without prices may be busy or forgetful — or may be counting on your reluctance to look cheap in front of your friends or family. Always ask, and no $23 plate of noodles (true story) will ever sneak up on you. And if you're with a large group (six, eight, or more, depending on the restaurant), the check may include a service charge, typically 15 to 18 percent. Examine the total before accidentally tipping twice.

A final thought: A fancy dinner every night is no vacation for anyone but a hard-core foodie. Give yourself a break, dip into the less expensive categories, and chow down.

Boston's Best Restaurants

Hungry? If you're not already, you probably will be soon. This section lists and reviews my favorite restaurants. I also suggest neighborhoods to seek out when you're in the mood for something ethnic.

The Kid Friendly icon indicates restaurants that your family will like and that will like your family. Most have children's menus; all offer friendly service and not-too-challenging fare that can make any homesick youngster feel a little more settled. (Adventurous palates will find reasonable options, too.) As with hotels, the absence of the icon doesn't mean kids are unwelcome — but think twice if your youngsters tend to get rambunctious. If you're unsure, ask someone at the restaurant before you make a reservation.

The dollar symbols ($) that accompany each review give an idea of the price of dinner for one. That covers an appetizer, main course, dessert, and one nonalcoholic drink, not including tax and tip. The listings also include a price range (see Table 10-1) for main courses. The price ranges are estimates — adjust accordingly if you order truffles, lobster, and wine from Château d'Expensive or if you split an appetizer, drink water, stick to pasta, and skip dessert.

Table 10-1	Key to Restaurant Dollar Signs
Dollar Sign(s)	*Price Range*
$	Less than $20
$$	$20–$30
$$$	$31–$45
$$$$	$46 and up

For restaurant locations, see the "Boston Dining" or "Cambridge Dining" maps in this chapter.

The Blue Room
$$$$ **Cambridge/Kendall Square ECLECTIC**

The trek to the Blue Room is more like a pilgrimage for diners who seek unusual cuisine in unusual locations. Tech-heavy East Cambridge is not a fine-dining mecca, but the Blue Room is a revelation: The kitchen grills, roasts, and braises up a storm, creating gutsy, flavorful food in a sleek but comfortable setting. You'll find the best roast chicken in town among the inventive main courses, which always include admirable vegetarian options. In warm weather, seating on the brick patio is available.

See map p. 128. 1 Kendall Sq. (off Hampshire Street). ☎ **617-494-9034.** www. theblueroom.net. *Reservations recommended. T: Kendall (Red Line); cross through the Marriott lobby, turn left, follow Broadway 2 long blocks (across the train tracks), bear right onto Hampshire Street, and walk ½ block. Main courses: $18–$24. AE, DC, DISC, MC, V. Open: Sun–Thurs 5:30–10 p.m., Fri–Sat 5:30–11 p.m. (dinner); Sun 11 a.m.–2:30 p.m. (brunch).*

Bob the Chef's Jazz Cafe
$$ **South End AMERICAN**

Southern food and jazz are a match made in heaven, so I guess that makes Bob the Chef's heavenly. Here, you'll find "glorifried" chicken, meatloaf, pan-fried catfish, barbecued ribs, and more, served with your choice of two side dishes. I like the mac-and-cheese and the collard greens; your friendly server can help you decide. The sophisticated setting brings to mind a jazz club, and that's the soundtrack here — live Thursday though Saturday nights and at Sunday brunch.

See map p. 126. 604 Columbus Ave. (at Northampton Street). ☎ **617-536-6204.** www.bobthechefs.com. *Reservations (accepted only for parties of four or more) suggested on weekends. T: Massachusetts Avenue (Orange Line); turn right, follow Mass. Ave. to Columbus Avenue, turn right, and walk 1 block. Main courses: $9–$15; brunch $19. AE, DISC, MC, V. Open: Mon–Thurs 5–10 p.m; Fri–Sat 11:30am–midnight; Sun 10 a.m.–10 p.m. (brunch until 2:30 p.m.).*

Border Café
$$ **Cambridge/Harvard Square   SOUTHWESTERN**

Huge crowds don't necessarily mean high quality, unless the crowds have been huge since the mid-'80s. The nonstop party at the Border Café runs on heaping portions of Tex-Mex, Cajun, and occasionally Caribbean food — and, of course, beer and margaritas. The cheerful but frantic staff keeps the peace with plenty of chips and salsa. Except at off hours, there are no quick meals (the wait for a table can stretch out), so be in the mood to linger and join the party.

See map p. 128. 32 Church St. (at Palmer Street). ☎ *617-864-6100. Reservations not accepted. T: Harvard (Red Line); use Church Street exit (at front of Alewife-bound train), go right at turnstiles, and walk 1 block. Main courses: $7–$15. AE, MC, V. Open: Daily 11 a.m.–11 p.m.*

Brasserie Jo
$$–$$$ **Back Bay   FRENCH**

Traditional French brasserie fare (*choucroute garnie,* onion tart, shellfish so fresh you want to slap it) contrasts deliciously with the sleek dining room off the lobby of this contemporary hotel. The long hours and great location — between the Copley Place and Shops at Prudential Center malls, not far from Symphony Hall and Newbury Street — make Brasserie Jo a tasty destination throughout the day.

See map p. 126. In the Colonnade Hotel, 120 Huntington Ave. ☎ *617-425-3240.* www. brasseriejoboston.com. *Reservations recommended at dinner. T: Green Line E to Prudential. Parking: Valet and garage. Main courses $15–$27; plats du jour $18–$32. AE, DC, DISC, MC, V. Open: Mon–Fri 6:30 a.m.–11 p.m.; Sat 7 a.m.–11 p.m.; Sun 7 a.m.–10 p.m.; late-night menu daily until 1 a.m.*

Buddha's Delight
$ **Chinatown   VEGETARIAN VIETNAMESE**

It's hard to believe that food this good is actually good for you. Buddha's Delight looks like a run-of-the-mill Asian restaurant, but it doesn't serve meat, poultry, fish, or dairy. (Some beverages are made with condensed milk.) Instead, the chefs transform tofu and gluten into chicken, pork, beef, shrimp, and even lobster taste-alikes. Head here for bounteous portions of unusual but delicious food. Try the delightful fresh spring roll appetizer; then start experimenting.

See map p. 126. 5 Beach St. (at Washington Street). ☎ *617-451-2395. Reservations not required. T: Chinatown (Orange Line); follow Washington Street (past the China Trade Center) 1 block and turn left onto Beach Street. Main courses: $6–$13. MC, V. Open: Sun–Thurs 11 a.m.–9:30 p.m.; Fri–Sat 11 a.m.–10:30 p.m.*

Café Jaffa
$ **Back Bay** **MIDDLE EASTERN**

Newbury and Boylston streets are consumer central, and the last thing you want in the middle of a shopping spree is a meal that weighs you down — physically or financially. Café Jaffa is a favorite with shoppers and students, who come here for low prices, high quality, and good-sized portions. Traditional Middle Eastern dishes such as falafel, baba ghanoush, and hummus make a not-too-filling break from bargain hunting; lamb, beef, and chicken kabobs, burgers, and steak tips are heartier and equally tasty. The exposed-brick, glass-fronted room makes a good setting for midafternoon coffee, too.

See map p. 126. 48 Gloucester St. (between Boylston and Newbury streets). ☎ *617-536-0230. Reservations not required. T: Hynes/ICA (Green Line B, C, or D); use Newbury Street exit, turn right, walk 2 blocks, and turn right. Main courses: $5–$16. AE, DC, DISC, MC, V. Open: Mon–Thurs 11 a.m.–10:30 p.m.; Fri–Sat 11 a.m.–11 p.m.; Sun noon to 10 p.m.*

Casa Romero
$$$ **Back Bay** **CLASSIC MEXICAN**

Hidden in an alley, Casa Romero is a romantic destination a stone's throw from busy Newbury Street. The peaceful atmosphere and dimly lit rooms almost make the food secondary, but this food demands attention. The authentic cuisine is nothing like what you find at Tex-Mex drive-throughs — the food is fresh, savory, and not too heavy. Unusual ingredients (cactus salad is an unexpectedly good starter) and flavor-layered sauces make meat, poultry, and seafood shine. The enclosed garden is pleasant in warm weather.

See map p. 126. 30 Gloucester St. (off Newbury Street; entrance in alley). ☎ *617-536-4341. Reservations recommended. T: Hynes/ICA (Green Line B, C, or D); turn right onto Mass. Ave. and right onto Newbury Street, walk 2 blocks, and turn left. Main courses: $14–$27. DISC, MC, V. Open: Sun–Thurs 5–10 p.m.; Fri–Sat 5–11 p.m.*

Chacarero
$ **Downtown Crossing** **CHILEAN SANDWICHES**

If you serve only one thing, that one thing had better be pretty darn good, and the sandwiches at this takeout window are scrumptious. You choose one of five fillings — grilled or barbecued chicken, grilled or barbecued beef, or vegetarian — on a homemade roll. For the full experience, order yours "with everything," which means tomatoes, Muenster cheese, avocado, hot sauce, and green beans. The logistics: Order and pay at the right-hand window and then join the line trailing away from the left-hand window, which allows a front-row view of the prep area. At lunchtime in warm weather, the whole process can take as long as 20 minutes. The sandwiches are totally worth it.

Boston Dining

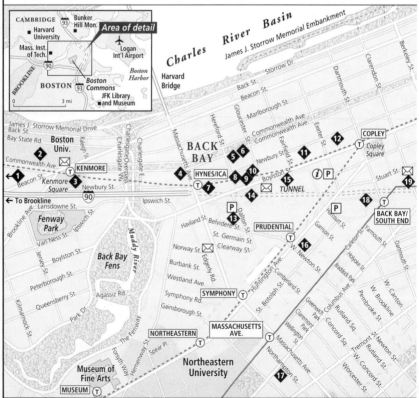

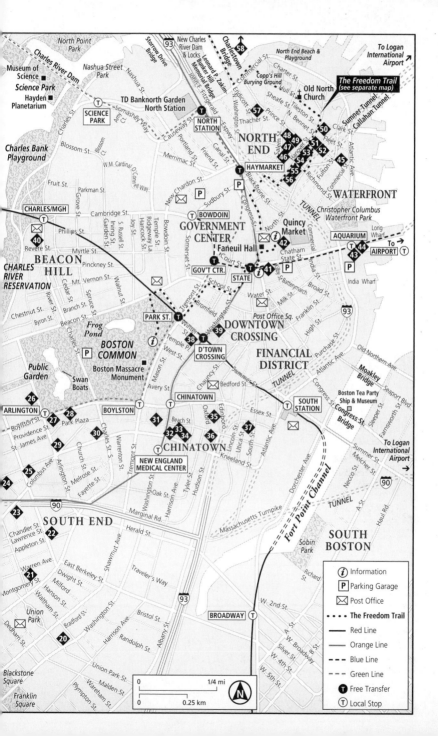

Cambridge Dining

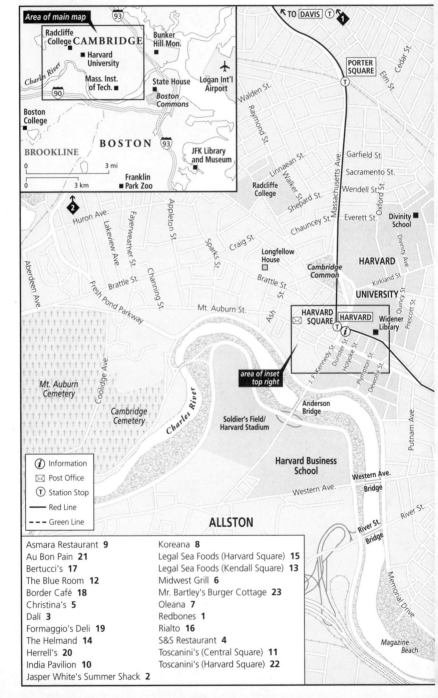

Asmara Restaurant **9**
Au Bon Pain **21**
Bertucci's **17**
The Blue Room **12**
Border Café **18**
Christina's **5**
Dalí **3**
Formaggio's Deli **19**
The Helmand **14**
Herrell's **20**
India Pavilion **10**
Jasper White's Summer Shack **2**

Koreana **8**
Legal Sea Foods (Harvard Square) **15**
Legal Sea Foods (Kendall Square) **13**
Midwest Grill **6**
Mr. Bartley's Burger Cottage **23**
Oleana **7**
Redbones **1**
Rialto **16**
S&S Restaurant **4**
Toscanini's (Central Square) **11**
Toscanini's (Harvard Square) **22**

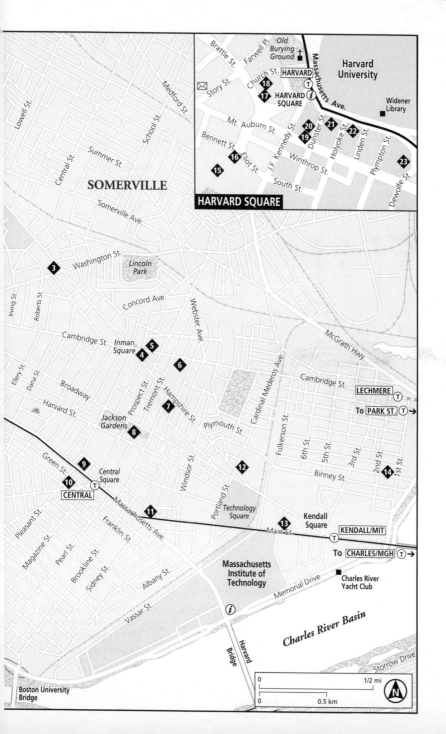

See map p. 126. 426 Washington St. (at Franklin Street). ☎ *617-542-0392.* www.chacarero.com. *Reservations not accepted. T: Downtown Crossing (Red or Orange Line); with Filene's on your right, walk 1 block, and turn right. Main courses: $4–$7. No credit cards. Open: Mon–Fri 11 a.m.–7 p.m.*

Daily Catch
$$ Downtown/North End   SEAFOOD AND SOUTHERN ITALIAN

For a true North End experience, try this tiny storefront under an awning that reads "Calamari Café." The open kitchen cranks out hearty, garlicky food that often revolves around squid, right down to the garlic-and-oil pasta sauce (which includes chopped calamari) and the black pasta (the color comes from squid ink). The casual atmosphere — some dishes land on the table still in the cooking skillet — is part of the fun.

See map p. 126. 323 Hanover St. (between Richmond and Prince streets). ☎ *617-523-8567.* www.dailycatch.com. *Reservations not accepted. T: Haymarket (Green or Orange Line); follow signs to North End, turn right, follow Cross Street to Hanover Street, turn left, and go 1½ blocks. Main courses: $12–$19. No credit cards. Open: Sun–Thurs 11:30 a.m.–10 p.m.; Fri–Sat 11:30 a.m.–11 p.m.*

Dalí
$$ Cambridge/Somerville   SPANISH

Appetizers with no main course make a good dinner-party menu at home — and they can be even better at a restaurant. The main attraction at this boisterous place is delectable *tapas*. The appetizer-like plates of hot or cold meat, seafood, vegetables, and cheese are so tasty that you won't miss the big platter of one boring thing. Instead, you'll want to ask for another order or two of sausages, cold potato salad, salmon croquettes, or whatever catches your fancy. The wait at the bar can be long, but the atmosphere is festive and the payoff huge — unlike the bill. (A conventional meal of Spanish classics will push the tab into $$$ territory.)

See map p. 128. 415 Washington St., Somerville. ☎ *617-661-3254.* www.dalirestaurant.com. *Reservations not accepted. T: Harvard (Red Line); cross through Harvard Yard and follow Kirkland Street from the back of Memorial Hall to the intersection of Washington and Beacon streets. It's a $5 cab ride. Tapas: $3–$9. Main courses: $17–$24. AE, DC, MC, V. Open: Daily 6–11 p.m. in summer; 5:30–11 p.m. in winter.*

Durgin-Park
$$ Downtown/Faneuil Hall Marketplace   NEW ENGLAND

If you prefer hearty food and sassy service to fancy ingredients and unpronounceable dishes, Durgin-Park is the classic New England experience. Bostonians and out-of-towners come to the long, multiple-party tables (smaller ones are available) for generous helpings of delicious, down-to-earth fare. The cornbread and baked beans are famous, the prime rib and fresh seafood are delicious, and the strawberry shortcake is as fresh as some of the waitresses. That's right — like a 19th-century theme restaurant, Durgin-Park (founded in 1827) has a shtick: borderline-belligerent service. Far from being cranky, many waitresses are actually pleasant, but a trip into the orbit of someone who takes the job seriously can be an eye-opening experience.

See map p. 126. 340 Faneuil Hall Marketplace (in the North Market building). ☎ *617-227-2038.* www.durgin-park.com. *Reservations accepted for parties of 15 or more. T: Government Center (Green or Blue Line) or Haymarket (Orange Line); follow the crowds. Main courses: $5–$25; specials $19–$40. AE, DC, DISC, MC, V. Open: Mon–Sat 11:30 a.m.–10 p.m., Sun 11:30 a.m.–9 p.m. (lunch menu until 2:30 p.m.).*

The Elephant Walk
$$$ **Back Bay/Kenmore Square** **FRENCH AND CAMBODIAN**

The Elephant Walk is the worst-kept "secret" on the Boston culinary scene, but it does feel like a great find. The unique combination of French and Cambodian isn't the mishmash that plagues fusion cuisine; rather, each side of the menu stands alone and complements the other. On the French side, you may find pan-seared filet mignon. On the Cambodian side, *curry de crevettes* (yup, that's French) is a perfect shrimp dish. The accommodating staff offers excellent advice, and tofu can replace animal protein in many dishes.

See map p. 126. 900 Beacon St. (at St. Mary's Street; 4 blocks past Kenmore Square). ☎ *617-247-1500.* www.elephantwalk.com. *Reservations suggested at dinner Sun–Thurs, not accepted Fri–Sat. T: St. Mary's (Green Line C). Parking: Valet at dinner only. Main courses: $10–$24. AE, DISC, MC, V. Open: Mon–Fri 11:30 a.m.–2:30 p.m.; Sun–Thurs 5–10 p.m.; Fri–Sat 5–11 p.m.*

Giacomo's Ristorante
$$ **Downtown/North End** **SEAFOOD AND SOUTHERN ITALIAN**

For pure inconvenience — long lines, no credit cards, improbably cramped space — you'll have a hard time beating Giacomo's. So why the crowds? You can't beat the food. Go early, before the queue gets too long. Check the board for outstanding daily specials, take the chef's advice, or create your own dish from the list of ingredients and sauces. Salmon with sundried tomatoes over fettuccine is my favorite, but I've never had anything short of fabulous. Portions are large, and even dainty eaters who declare themselves stuffed can't help trying just one more mouthful.

See map p. 126. 355 Hanover St. (near Fleet Street). ☎ *617-523-9026. Reservations not accepted. T: Haymarket (Green or Orange Line); follow signs to North End, turn right, follow Cross Street to Hanover Street, turn left, and walk 3 full blocks. Main courses: $11–$20. No credit cards. Open: Mon–Thurs 5–10 p.m.; Fri–Sat 5–10:30 p.m.; Sun 4–10 p.m.*

Grill 23 & Bar
$$$$ Back Bay   AMERICAN

The best steakhouse in Boston earns that title with an irresistible mix of macho atmosphere and splendid food. Grill 23 is a favorite business destination with a raucous crowd that seems to have sealed a deal minutes before. If they're smart, the young (and old) turks give a moment's thought to their plates. The steak and chops are magnificent, and the more inventive options — for example, top-notch meatloaf — are equally satisfying but not as *Flintstones*-like. As at any self-respecting steakhouse, the side dishes (à la carte) and desserts are diet-busting delights.

See map p. 126. 161 Berkeley St. (at Stuart Street). ☎ *617-542-2255.* www.grill123. com. *Reservations recommended. T: Arlington (Green Line); follow Boylston Street 1 block away from the Public Garden, turn left, and walk 2 full blocks. Parking: Valet. Main courses: $22–$44; Kobe beef $44 and up. AE, DC, DISC, MC, V. Open: Mon–Thurs 5:30–10:30 p.m.; Fri–Sat 5:30–11 p.m.; Sun 5:30–10 p.m.*

The Helmand
$$ Cambridge/Kendall Square   AFGHAN

In Cambridge's United Nations of dining, the Helmand stands out. This restaurant offers the tasty food, friendly service, and reasonable prices for an ethnic restaurant in an elegant setting that may make you wonder what the catch is. (The Helmand is *too* popular, would be my grumpy answer — as was the case even before the world turned its attention to Afghanistan.) Afghan cuisine is Middle Eastern with Indian and Pakistani influences, filling but not heavy, redolent of spices. Vegetarians will be happy; meat accents many dishes instead of dominating, and many meatless choices are available. My pick is baked pumpkin with meat sauce, but that's a tough decision — everything is flat-out delicious.

See map p. 128. 143 First St. (at Bent Street). ☎ **617-492-4646**. *Reservations recommended. T: Lechmere (Green Line); walk past rear of trolley, pass through tunnel on right, and go 6½ short blocks on First Street, passing CambridgeSide Galleria mall. Main courses: $12–$20. AE, MC, V. Open: Sun–Thurs 5–10 p.m.; Fri–Sat 5–11 p.m.*

Icarus
$$$$ South End   ECLECTIC

This subterranean hideaway is the most romantic restaurant in town (an insanely competitive category), a grand space that abounds with personal touches like mismatched chairs and antique lighting. The regularly changing menu is equally quirky and equally enjoyable. Chef–owner Christopher Douglass simply transforms his fresh local ingredients. The no-nonsense descriptions (lemony grilled chicken with garlic and herbs, polenta with braised exotic mushrooms) can't do justice to the imaginative interplay of flavors and textures. Save room for an unbelievable dessert; even chocolate fiends love the fruit sorbets.

See map p. 126. 3 Appleton St. (off Tremont Street). ☎ **617-426-1790**. www.icarus restaurant.com. *Reservations recommended. T: Arlington (Green Line); follow*

Arlington Street away from the Public Garden, across the Mass. Pike. (about 6 blocks), bear right onto Tremont Street, and go 1 long block. Or Back Bay (Orange Line); use Clarendon Street exit (at back of Forest Hills–bound train), turn right, walk 4 blocks, turn left onto Appleton Street, and go 2 blocks. Parking: Valet. Main courses: $24–$33. AE, DC, DISC, MC, V. Open: Mon–Thurs 6–10 p.m.; Fri 6–10:30 p.m.; Sat 5:30–10:30 p.m.; Sun 5:30–10 p.m.

La Summa

$$ Downtown/North End   SOUTHERN ITALIAN

As newcomers push the North End up the *nouveau* scale, neighborhood favorites such as La Summa tick along, offering homey food in a welcoming atmosphere. House-made pasta and desserts attract locals and savvy passersby to a restaurant that also serves terrific seafood and meat dishes. Check the specials board on the way in, and if lobster ravioli is on there, don't hesitate. Just be sure to save room for sweets.

See map p. 126. 30 Fleet St. ☎ 617-523-9503. Reservations recommended on weekends. T: Haymarket (Green or Orange Line); follow signs to the North End, turn right, and follow Cross Street to Hanover Street. Follow Hanover Street to Fleet Street, turn right, and go 1½ blocks. Main courses: $11–$24. AE, DC, DISC, MC, V. Open: Sun–Fri 4:30–10:30 p.m., Sat 4:30–11 p.m.

Legal Sea Foods

$$$ Back Bay, Downtown/Waterfront, other locations   SEAFOOD

Out-of-towners arrive in Boston, unpack, and demand seafood. The ones who wind up here are in for a treat: the freshest seafood around. From its roots as a counter in a fish store, "Legal's" has grown into a sprawling chain that incorporates no-frills filets and inventive preparations. This is the place for perennial favorites (lobsters the size of a laptop, every species of fish that's available fresh that day) and seasonal specials (shad roe, soft-shell crabs). Legal Sea Foods is the place for do-believe-the-hype clam and fish chowder, sublime raw-bar offerings, and even scrumptious desserts. The restaurants are never quiet, and service is pleasant but can be somewhat slapdash — that's part of the experience.

Until recently, the long wait for a table was also part of the experience. The Prudential Center branch takes reservations at lunch only, so go there then if you can't abide waiting. Another good strategy: Go for a late lunch or early dinner. Or put your name on the list and see what *not* being an out-of-towner feels like.

See map p. 126. 800 Boylston St., in the Prudential Center. ☎ 617-266-6800. www. legalseafoods.com. *Reservations recommended; accepted only at lunch. T: Copley (Green Line); follow Boylston Street 3 blocks, past the Boston Public Library. Or Prudential (Green Line E); inside shopping mall, follow main concourse toward Boylston Street. Main courses: Dinner $11–$35; lobster market price (at least $15 a pound). AE, DC, DISC, MC, V. Open: Mon–Thurs 11 a.m.–10:30 p.m.; Fri–Sat 11 a.m.–11:30 p.m.; Sun noon to 10 p.m.*

See map p. 126. Also at 255 State St., 1 block from the New England Aquarium, Waterfront (☎ 617-227-3115; T: Aquarium [Blue Line]); 36 Park Sq., between Columbus Avenue and Stuart Street, Back Bay (☎ 617-426-4444; T: Arlington [Green Line]); Copley Place, second level, Back Bay (☎ 617-266-7775); 20 University Rd., in the courtyard of the Charles Hotel, Harvard Square, Cambridge (☎ 617-491-9400; T: Harvard [Red Line]); and 5 Cambridge Center, Kendall Square, Cambridge (☎ 617-864-3400; T: Kendall/MIT [Red Line]).

L'Espalier
$$$$ Back Bay   NEW ENGLAND AND FRENCH

Diners disappear into this elegant townhouse off Newbury Street like guests arriving at a dinner party, and in a way, that's just what they are (well, except for the pesky matter of money). The gorgeous 19th-century dining rooms make a lovely backdrop for chef and co-owner Frank McClelland's innovative, deliriously good food. French techniques and fresh local ingredients — seafood, game, unusual produce, artisan cheeses — collide to produce unusual dishes that never cross the line into brain-teaser territory. The dessert cart is worth a look, and this is one of the only places in town where the after-dinner cheese tray gets deserved attention.

See map p. 126. 30 Gloucester St. (off Newbury Street). ☎ 617-262-3023. www. lespalier.com. Reservations required. T: Hynes/ICA (Green Line B, C, or D); turn right onto Mass. Ave. and right onto Newbury Street, walk 2 blocks, and turn left. Parking: Valet. Prix fixe: $68 (three courses). Degustation menu (seven courses): $85. AE, DC, DISC, MC, V. Open: Mon–Sat 5:30–10 p.m.

Les Zygomates
$$$ Downtown   FRENCH BISTRO

A friend who used to live in Paris is in town from the suburbs. I mention Les Zygomates (lay *zee*-go-mat), and suddenly she *does* have time for dinner. Primarily a wine bar, this bistro serves an excellent selection of vintages by the bottle, glass, and 2-ounce taste. Classic but original, the food is an artful mix of local ingredients and bistro favorites, such as braised lamb shank with garlic puree. The quirky neighborhood (technically, the Leather District) attracts business lunchers and a stylish dinner crowd that lingers for live jazz in its own dining room.

See map p. 126. 129 South St. (between Tufts and Beach streets; 2 blocks from South Station). ☎ 617-542-5108. www.winebar.com. Reservations recommended. T: South Station (Red Line); cross Atlantic Avenue, turn left, walk 1 block to East Street, turn right, and walk 1 block to South Street. Or ask a construction worker. Parking: Valet at dinner only. Main courses: $17–$26; prix-fixe lunch: $15; prix-fixe dinner: $29. AE, DC, DISC, MC, V. Open: Mon–Fri 11:30 a.m.–1 a.m. (lunch menu until 2 p.m., dinner menu until 10:30 p.m.); Sat 6 p.m.–1 a.m. (dinner until 11:30 p.m.).

Mamma Maria
$$$$ Downtown/North End   NORTHERN ITALIAN

A fine-dining destination in a pasta-and-pizza neighborhood, Mamma Maria is the best restaurant in the North End. Plenty of competitors serve excellent food in no-frills settings, but this elegant townhouse a stone's throw from the Paul Revere House is the champ. The romantic atmosphere makes it a popular place for marriage proposals and anniversary dinners. The exquisite cuisine, which changes seasonally, always includes fabulous seafood dishes, daily pasta specials, and fork-tender osso buco. You won't even miss the pizza.

See map p. 126. 3 North Sq. (at Prince Street). ☎ *617-523-0077.* www.mamma maria.com. *Reservations recommended. T: Haymarket (Green or Orange Line); follow signs to the North End, turn right, follow Cross Street to Hanover Street, and turn left. Walk 2 full blocks, go right onto Prince Street, and walk 1 block. Parking: Valet. Main courses: $19–$35. AE, DC, DISC, MC, V. Open: Sun–Thurs 5–9:30 p.m.; Fri–Sat 5–10:30 p.m.*

Mr. Bartley's Burger Cottage
$ Cambridge/Harvard Square   AMERICAN

Down-to-earth burger joints are scarce in Harvard Square, which is more retail haven than college campus. But even Harvard students need ground beef (and turkey), and this place is great for both. The college-town atmosphere is authentic, from the vintage posters to the chummy wait staff. Although meat is the main event, vegetarians can eat surprisingly well. Sublime onion rings round out a perfect burger-joint meal.

See map p. 128. 1246 Massachusetts Ave. (between Plympton and Bow streets). ☎ *617-354-6559.* www.mrbartleys.com. *Reservations not required. T: Harvard (Red Line); with the Harvard Coop at your back, follow Mass. Ave. 3½ blocks. Main courses: $9 or less. No credit cards. Open: Mon–Sat 11 a.m.–9 p.m.*

Nashoba Brook Bakery
$ South End   SANDWICHES/LIGHT FARE

An unassuming storefront conceals a mouthwatering display of sandwiches on artisan breads, soups, salads, and amazing pastries, all fresh from the original location in suburban Concord (see Chapter 14). It's a cozy neighborhood place where you can linger over a cup of coffee and maybe just one more taste of that delicious cookie.

See map p. 126. 288 Columbus Ave. (between Clarendon and Dartmouth streets). ☎ *617-236-0777.* www.slowrise.com. *Reservations not necessary. T: Orange Line to Back Bay; turn left and follow Dartmouth Street 1 block, cross Columbus Avenue, turn left, and walk ½ block. Main courses: Most less than $7. MC, V. Mon–Fri 7 a.m.– 6 p.m.; Sat 8 a.m.–5 p.m.; Sun 8 a.m.–4 p.m.*

Oleana
$$$ Cambridge/Inman Square MEDITERRANEAN

Oleana is a sunny destination on even the dreariest night. The menu of seasonal offerings and timeless classics has something for everyone — adventurous or timid, vegetarian or meat-lover. Flavors are bold but not overwhelming, and the kitchen pays just as much attention to the little things (delectable deviled eggs) as to the more complicated creations (traditional Portuguese clams cataplana). In the summer, ask for a table on the peaceful patio.

See map p. 128. 134 Hampshire St. (at Columbia Street). ☎ *617-661-0505.* www. oleanarestaurant.com. *Reservations recommended. T: Central (Red Line); turn right on Prospect Street (at Starbucks), go 4 blocks, turn right onto Inman Street and go 5 blocks (a 10-minute walk). Main courses: $17–$24; vegetarian tasting menu: $38. AE, MC, V. Open: Sun–Thurs 5:30–10 p.m.; Fri–Sat 5:30–11 p.m.*

Piccola Venezia
$$ Downtown/North End SOUTHERN ITALIAN

Piccola Venezia probably loses some business because of its location: on the first block of the North End's main drag. Banish "maybe we'll find something better" from your mind — you won't be sorry. The menu combines home-style specialties with less red-sauce-intensive options, all in generous quantities. To give you some idea of the scope, tripe is a house specialty, polenta with mushrooms is a great starter, and a recent special of seafood lasagna made a delectable dinner *and* a filling lunch the next day. It's a cliché, but spaghetti and meatballs is a good choice, too.

See map p. 126. 263 Hanover St. ☎ *617-523-3888. Reservations suggested at dinner. T: Haymarket (Green or Orange Line); follow signs to the North End, turn right, follow Cross Street to Hanover Street, turn left, and walk ½ block. Main courses: $11–$21; lunch specialties: $5–$10. AE, DISC, MC, V. Open: Daily 11 a.m.–10 p.m. (lunch menu weekdays until 4 p.m.).*

Pizzeria Regina
$ North End ITALIAN

Regina's is the only Boston pizza place that competes with New York in quality and ambience. True, it's hard to find, and the line can be long (though it moves quickly). The too-good-to-be-true atmosphere is the real thing, right down to waitresses who call you "honey" while warning you not to burn your mouth on the bubbling-hot pie that just arrived. The pizza, fresh from the brick oven, is that hot. And that good.

See map p. 126. 11½ Thacher St. (at North Margin Street). ☎ *617-227-0765.* www. pizzeriaregina.com. *Reservations not accepted. T: Haymarket (Green or Orange Line); follow signs to North End, go straight onto Salem Street for 3 blocks, turn left onto Cooper Street, take next right onto North Margin Street, and go 2 blocks to Thacher Street. Pizza: $9–$16. No credit cards. Open: Mon–Thurs 11 a.m.– 11:30 p.m.; Fri–Sat 11 a.m.–midnight; Sun noon to 11 p.m.*

Redbones

$$ Cambridge/Somerville BARBECUE

"New England barbecue" doesn't exactly roll off the tongue. But you'll want these treats rolling right into your mouth after just one whiff of this place. The festive crowd and whimsical decor make an appealing first impression, and the down-home food backs it up. Expatriate Southerners, ravenous college students, and celebratory families relish the lively atmosphere and authentic fare. Barbecue in all incarnations shares the menu with Southern specialties such as catfish and pecan pie, all in abundant portions. Try to get a table at street level, not in the barlike space downstairs. Suck down a beer, make a dent in a pile of pulled pork or baby-back ribs, and you'll understand why there's a stack of paper napkins on every table.

See map p. 128. 55 Chester St. (off Elm Street), Somerville. ☎ *617-628-2200.* www. redbonesbbq.com. *Reservations suggested; accepted Sun–Thurs only. T: Davis (Red Line); right at turnstiles, right at exit, walk 3 blocks on Elm Street, and turn right onto Chester Street. Main courses: $6–$19. No credit cards. Open: Mon–Sat 11:30 a.m.–10:30 p.m., Sun noon to 10:30 p.m. (lunch menu until 4 p.m., late-night menu until 12:30 a.m.).*

Rialto

$$$$ Cambridge/Harvard Square MEDITERRANEAN

Rialto has the sleek-chic vibe you'd expect at the Charles Hotel, but never to the point of feeling snooty. The restaurant assembles the elements that make a memorable dining experience unforgettable: a glamorous but comfortable space, attentive service, and, most important, Jody Adams's amazing food. She makes good use of seasonal local products, creating an overall effect of a sun-drenched field overlooking the Mediterranean. Try any seafood dish, any vegetarian option — anything, really. Now you're *so* cutting edge.

See map p. 128. 1 Bennett St. (in the Charles Hotel). ☎ *617-661-5050.* www.rialto-restaurant.com. *Reservations suggested. T: Harvard (Red Line); follow Brattle Street 2 blocks, bear left onto Eliot Street, and go 2 blocks. Parking: Valet and validated. Main courses: $22–$37. AE, DC, MC, V. Open: Mon–Fri 5:30–10 p.m.; Sat 5:30–11 p.m.; Sun 5:30–9 p.m.*

S&S Restaurant

$ Cambridge/Inman Square AMERICAN

The best brunch in the area draws huge weekend crowds to this Inman Square standby, which is also a fine place for a tasty meal during the week. Never mind the long walk from the T — on the way back, you'll be working off calories from the huge omelets, inventive pancakes and waffles, and excellent baked goods. On weekends, arrive early, or schedule your day to allow for waiting time (and people watching). During nonbrunch hours, the traditional deli menu includes breakfast any time.

Around the world in 80 plates: Ethnic dining

Boston and Cambridge boast a virtual United Nations of ethnic restaurants. Space doesn't allow me to suggest more than a few restaurants here, but the following neighborhoods are all good places to wander around and follow your nose. You don't want to be the first one through the door (trust me, the empty places are empty for a reason), but if the menu looks promising, don't let a less-than-full room stop you, especially on a weeknight. Here's a brief guide of what to expect in these area's eateries:

✔ If you head to the **North End** (Haymarket stop on the Green or Orange Line), you'll find Italian food of every description in every price range. Ordinarily, I can't abide waiting, but in this area, lines are good. You'll see some locals in restaurants on high-traffic Hanover and Salem streets, but the neighborhood places are on the side streets. Check out **Artú**, 6 Prince St. (☎ 617-742-4336), for excellent sandwiches, pastas, and roasted meats; and **DiMio**, 261 North St. (☎ 617-725-8880), for thin-crust pizza with the full range of yuppie toppings.

✔ **Chinatown** (which has an Orange Line stop) is another promising neighborhood, and not just for Chinese food. Reasonably priced Asian cuisine of all descriptions abounds on Beach Street and the narrow streets that branch off between Washington Street (where the T stop is) and the Surface Artery (where the landmark Chinatown Arch is). **Pho Pasteur**, 682 Washington St. (☎ 617-482-7467), is the original location of a local Vietnamese minichain that specializes in authentic noodle soup, and **Penang**, 685–691 Washington St. (☎ 617-451-6373), is part of a New York–based chain of Malaysian restaurants.

✔ Cambridge's **Central Square** is a social and culinary melting pot, with food from almost every corner of the globe. Follow Mass. Ave. in either direction from the T stop (Red Line to Central), and you'll probably find something that gets your nose's attention. I generally head straight for either **India Pavilion,** 17 Central Sq. (☎ 617-547-7463), the oldest Indian restaurant in Cambridge, or **Asmara Restaurant,** 739 Mass. Ave. (☎ 617-864-7447), for Ethiopian and Eritrean food.

✔ Try taking take the Red Line to Central, turn the corner at Starbucks, and walk up Prospect Street to **Inman Square,** where you'll find everything from Brazilian barbecue (at the **Midwest Grill**, 1124 Cambridge St. [☎ 617-354-7536]) to bibimbap and sushi (at **Koreana**, 154–158 Prospect St. [☎ 617-576-8661]) within about 5 blocks.

See map p. 128. 1334 Cambridge St. (at Hampshire Street). ☎ *617-354-0777.* www. sandsrestaurant.com. *Reservations not accepted. T: Central (Red Line); turn right on Prospect Street (at Starbucks), go 5 blocks to Cambridge Street, and turn left. Or Harvard (Red Line); use Church Street exit (at front of Alewife-bound train), and turn left at turnstiles; then take Number 69 (Harvard-Lechmere) bus to Inman Square, walk ¹⁄₁₀ mile up Cambridge Street, or take a $5 cab ride. Main courses: $4–$14. AE, MC, V. Open: Mon–Wed 7 a.m.–11 p.m., Thurs–Fri 7 a.m.–midnight; Sat 8 a.m.–midnight; Sun 8 a.m.–10 p.m. (brunch weekends until 4 p.m.).*

Sel de la Terre

$$$ Downtown/Waterfront   MEDITERRANEAN

The atmosphere at this upscale-but-not-too-upscale cousin of L'Espalier may be the neatest trick in town: Although Sel de la Terre is on the edge of the remains of the Big Dig, you'd never know it. Not that you'll imagine you're in Provence, but that's clearly where executive chef Geoff Gardner's heart is. He transforms fresh local ingredients (especially seafood) into flavor-packed cuisine that's never overwhelming. The crowd is businesslike at lunch, chic at dinner. And you don't even need to ruin your appetite by filling up on the delicious breads — they're for sale at the *boulangerie* near the entrance.

See map p. 126. 255 State St. (at Atlantic Avenue; 1 block from the New England Aquarium). ☎ *617-720-1300.* www.seldelaterre.com. *Reservations suggested. T: State (Blue or Orange Line) or Aquarium (Blue Line), if open; walk 4 blocks toward the harbor on State Street. Main courses: All $24. AE, DC, DISC, MC, V. Open: Mon–Fri 11:30 a.m.–2:30 p.m.; Sat–Sun 11 a.m.–3:30 p.m.; daily 5–10 p.m.*

Dining and Snacking on the Go

Multiple courses, starched tablecloths, and courtly service have their time and their place; that's usually *not* in the middle of a busy day of sightseeing. In this section, you get the scoop on grabbing a bite (outdoors and indoors), plus pointers on afternoon tea, dim sum, coffee, and ice cream.

Picking the picnic option

With the harbor here and the river there, acres of waterfront space offer perfect opportunities for picnicking, and you can find plenty of places in Boston and Cambridge to fill up your metaphorical picnic basket. Here are some airy options:

- ✔ Gathering food for your outdoor feast is a picnic (ouch!) at the **Colonnade food court** at Faneuil Hall Marketplace (T: Government Center [Green or Blue Line] or Haymarket [Orange Line]), which has plenty of variety, including enough to satisfy a large group. When you're set, cross Atlantic Avenue and seek out the plaza at the end of **Long Wharf** or the benches and lawns of **Christopher Columbus Waterfront Park.**

- ✔ In the North End, **Il Panino Express,** 266 Hanover St. (T: Haymarket [Green or Orange Line]; ☎ 617-720-5720), cranks out superb sandwiches, pasta, and pizza. Cross Hanover Street to Richmond Street and follow it 4 blocks downhill to **Christopher Columbus Park.**

- ✔ At the foot of Beacon Hill (near the Esplanade, a destination for concerts and movies all summer), **Savenor's Market,** 160 Charles St. (T: Charles/MGH [Red Line]; ☎ 617-723-6328) lets you load up on gourmet provisions before heading across the footbridge to the

Charles River Basin. From the Back Bay, gain access to the river-bank from Mass. Ave. after hitting **Trader Joe's,** 899 Boylston St. (☎ 617-262-6505), for the makings of your alfresco feast.

✔ Harvard Square also affords easy access to the Charles. **Formaggio's Deli,** 81 Mount Auburn St., in the Garage mall (T: Harvard [Red Line]; ☎ 617-547-4795), is more gourmet-sandwich mecca than tra-ditional deli, with sandwiches that are stuffed yet sophisticated. Stake out a bench on the riverbank or a comfy spot at **John F. Kennedy Park** at Kennedy Street and Memorial Drive.

Checking out the chains

National chains abound, but really, can't you do that at home? One exception that's especially useful if you're traveling with teenagers is the **Hard Rock Cafe,** 131 Clarendon St. (off Stuart Street), Back Bay (T: Back Bay [Orange Line] or Copley [Green Line]; ☎ 617-424-ROCK; www.hardrock.com). If you don't know what to expect, ask the kids.

Local chains offer a less generic experience. Check out my favorite picks:

✔ The upscale pizzerias of **Bertucci's** appeal to adults and kids alike. The little ones can concentrate on the wood-burning brick ovens, and their caddies can exclaim over the plain and fancy pizzas and pastas. Handy branches are at Faneuil Hall Marketplace, Merchants Row, off State Street (☎ 617-227-7889); 43 Stanhope St., around the corner from the Hard Rock Cafe, Back Bay (T: Back Bay [Orange Line] or Copley [Green Line]; ☎ 617-247-6161); 533 Common-wealth Avenue, Kenmore Square (T: Kenmore [Green Line B, C, or D]; ☎ 617-236-1030); and 21 Brattle St., Harvard Square, Cambridge (T: Harvard [Red Line]; ☎ 617-864-4748).

✔ The fresh, tasty sandwiches and baked goods at **Au Bon Pain** are never particularly unusual or disappointing. Locations are all over town, including the Prudential Center, 800 Boylston St., Back Bay (T: Prudential [Green Line E] or Hynes/ICA [Green Line B, C, or D]; ☎ 617-421-9593); and 53 State St. (T: State [Blue or Orange Line]; ☎ 617-723-8483). The patio at the Harvard Square location, in Holyoke Center, 1350 Mass. Ave., Cambridge (T: Harvard [Red Line]; ☎ 617-497-9797) is one of the best people-watching perches in New England.

Taking tea time

The original Boston Tea Party, a colonial rebellion, couldn't be further from the experience of a proper afternoon tea in a posh hotel. Finger sandwiches, pastries, scones, clotted cream, and other niceties make this the most polite way I know to make a pig of yourself. These hotels are within walking distance of the Arlington T stop (Green Line). You'll need a reservation, especially on weekends. Put on your daintiest attitude at:

✔ The Four Seasons Hotel, 200 Boylston St. **The Bristol** (☎ **617-351-2037**) serves tea daily from 3 to 4:30 p.m. Expect to pay $24 per person, more if you spring for the signature kir royale (a champagne cocktail).

✔ The Ritz-Carlton, Boston, 15 Arlington St. (☎ **617-536-5700**). The legendary **Lounge** serves tea Wednesday through Sunday at 2:30 and 4 p.m. for about $25 a person.

Bao, wow: Dim sum

Dim sum, a Chinese midday meal, is a perfect way to sample a variety of small dishes. To enjoy the most options, go on a weekend with at least one other person. Waitresses make the rounds, pushing carts loaded with *bao* (steamed buns), steamed and fried dumplings, spring rolls, sweets, and more. Point at what you want (unless you speak Chinese), and the server stamps your check with the symbol of the dish; most cost $1 to $3. For around $10 per person, this option is a thoroughly satisfying experience.

If you don't care for fried food, pork, or shrimp, dim sum may leave you feeling more deprived than satisfied.

The top dim sum destinations, all near the Chinatown T stop (Orange Line), include the following:

✔ **Empire Garden Restaurant,** 690–698 Washington St., 2nd floor (☎ **617-482-8898**)

✔ **China Pearl,** 9 Tyler St., 2nd floor (☎ **617-426-4338**)

✔ **Chau Chow City,** 81 Essex St. (☎ **617-338-8158**)

Espresso express

Boston and Cambridge overflow with congenial coffee outlets (college and stimulants seem to go together), but the classic caffeine-related experience is a spell in a North End *caffè*. Check out the pastries, order an espresso or cappuccino (decaf, if you insist), sit back, and watch the world go by. To get to the North End, take the T to Haymarket (Green or Orange Line) and follow signs.

My favorite destinations include **Caffè dello Sport,** 308 Hanover St. (☎ **617-523-5063**), and **Caffè Vittoria,** 296 Hanover St. (☎ **617-227-7606**). **Caffè Paradiso,** 255 Hanover St. (☎ **617-742-1768**), is *the* place to watch big European soccer matches. **Mike's Pastry,** 300 Hanover St. (☎ **617-742-3050**), is a popular bakery with table service. Find what you want in the case and then sit down and order — or try something tasty to go and head down to the harbor for a dessert picnic.

I scream, you scream

The New Yorker in me still can't believe the year-round popularity of ice cream in the Boston area. (For the record, that's not a complaint.) After encyclopedic research and great personal sacrifice, I can attest to the quality of the following.

In Cambridge:

- ✔ **Herrell's,** 15 Dunster St., Harvard Square (T: Harvard [Red Line]; ☎ 617-497-2179)

- ✔ **Toscanini's,** 899 Main St., Central Square (T: Central [Red Line]; ☎ 617-491-5877), and 1310 Mass. Ave., Harvard Square (T: Harvard [Red Line]; ☎ 617-354-9350)

- ✔ **Christina's,** 1255 Cambridge St., Inman Square (T: Central [Red Line], turn right onto Prospect Street (at Starbucks) and go 5 blocks; ☎ 617-492-7021)

In the Back Bay:

- ✔ **Emack & Bolio's,** 290 Newbury St. (T: Hynes/ICA [Green Line B, C, or D]; ☎ 617-247-8772)

- ✔ **Herrell's,** 224 Newbury St. (T: Hynes/ICA [Green Line B, C, or D]; ☎ 617-236-0857)

- ✔ **JP Licks,** 352 Newbury St. (T: Hynes/ICA [Green Line B, C, or D]; ☎ 617-236-1666)

- ✔ **Ben & Jerry's,** 174 Newbury St. (T: Copley [Green Line]; ☎ 617-536-5456)

Index of Restaurants by Neighborhood

Back Bay

Au Bon Pain (Sandwiches, $)
Bertucci's (Pizza, $)
Brasserie Jo (French, $$–$$$)
The Bristol (American, $$$)
Café Jaffa (Middle Eastern, $)
Casa Romero (Classic Mexican, $$$)
Clio (French, $$$$)
The Elephant Walk (French and Cambodian, $$$)
Excelsior (American, $$$$)
Great Bay (Seafood, $$$$)
Grill 23 & Bar (American, $$$$)
Hamersley's Bistro (American, $$$)
Hard Rock Cafe (American, $–$$)

Legal Sea Foods (Seafood, $$$)
L'Espalier (New England and French, $$$$)
The Lounge at the Ritz-Carlton (American, $$$)
Summer Shack (Seafood, $$$)

Cambridge

Asmara Restaurant (Central Square, Ethiopian and Eritrean, $)
Au Bon Pain (Harvard Square, Sandwiches, $)
Bertucci's (Harvard Square, Pizza, $)
The Blue Room (Kendall Square, Eclectic, $$$)

Border Café (Harvard Square, Southwestern, $$)
Dalí (Central Cambridge, Spanish, $$)
Formaggio's Deli (Harvard Square, Sandwiches, $)
The Helmand (East Cambridge, Afghan, $$)
India Pavilion (Central Square, Indian, $)
Kingfish Hall (Downtown, $$$–$$$$)
Koreana (Inman Square, Korean and Sushi, $$–$$$)
Legal Sea Foods (Harvard and Kendall squares, Seafood, $$$)
Midwest Grill (Inman Square, Brazilian, $$)
Mr. Bartley's Burger Cottage (Harvard Square, American, $)
Oleana (Inman Square, Mediterranean, $$$)
Redbones (Davis Square, Barbecue, $$)
Rialto (Harvard Square, Mediterranean, $$$$)
S&S Restaurant (Inman Square, American, $)
Summer Shack (Seafood, $$$)

Chinatown

Buddha's Delight (Vegetarian Vietnamese, $)
Chau Chow City (Dim Sum, $)
China Pearl (Dim Sum, $)
Empire Garden Restaurant (Dim Sum, $)
Penang (Malaysian, $$)
Pho Pasteur (Vietnamese, $)

Downtown

Au Bon Pain (Sandwiches, $)
Bertucci's (Pizza, $)
Chacarero (Chilean Sandwiches, $)
Durgin-Park (New England, $$)
Kingfish Hall (Seafood, $$$–$$$$)
Legal Sea Foods (Seafood, $$$)
Les Zygomates (French Bistro, $$$)
Locke-Ober (American, $$$$)
Sel de la Terre (Mediterranean, $$$)

North End

Artú (Southern Italian and Sandwiches, $–$$)
Daily Catch (Seafood and Southern Italian, $$)
DiMio (Pizza, $–$$)
Giacomo's Ristorante (Seafood and Southern Italian, $$)
Il Panino Express (Sandwiches and Pizza, $)
La Summa (Southern Italian, $$)
Mamma Maria (Northern Italian, $$$$)
Piccola Venezia (Southern Italian, $$)
Pizzeria Regina (Italian, $)

South End

Bob the Chef's Jazz Cafe (American, $$)
Icarus (Eclectic, $$$$)
Nashoba Brook Bakery (Sandwiches, $)
Union Bar and Grille (Contemporary American, $$$$)

Index of Restaurants by Cuisine

American

Bob the Chef's Jazz Cafe (South End, $$)
Bonfire (Downtown, $$$$)
The Bristol (Back Bay, $$$)
Durgin-Park (Downtown, $$)
Excelsior (Back Bay, $$$$)

Grill 23 & Bar (Back Bay, $$$$)
Hamersley's Bistro (Back Bay, $$$)
Hard Rock Cafe (Back Bay, $–$$)
L'Espalier (Back Bay, $$$$)
Locke-Ober (Downtown, $$$$)
The Lounge at the Ritz-Carlton (Back Bay, $$$)

Mr. Bartley's Burger Cottage
(Cambridge/Harvard Square, $)
Olives (Charlestown, $$$–$$$$)
Redbones (Cambridge/Somerville, $$)
S&S Restaurant (Cambridge/
Inman Square, $)
Union Bar and Grille (South End, $$$$)

Asian

Buddha's Delight (Chinatown, $)
Chau Chow City (Chinatown, $)
China Pearl (Chinatown, $)
The Elephant Walk (Back Bay/
Kenmore Square, $$$)
Empire Garden Restaurant
(Chinatown, $)
India Pavilion (Cambridge/
Central Square, $)
Koreana (Cambridge/
Inman Square, $$–$$$)
Penang (Chinatown, $$)
Pho Pasteur (Chinatown, $)

Eclectic

The Blue Room (Cambridge/
Kendall Square, $$$)
Icarus (South End, $$$$)

French

Brasserie Jo (Back Bay, $$–$$$)
Clio (Back Bay, $$$$)
The Elephant Walk (Back Bay/
Kenmore Square, $$$)
L'Espalier (Back Bay, $$$$)
Les Zygomates (Downtown, $$$)

Italian

Artú (North End, $–$$)
Bertucci's (Downtown and other
locations, $)
Daily Catch (North End, $$)
DiMio (North End, $–$$)
Giacomo's Ristorante (North End, $$)
Il Panino Express (North End, $)

La Summa (North End, $$)
Mamma Maria (North End, $$$$)
Piccola Venezia (North End, $$)
Pizzeria Regina (North End, $)

Mediterranean

Dalí (Cambridge/Somerville, $$)
Oleana (Cambridge, $$$)
Rialto (Cambridge/
Harvard Square, $$$$)
Sel de la Terre (Downtown, $$$)

Sandwiches

Artú (North End, $–$$)
Au Bon Pain (Back Bay and other
locations, $)
Chacarero (Downtown Crossing, $)
Formaggio's Deli (Cambridge/Harvard
Square, $)
Nashoba Brook Bakery (South End, $)

Seafood

Daily Catch (North End, $$)
Giacomo's Ristorante (North End, $$)
Great Bay (Back Bay, $$$$)
Kingfish Hall (Downtown, $$$–$$$$)
Legal Sea Foods (Back Bay and other
locations, $$$)
Summer Shack (Back Bay, $$$)

South of the Border

Border Café (Cambridge/
Harvard Square, $$)
Casa Romero (Back Bay, $$$)

Other Ethnic

Asmara Restaurant (Ethiopian and
Eritrean, Cambridge/Central Square, $)
Café Jaffa (Middle Eastern, Back Bay, $)
The Helmand (Afghan,
Cambridge/Kendall Square, $$)
Midwest Grill (Brazilian,
Cambridge/Inman Square, $$)

Index of Restaurants by Price

$

Artú (Southern Italian and Sandwiches, North End)
Asmara Restaurant (Ethiopian and Eritrean, Cambridge/Central Square)
Au Bon Pain (Sandwiches, Back Bay and other locations)
Bertucci's (Pizza, Downtown and other locations)
Buddha's Delight (Vegetarian Vietnamese, Chinatown)
Café Jaffa (Middle Eastern, Back Bay)
Chacarero (Chilean Sandwiches, Downtown Crossing)
Chau Chow City (Dim Sum, Chinatown)
China Pearl (Dim Sum, Chinatown)
DiMio (Pizza, North End)
Empire Garden Restaurant (Dim Sum, Chinatown)
Formaggio's Deli (Sandwiches, Cambridge/Harvard Square)
Hard Rock Cafe (American, Back Bay)
Il Panino Express (Sandwiches and Pizza, North End
Mr. Bartley's Burger Cottage (American, Cambridge/ Harvard Square)
Nashoba Brook Bakery (Sandwiches, South End)
Pho Pasteur (Vietnamese, Chinatown)
Pizzeria Regina (Italian, North End)
S&S Restaurant (American, Cambridge/Inman Square)

$$

Artú (Southern Italian and Sandwiches, North End)
Bob the Chef's Jazz Cafe (American, South End)
Border Café (Southwestern, Cambridge/Harvard Square)
Brasserie Jo (French, Back Bay)
Daily Catch (Seafood and Southern Italian, North End)
Dalí (Spanish, Cambridge/Somerville)
DiMio (Pizza, North End)

Durgin-Park (New England, Downtown)
Giacomo's Ristorante (Seafood and Southern Italian, North End)
Hard Rock Cafe (American, Back Bay)
The Helmand (Afghan, Cambridge/ Kendall Square)
Koreana (Korean and Sushi, Cambridge)
La Summa (Southern Italian, North End)
Midwest Grill (Brazilian, Cambridge/Inman Square)
Penang (Malaysian, Chinatown)
Piccola Venezia (Southern Italian, North End)
Redbones (Barbecue, Cambridge/Somerville)

$$$

The Blue Room (Eclectic, Cambridge/ Kendall Square)
Brasserie Jo (French, Back Bay)
The Bristol (American, Back Bay)
Casa Romero (Classic Mexican, Back Bay)
The Elephant Walk (French and Cambodian, Back Bay/Kenmore Square)
Hamersley's Bistro (American, Back Bay)
Kingfish Hall (Seafood, Downtown)
Koreana (Korean and Sushi, Cambridge)
Legal Sea Foods (Seafood, Back Bay and other locations)
Les Zygomates (French Bistro, Downtown)
The Lounge at the Ritz-Carlton (American, Back Bay)
Oleana (Mediterranean, Cambridge/Inman Square)
Olives (American, Charlestown)
Sel de la Terre (Mediterranean, Downtown/Waterfront)
Summer Shack (Seafood, Back Bay/ Cambridge)

$$$$

Bonfire (American, Back Bay)
Clio (French, Back Bay)
Excelsior (American, Back Bay)
Great Bay (Seafood, Back Bay)
Grill 23 & Bar (American, Back Bay)
Icarus (Eclectic, South End)
Kingfish Hall (Seafood, Downtown)
L'Espalier (New England and French,
Back Bay)

Locke-Ober (American, Downtown)
Mamma Maria (Northern Italian,
North End)
Olives (American, Charlestown)
Rialto (Mediterranean, Cambridge/
Harvard Square)
Union Bar and Grille (Contemporary
American, South End)

Part IV
Exploring Boston

The 5th Wave   By Rich Tennant

@RICHTENNANT

"Only at a jazz club in the biotech section of Cambridge could you hear one of the great baritone test tube players of all time."

In this part . . .

*I*n this part, I reach the heart of the matter: the experiences and activities that led you to choose Boston over every other potential destination. (If the meeting planners or the bride and groom or your parents chose for you, think of this part as the "maybe they know what they're doing" section.)

You can approach Boston as a history lesson, an art gallery, a seafood buffet, or even a giant shopping center. You can concentrate on a specific interest or skip around. You can spend a day, a weekend, or a month and still only scratch the surface. You can pick a neighborhood and settle in or head out for a day trip. Weigh the innumerable options, don't try to do too much, and soon you'll be on your way to a good time. The information in this part helps you mix and match a trip that's just right for you.

Chapter 11

Discovering Boston's Best Attractions

In This Chapter

▶ Finding the best destinations and most entertaining activities
▶ Planning a rewarding visit
▶ Mapping the Freedom Trail

*B*oston stimulates all your senses: You see great paintings and sculpture, hear classical and popular music, taste ocean-fresh seafood, smell the perfume of Public Garden flowerbeds, and feel the breeze off the harbor in your hair. The preceding chapters address getting to Boston and finding shelter and food. This chapter describes the most popular attractions and contains separate sections on the world-famous Freedom Trail and guided tours.

The best thing you can do at this stage is to forget that you know the words *should* and *ought*. Listen to yourself (and me, of course), not to the friends who say you *must* see or do something that sounds, to you, as dull as watching paint dry. If you think it's boring, it is — and there's no reason to be bored in Boston.

The Top Attractions

Many Boston-area attractions are government (federal, state, and city) property, with the same concern for security Americans have come to expect at other government institutions. You may have to pass through a checkpoint, have your bag inspected, clear a metal detector, or stay a certain distance from some buildings or public spaces.

For locations of the various attractions described here, see the "Boston Attractions" and "Cambridge Attractions" maps in this chapter, unless otherwise noted.

Faneuil Hall Marketplace
Downtown

This is one of the city's most popular attractions for a reason: It promises an agreeable amalgam of recreation, retail, and restaurants. Brick plazas and plenty of outdoor seating surround the five-building "festival market" complex, which buzzes with activity from just past dawn till well past dark in pleasant weather year-round. Dozens of stores, shops, boutiques, and pushcarts share space with restaurants, bars, and food counters.

The marketplace is busiest in summer and fall, which are peak travel times when street performers and musicians make the rounds. The shopping ranges from generic to quirky, while the dining ranges from fast to fancy. The central building, **Quincy Market,** contains a food court that runs the length of the building. You don't need to spend a penny to enjoy the fun, though. Between entertainers on the streets and visitors from all over the world, the marketplace also offers great people-watching. True, this spot is touristy, especially in warm weather — but sometimes you just need to relax and let your inner tourist look around.

See "The Freedom Trail" section, later in this chapter, for information about **Faneuil Hall.**

Between North, Congress, and State streets and I-93. ☎ *617-338-2323. T: Government Center (Green or Blue Line); cross the plaza, walk down the stairs, and cross Congress Street. Or Haymarket (Orange Line); follow Congress Street (with City Hall Plaza on your right) for 2 to 3 blocks. Open: Marketplace Mon–Sat 10 a.m.–9 p.m.; Sun noon to 6 p.m. Food court opens earlier; restaurant hours vary.*

Harvard University
Cambridge

It's not just old, famous, and known for educating many notable people — as are dozens of similar institutions. Harvard is the country's *oldest* (established in 1636) and *best-known* college, as well as the alma mater of five American presidents. The heart of the campus, two hopelessly picturesque quadrangles known as **Harvard Yard** (or just "the Yard"), sits behind the brick walls that run along Mass. Ave. and Quincy and Cambridge streets.

The Yard is the oldest part of the campus and contains Harvard's oldest building, **Massachusetts Hall** (1720), home to the university president's office. Also in the Yard, in front of University Hall, you find the **John Harvard Statue** (1884), a magnet for photographers from all over the world. Campus legend nicknames it "the Statue of Three Lies" because its inscription reads "John Harvard — Founder — 1638." The truth: The college dates to 1636; Harvard bestowed money and his library on the fledgling institution but wasn't *the* founder; and sculptor Daniel Chester French's model reputedly was either a descendant of Harvard's or a student.

Time- and money-saving suggestions

Here are two good options for visitors spending more than a day or two:

✔ The **Boston CityPass** includes tickets to the John F. Kennedy Library, Harvard Museum of Natural History, Museum of Fine Arts, Museum of Science, New England Aquarium, and Prudential Center Skywalk. The price is subject to change as museum fees skyrocket. At press time, adults pay $34; children ages 3 to 17 pay $20. For adults, that's a 50 percent savings if you visit all six attractions (and you don't need to wait in line!). The passes, good for nine days from the date of purchase, are sold at participating attractions, as well as at the Boston Common and Prudential Center visitor information centers, through the Greater Boston Convention & Visitors Bureau (☎ **800-SEE-BOSTON**), at some hotel concierge desks, and online at www.citypass.net.

✔ The **Go Boston card** (☎ **617-848-5900**; www.gobostoncard.com) includes admission to more than 30 Boston-area museums and attractions, dining and shopping discounts, a guidebook, and a two-day Beantown Trolley ticket. It's expensive — $39 for one day, $69 for two days, $89 for three days, or $109 for five days, with discounts for children and for winter travelers — but if you strategize wisely, it's a great value. The Go Boston Card is available through the Web site, at the Transportation Building located at 16 Charles St. S., at many concierge desks, and as part of some hotel packages.

Across Mass. Ave., the Events & Information Center distributes maps and self-guided tour directions and has a bulletin board that lists campus activities. You may also want to visit the university's art and science museums; see the listings later in this chapter.

Events & Information Center: Holyoke Center, 1350 Mass. Ave. ☎ **617-495-1573.** www.harvard.edu. *T: Harvard (Red Line). Open: Information Center Mon–Sat 9 a.m.–5 p.m.; Sun noon to 5 p.m. Free guided tours four times a day Mon–Sat during the summer; during school year (except vacations), twice a day on weekdays, and once on Sat. Call for exact times; reservations aren't necessary.*

Isabella Stewart Gardner Museum
Fenway

Arts patron Isabella Stewart Gardner (1840 to 1924) designed this magnificent home in the style of a 15th-century Venetian palace. After Gardner's death, the home became a gorgeous museum — and a testament to the timeless judgment of a fascinating, iconoclastic woman. The collections include European, American, and Asian painting and sculpture, and furniture and architectural details from European churches and palaces. Allow at least two hours to peruse works by Titian, Botticelli, Raphael, Rembrandt, Matisse, James McNeill Whistler, and John Singer Sargent. Under the terms of Gardner's will, the arrangement of the galleries does not change; special shows go up in a separate space two or three times a year.

Boston Attractions

Boston Public Library **7**
Boston Tea Party Ship & Museum
  (closed indefinitely) **23**
Children's Museum **24**
Faneuil Hall Marketplace **19**
Fenway Park **1**
FleetCenter **17**
Foster's Rotunda **21**
Gibson House Museum **9**
Harrison Gray Otis House **15**
Independence Wharf **22**
Institute of Contemporary Art **5**
Isabella Stewart Gardner Museum **2**
John F. Kennedy Library and Museum **25**

Make Way for Ducklings **12**
Mapparium / Mary Baker Eddy Library **4**
Museum of Afro-American History **14**
Museum of Fine Arts **3**
Museum of Science **16**
New England Aquarium **20**
Nichols House Museum **13**
Paul Revere House **18**
Prudential Center Skywalk **6**
Public Garden **10**
Sports Museum of New England **17**
Swan Boats **11**
Trinity Church **8**

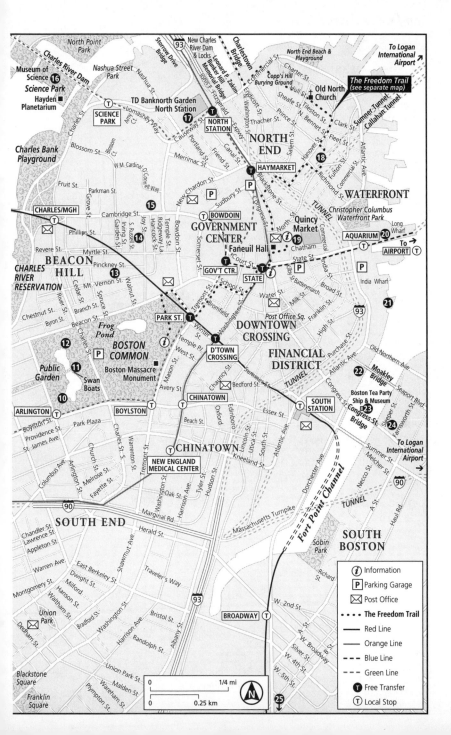

North Point Park

Museum of Science **16**
Science Park
Hayden
Planetarium

Charles River Dam

Nashua Street Park

New Charles River Dam & Locks

Charlestown Bridge

Copp's Hill Burying Ground

North End Beach & Playground

Charter St.

Commercial St.

To Logan International Airport

Old North Church

The Freedom Trail
(see separate map)

Sumner Tunnel
Callahan Tunnel

Storrow Drive

Leonard P. Zakim Bunker Hill Memorial Bridge

John F. Fitzgerald Expwy.

Hull St.

Sheafe St. Tileston St.

Prince St.

N. Bennet St.

Clark St.

Fleet St.

Atlantic Ave.

TD Banknorth Garden North Station

SCIENCE PARK

Lomasney Way

Army Ct.

NORTH STATION **17**

Causeway St.

Portland St.

Canal St.

Friend St.

Thacher St.

Washington St.

Hanover St.

NORTH END

Salem St.

Richmond St.

Commercial St.

Fulton St.

18

WATERFRONT

Charles Bank Playground

Blossom St.

Blossom St.

W.M. Cardinal / O'Connell Way

Merrimac St.

New Chardon St.

Sudbury St.

Congress St.

Blackstone St.

HAYMARKET

TUNNEL

Christopher Columbus Waterfront Park

Long Wharf

Fruit St.

Parkman St.

15

BOWDOIN

GOVERNMENT CENTER

Quincy Market

North St.

CHARLES/MGH

Cambridge St.

Temple St.

Ridgeway La.

Bowdoin St.

Somerset St.

Chatham

Commercial St.

AQUARIUM **20**

To AIRPORT

Phillips St.

Joy St.

S. Russell St.

Hancock St.

Irving St.

Garden St.

14

Faneuil Hall

Court St.

State St.

India St.

Revere St.

Myrtle St.

BEACON

GOV'T CTR.

STATE

S. Battenmarch

Broad St.

India Wharf

CHARLES RIVER RESERVATION

HILL

Pinckney St.

13

Mt. Vernon St.

Walnut St.

School St.

Water St.

Milk St.

Franklin St.

High St.

21

Chestnut St.

Branch St.

Spruce St.

Cedar St.

River St.

Beacon St.

Tremont St.

Bromfield St.

Post Office Sq.

Old Northern Ave.

Byron St.

Charles St.

Frog Pond

PARK ST.

Winter St.

Washington St.

DOWNTOWN CROSSING

Purchase Ave.

Atlantic Ave.

Congress St.

22

Moakley Bridge

Seaport Blvd.

12

BOSTON COMMON

Temple Pl.

West St.

FINANCIAL DISTRICT

Summer St.

Public Garden

11

Boston Massacre Monument

Mason St.

D'TOWN CROSSING

Chancy St.

Bedford St.

Boston Tea Party Ship & Museum

Congress St. Bridge

23

Farnsworth St.

Swan Boats

Avery St.

CHINATOWN

Oxford St.

Lincoln St.

Utica St.

Atlantic Ave.

SOUTH STATION

24

10

ARLINGTON

BOYLSTON

Beach St.

Edinboro

Essex St.

To Logan International Airport

Boylston St.

Park Plaza

Charles St. S.

CHINATOWN

Kneeland St.

Melcher St.

Providence St.

St. James Ave.

Church St.

Warrenton St.

Tremont St.

NEW ENGLAND MEDICAL CENTER

Washington St.

Tyler St.

Hudson St.

Sumner Tunnel

Necco St.

Arlington St.

Melrose St.

Fayette St.

Oak St.

Harrison Ave.

Marginal Rd.

TUNNEL

90

Columbus Ave.

90

Massachusetts Turnpike

Haul Rd.

Chandler St.

Herald St.

Fort Point Channel

SOUTH BOSTON

Lawrence St.

Appleton St.

SOUTH END

Shawmut Ave.

Traveler's Way

Sobin Park

Richard St.

Warren Ave.

East Berkeley St.

Dwight St.

Milford St.

(i) Information

Montgomery St.

Hanson St.

P Parking Garage

Waltham St.

Bristol St.

93

W. 2nd St.

✉ Post Office

Union Park

Bradford St.

Albany St.

W. Broadway

• • • **The Freedom Trail**

Dedham St.

Washington St.

Harrison Ave.

Randolph St.

BROADWAY

Silver St.

W. 3rd St.

——— Red Line

╍╍╍╍ Orange Line

Blackstone Square

Union Park St.

Malden St.

Plympton St.

Wareham St.

W. 4th St.

╍ ╍ ╍ Blue Line

Franklin Square

0   1/4 mi

0   0.25 km

W. 5th St.

25

╍ ╍ ╍ Green Line

T Free Transfer

(T) Local Stop

Cambridge Attractions

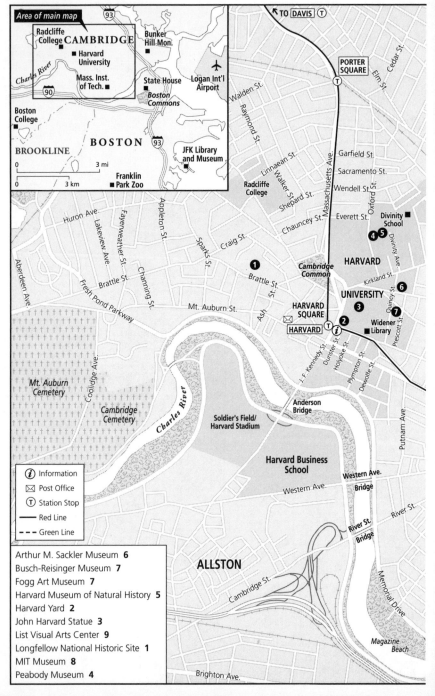

Arthur M. Sackler Museum **6**
Busch-Reisinger Museum **7**
Fogg Art Museum **7**
Harvard Museum of Natural History **5**
Harvard Yard **2**
John Harvard Statue **3**
List Visual Arts Center **9**
Longfellow National Historic Site **1**
MIT Museum **8**
Peabody Museum **4**

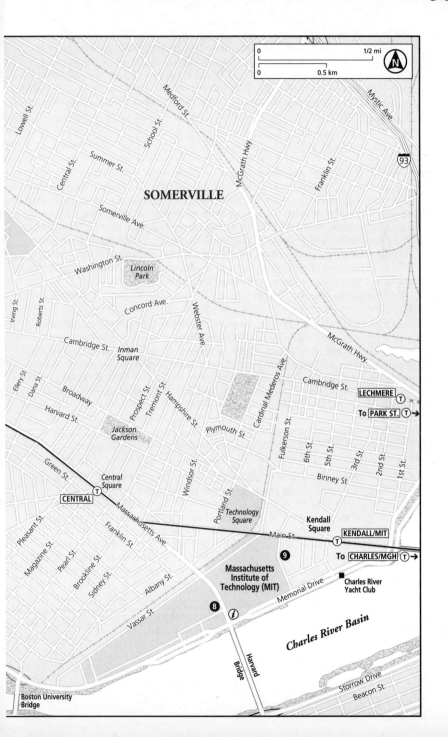

280 The Fenway (at Museum Road, off Huntington Avenue). ☎ **617-566-1401.** www. gardnermuseum.org. *T: Museum (Green Line E); walk 2 blocks straight ahead (away from Huntington Avenue, with the Museum of Fine Arts on your right). Admission: $11 adults weekends, $10 adults weekdays, $7 seniors, $5 college students with ID, and free for children under age 18 and adults named Isabella with ID. Open: Tues–Sun 11 a.m.–5 p.m. and some Mon holidays. Closed Thanksgiving, Dec 25, and Dec 31.*

John F. Kennedy Library and Museum
Dorchester

A magnificent building designed by I. M. Pei, the Kennedy Library celebrates the life and legacy of the 35th president. History buffs will want to spend at least 90 minutes exploring exhibits that recall "Camelot." The displays include audio and video recordings, replicas of the Oval Office and the office of Attorney General Robert F. Kennedy, a film about the Cuban missile crisis, and imaginatively displayed documents and memorabilia. A 17-minute film about Kennedy's early life introduces the museum, which regularly updates displays and schedules special exhibits, lectures, and other events. Allow for travel time — 30 minutes from or to downtown Boston.

Columbia Point (off Morrissey Boulevard). ☎ **877-616-4599** or *617-514-1600.* www. jfklibrary.org. *T: JFK/UMass (Red Line); then take the free shuttle bus, which runs every 20 minutes. By car: Take I-93/Route 3 south to Exit 15 (Morrissey Boulevard/JFK Library), turn left onto Columbia Road, and follow the signs to the free parking lot. Admission: $10 adults; $8 seniors, students with ID, and youths 13–17; free for children under 13. Open: Daily 9 a.m.–5 p.m. (last film at 3:55). Closed Jan 1, Thanksgiving, and Dec 25.*

Museum of Fine Arts
Fenway

Out-of-towners typically hear about the MFA because of special exhibitions and traveling shows, not because of the real appeal: an unbeatable combination of the familiar and the unexpected. The galleries contain so many classic pieces that you'll probably feel as if you've bumped into an old friend at least once during your visit. The collections span the centuries and the globe — from Old Kingdom Egyptian collections (that means mummies, kids) to contemporary photography. The celebrated Impressionist paintings include dozens of Monets. And you'll always run across something, ancient or modern, that leaves you glad you made the trip.

Schedule at least half a day to explore; art fiends should allow more time. The best way to get an overview is to take a free **guided tour.** They start on weekdays (except Monday holidays) at 10:30 a.m. and 1:30 p.m.; Wednesdays at 6:15 p.m.; and Saturdays at 10:30 a.m. and 1 p.m. If you prefer to explore the sprawling galleries on your own, pick up a floor plan or family-activity booklet at the information desk. Check ahead for special family- and child-friendly activities, which take place year-round.

The MFA is one of the most expensive museums in the country; if your plans allow, a Boston CityPass can be a great investment.

465 Huntington Ave. (at Museum Road). ☎ *617-267-9300.* www.mfa.org. *T: Museum (Green Line E). Or Ruggles (Orange Line); walk 2 blocks on Ruggles Street. Admission, good for 2 visits within 30 days of purchase: Adults $15 entire museum, $13 when only West Wing is open; students and seniors $13 entire museum, $11 when only West Wing is open. Children under 18 $5 on school days before 3 p.m., otherwise free. Voluntary contribution ($15 suggested), Wed 4:00–9:45 p.m. Surcharges may apply for special exhibitions. No fee to visit only shop, library, or auditoriums. Open: Entire museum Sat–Tues 10 a.m.–4:45 p.m.; Wed 10 a.m.–9:45 p.m.; Thurs–Fri 10 a.m.–5 p.m. West Wing only Thurs–Fri 5–9:45 p.m. Closed Jan 1, Patriots Day, July 4, Thanksgiving, and Dec 25.*

Museum of Science
Science Park (between Boston and East Cambridge)

A superb destination for children and adults, the Museum of Science introduces principles and theories so painlessly that the intro is almost sneaky. Hands-on displays and exhibits explore every scientific field you can imagine, but — I can't emphasize this enough — always in a fun, accessible way.

Allow at least a couple of hours; if you plan to take in a show (see the next paragraph), you may want to set aside a day. The Virtual FishTank, acquired when the science museum joined forces with the Computer Museum, is one of the most popular exhibits. You can "build" your fish using your home computer (visit www.virtualfishtank.com) or on the scene and then watch as your new pet interacts with other people's creations.

A show at one of the museum's theaters, which charge separate admission, is well worth your time. The Mugar Omni Theater shows IMAX movies on a five-story domed screen; the Charles Hayden Planetarium schedules daily star shows, weekend rock-music laser extravaganzas, and shows on special astronomical topics.

Buy all of your tickets at once, not only because you save money but also because shows may sell out. You can buy tickets in person or order them in advance (subject to a service charge) over the phone or online using a credit card.

Science Park (off Route 28). ☎ *617-723-2500.* www.mos.org. *T: Science Park (Green Line); follow signs along elevated walkway onto bridge. Admission: Exhibit halls $13 adults, $11 seniors, $10 children 3–11, free for children under 3. Mugar Omni Theater, Hayden Planetarium, or laser shows $8.50 adults, $7.50 seniors, $6.50 children 3–11, free for children under 3. Discounted admission tickets for two or three attraction combinations. Open: Museum July 5–Labor Day Sat–Thurs 9 a.m.–7 p.m., Fri 9 a.m.–9 p.m.; day after Labor Day–July 4 Sat–Thurs 9 a.m.–5 p.m., Fri 9 a.m.–9 p.m. Shows during museum hours and some evenings; call or check the Web site for the schedule. Closed Thanksgiving and Dec 25.*

A room with a view, times two

A sensational view is its own reward, and it's so much more rewarding if it's free. Not far from the Aquarium are two buildings with public observation areas that overlook the harbor, the airport, and the South Boston waterfront. Admission is free, but be ready to show an ID and perhaps sign in. The viewing area on the 14th floor of Independence Wharf, 470 Atlantic Ave., at Northern Avenue, is open daily from 11 a.m. to 5 p.m. Foster's Rotunda, on the ninth floor of 30 Rowes Wharf (in the Boston Harbor Hotel complex), is open Monday to Friday from 11 a.m. to 4 p.m.

New England Aquarium
Waterfront

A sprawling complex that overlooks Boston Harbor, the Aquarium is home to more than 15,000 fish and aquatic mammals. The centerpiece is the 200,000-gallon Giant Ocean Tank; other exhibits focus on local ecology, the Aquarium medical center, and a roster of regularly changing special topics. Allow at least 2½ hours for the Aquarium, plus an hour or so if you plan to take in a film in the state-of-the-art Simons IMAX Theatre.

"Science at Sea" harbor tours operate daily in the spring, summer, and fall. Tickets are $13 for adults, $10 for seniors and college students with ID, $9 for youths 12 to 18, and $9 for children under 12. IMAX tickets cost $8 for adults, $6 for seniors and children 3 to 11. Discounts are available when you combine a visit to the Aquarium with a harbor tour, an IMAX movie, or a whale watch.

At busy times, the Aquarium can be uncomfortably crowded and the lines unbearably long. The Boston CityPass is a good option — in time even more than money — on hot summer days when having a ticket allows you to go straight to the entrance. Seriously consider investing in the pass, especially if you're traveling with restless children. If you don't buy a pass, try to make this spot your first stop of the day and arrive when the doors open.

Central Wharf (off Atlantic Avenue at State Street). ☎ *617-973-5200. Simons IMAX Theatre:* ☎ *866-815-4629.* www.newenglandaquarium.org. *T: Aquarium (Blue Line). Admission: Aquarium $16 adults, $14 seniors, $9 children 3–11, free for children under 3. Simons IMAX Theatre $9 adults, $7 seniors and children 3–11. No fee to visit outdoor exhibits, cafe, and gift shop. Open: Aquarium July–Labor Day Mon–Thurs 9 a.m.–6 p.m.; Fri–Sun and holidays 9 a.m.–7 p.m. Day after Labor Day–June Mon–Fri 9 a.m.–5 p.m.; Sat–Sun and holidays 9 a.m.–6 p.m. Simons IMAX Theatre year-round daily 10 a.m.–9 p.m. Closed Dec 25 and until noon Jan 1.*

Prudential Center Skywalk
Back Bay

The 50-story Prudential Tower boasts Boston's only 360-degree view. The interactive displays are interesting, and the panorama can't be beat. Visit at twilight on slightly overcast days to enjoy spectacular sunsets. The 52nd floor holds the Top of the Hub restaurant and lounge (see Chapter 16).

Note: Adults must show a photo ID to enter the Prudential Tower.

800 Boylston St. (at Fairfield Street). ☎ *617-859-0648. T: Prudential (Green Line E) or Copley (Green Line B, C, or D); walk toward tower. Admission: $7 adults, $4 seniors and children 4–10. Open: Daily 10 a.m.–10 p.m.*

Public Garden/Swan Boats
Back Bay

One of the most pleasant spots in the city, the Public Garden is 8 square blocks of peaceful greenery surrounding an agreeable body of water. The oldest botanical garden in the country boasts thriving blooms from spring through late fall, and the action on the lagoon is always diverting. Children love to feed the geese, ducks, and swans. Adults get a kick out of the sculptures and monuments, which commemorate George Washington, the first use of ether as an anesthetic, and other apparently random people and events.

The **Swan Boats** have been synonymous with Boston since 1877. Still operated by the same family, the fiberglass birds on pedal boats (the attendants pedal, not the passengers) make a great low-tech break. Fans of *The Trumpet of the Swan* (HarperCollins, Collector's edition, 2000), by E. B. White, can't miss these vessels. Allow 30 minutes.

Near the corner of Charles and Beacon streets, nine little bronze figures immortalize Robert McCloskey's book *Make Way for Ducklings* (Viking Press, 1941; Puffin Books, Reprint edition, 1999). Nancy Schön's renderings of Mrs. Mallard and her babies inspire delighted shrieks from small visitors.

Between Arlington, Boylston, Charles, and Beacon streets. T: Arlington (Green Line). Or Charles/MGH (Red Line); follow Charles Street 5 blocks to Beacon Street. Open: Daily year-round. As in any park, be careful at night, especially if you're alone.

Swan Boats ☎ *617-522-1966.* www.swanboats.com. *Admission: $2 adults, $1.50 seniors, $1 children 2–15. Open: Daily, third Sat of April–mid-Sept.; summer 10 a.m.– 5 p.m.; spring 10 a.m.–4 p.m.; fall weekdays noon to 4 p.m.; fall weekends 10 a.m.– 4 p.m.*

The Freedom Trail

Saying "16 historic sights make up the 3-mile Freedom Trail" gives no sense of the role the trail (www.thefreedomtrail.org) plays for visitors to Boston. Not only are the attractions interesting, but the trail — a line of bricks or red paint on the sidewalk from Boston Common to Charlestown — also makes finding your way around considerably less confusing than it would be otherwise.

This section lists the stops along the trail, starting with Boston Common and ending with the Bunker Hill Monument. I cover them in the order that usually appears in pamphlets, maps, and other publications, but you don't have to speed-walk from one end to the other, go in exact order, or even see everything. Start in Charlestown and work backward, skip a stop or two, or even get "lost" — this area is too small for you to go too far astray. I insist on just one thing: Wear comfortable walking shoes.

The Freedom Trail takes at least two hours, even if you don't linger too long at any one stop. If that's too much time, consider a free 90-minute walking tour of the "heart" of the trail with a National Park Service ranger. The **Freedom Trail Foundation** (☎ **617-357-8300;** www.the freedomtrail.org) rents handheld digital audio players, for use with or without headphones, that allow visitors to take a narrated tour at their own pace. The two-hour narrative includes interviews, sound effects, and music. Players rent for $15 for the first adult, $12 for each additional adult, and $10 for each child; they're available at the Boston Common Visitor Center.

To head out on your own, start at the Visitor Information Center at 146 Tremont St., on Boston Common. Take the T to Park Street (Red or Green Line).

Boston Common
Downtown/Beacon Hill

In 1634, the town of Boston bought what's now the country's oldest park. In 1640, the land became common ground; it later served as a cow pasture (until 1830), military camp, and all-purpose municipal gathering place. Plaques and memorials abound. One of the loveliest is up the hill from the T station, on Beacon Street across from the State House. Augustus Saint-Gaudens designed the bas-relief **Robert Gould Shaw Memorial,** which honors Colonel Shaw and the Union Army's 54th Massachusetts Colored Regiment, which fought in the Civil War. (The 1989 movie *Glory,* with Matthew Broderick and Denzel Washington, told the story of the first American army unit made up of free black soldiers.)

Between Beacon, Park, Tremont, Boylston, and Charles streets. Visitor Information Center ☎ 800-SEE-BOSTON or 617-536-4100. T: Park Street (Red or Green Line).

The Freedom Trail

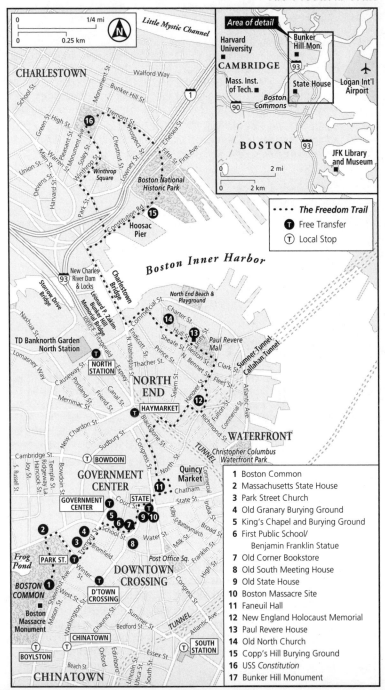

0   1/4 mi
0   0.25 km

Little Mystic Channel

Area of detail

Harvard University ■
CAMBRIDGE
Mass. Inst. of Tech. ■
Boston Commons

Bunker Hill Mon. ■
State House ■
Logan Int'l Airport ✈

BOSTON

JFK Library and Museum ■

0   2 mi
0   2 km

CHARLESTOWN

Walford Way

Bunker Hill St.

Tremont St.

Winthrop Square

Boston National Historic Park

Hoosac Pier

•••• **The Freedom Trail**
🅣 Free Transfer
🅣 Local Stop

Boston Inner Harbor

New Charles River Dam & Locks

Charlestown Bridge

North End Beach & Playground

TD Banknorth Garden North Station

NORTH STATION

Paul Revere Mall

NORTH END

HAYMARKET

WATERFRONT

Christopher Columbus Waterfront Park

BOWDOIN

GOVERNMENT CENTER

Quincy Market

GOVERNMENT CENTER

STATE

Frog Pond

PARK ST.

BOSTON COMMON

D'TOWN CROSSING

DOWNTOWN CROSSING

Boston Massacre Monument ■

CHINATOWN

BOYLSTON

SOUTH STATION

CHINATOWN

1   Boston Common
2   Massachusetts State House
3   Park Street Church
4   Old Granary Burying Ground
5   King's Chapel and Burying Ground
6   First Public School/ Benjamin Franklin Statue
7   Old Corner Bookstore
8   Old South Meeting House
9   Old State House
10   Boston Massacre Site
11   Faneuil Hall
12   New England Holocaust Memorial
13   Paul Revere House
14   Old North Church
15   Copp's Hill Burying Ground
16   USS *Constitution*
17   Bunker Hill Monument

Massachusetts State House
Beacon Hill

Governor Samuel Adams laid the cornerstone of the state capitol in 1795. The great Federal-era architect Charles Bulfinch designed the imposing central building and landmark golden dome. Free tours — guided and self-guided — leave from the second floor. Visit the rear of the building, off Bowdoin Street, to see a 60-foot monument that illustrates the hill's original height (material from the top went into 19th-century landfill projects).

Beacon St. (at Park Street). ☎ *617-727-3676.* www.mass.gov/statehouse. *T: Park Street (Red or Green Line); walk up Park Street 1 block. Admission: Free. Open: Weekdays 9 a.m.–5 p.m. Tours Mon–Fri 10 a.m.–3:30 p.m.*

Park Street Church
Downtown/Beacon Hill

Henry James described this 1809 structure as "the most interesting mass of bricks and mortar in America." Plaques arrayed around the entrance describe the storied history, which includes the first public performance of "America" ("My Country 'Tis of Thee") on July 4, 1831.

1 Park St. (at Tremont Street). ☎ *617-523-3383.* www.parkstreet.org. *T: Park Street (Red or Green Line). Admission: Free. Open: July–Aug Tues–Sat 9:30 a.m.–3:30 p.m. Year-round services Sun 8:30 a.m., 11 a.m., 4 p.m., 6 p.m.*

Old Granary Burying Ground
Downtown

This cemetery, which dates to 1660, was once part of Boston Common. The graveyard contains the final resting places of patriots Samuel Adams, Paul Revere, John Hancock, and James Otis; merchant Peter Faneuil (spelled "FUNAL"); the victims of the Boston Massacre; and Benjamin Franklin's parents. The wife of Isaac Vergoose, whom historians believe was "Mother Goose" of nursery-rhyme fame, is also buried here.

Gravestone rubbing is illegal in Boston's historic cemeteries (and pretty bad karma, if you ask me).

Tremont Street (at Bromfield Street). T: Park Street (Red or Green Line); walk 1 block on Tremont Street with Boston Common behind you. Open: Daily 8 a.m.–5 p.m. (until 3 p.m. in the winter).

King's Chapel and Burying Ground
Downtown

A squat granite structure, King's Chapel is historically and architecturally interesting. The first Anglican church in Boston, it replaced a wooden chapel, and construction (from 1749 to 1754) went on *around* the previous building. After the Revolution, in a rejection of the royal religion, King's Chapel became the first Unitarian church in America.

The **burying ground,** on Tremont Street, is the oldest in the city (1630). Elaborate colonial headstones dot the graveyard, which contains the graves of John Winthrop, the first governor of the Massachusetts Bay Colony; William Dawes, who rode with Paul Revere; and Mary Chilton, the first female colonist to step ashore on Plymouth Rock.

58 Tremont St. (at School Street). ☎ *617-523-1749. T: Government Center (Green or Blue Line); walk 1 block on Tremont Street. Admission: Donation requested from adults visiting chapel. Open: Chapel summer daily 9:30 a.m.–1 p.m.; winter Sat 10 a.m.–2 p.m. Services Wed 12:15 p.m., Sun 11 a.m. Burying ground daily 8 a.m.– 5:30 p.m. (until 3 p.m. in winter).*

First Public School/Benjamin Franklin Statue
Downtown

A colorful folk-art mosaic marks the site of the first public school in the country, which opened in 1634 (two years before Harvard). The school's illustrious alumni include John Hancock, Benjamin Franklin, Charles Bulfinch, Ralph Waldo Emerson, George Santayana, and Leonard Bernstein. Now called Boston Latin School, the structure still exists in the Fenway neighborhood.

A statue of Boston native **Benjamin Franklin** (1706 to 1790) is inside the fence. The plaques on the base describe Franklin's numerous accomplishments. The elegant granite building behind the statue is **Old City Hall,** built in 1865 and designed in Second Empire style by Arthur Gilman (who laid out the Back Bay) and Gridley J. F. Bryant.

School Street (at Province Street). T: State (Orange or Blue Line); walk 2 blocks on Washington Street and turn right.

Old Corner Bookstore Building
Downtown

This land once held the home of religious reformer Anne Hutchinson, who wasted no time in ticking off the church authorities — in 1638, a mere eight years after the establishment of Boston, they excommunicated her and expelled her from town. In the middle of the 19th century, the little brick building (which dates to 1712) held the publishing house of Ticknor & Fields. Publisher James "Jamie" Fields's wide circle of friends included Henry Wadsworth Longfellow, Henry David Thoreau, Ralph Waldo Emerson, Nathaniel Hawthorne, and Harriet Beecher Stowe.

3 School St. (at Washington Street). T: State (Orange or Blue Line); walk 2 blocks up Washington Street.

Old South Meeting House
Downtown

The Boston Tea Party started in this building, which remains a religious and political gathering place today. On December 16, 1773, revolutionaries protesting the royal tea tax assembled here and wound up dumping the cargo of three ships into the harbor. An interactive multimedia exhibit tells the building's fascinating story. This structure, with a landmark clock tower, dates to 1729; the original went up in 1670.

310 Washington St. ☎ *617-482-6439.* www.oldsouthmeetinghouse.org. *T: State (Orange or Blue Line); walk 3 blocks up Washington Street. Admission: $5 adults, $4 seniors and students, $1 children 6–18, free for children under 6. Open: Daily April–Oct 9:30 a.m.–5 p.m.; Nov–March daily 10 a.m.–4 p.m.*

Old State House
Downtown

Built in 1713, the Old State House served as the seat of the colony's government before the Revolution and as the state capitol until 1797. The gilded lion and unicorn that adorn the exterior are replicas — the original symbols of British rule went into a bonfire on July 18, 1776, the day Bostonians first heard the Declaration of Independence read from the balcony. Inside, you find the Bostonian Society's **museum of the city's history.** Displays include an introductory video on the history of the building and changing exhibits that showcase the society's enormous collection of documents, photographs, and artifacts. Plan on at least 45 minutes if you enjoy history, considerably less if you're more interested in architecture (or in getting to Faneuil Hall Marketplace for some shopping and eating).

206 Washington St. (at State Street). ☎ *617-720-3290.* www.bostonhistory.org. *T: State (Blue or Orange Line). Admission: $5 adults, $4 seniors and students, $1 children 6–18, free for children under 6. Open: Daily 9 a.m.–5 p.m.*

Boston Massacre Site
Downtown

Look for the ring of cobblestones on the traffic island in the middle of State Street alongside the Old State House. This spot marks the approximate site of the Boston Massacre, a conflict that took place March 5, 1770, and helped launch the colonial rebellion. Angered at the presence of royal troops in Boston, colonists threw snowballs, garbage, rocks, and other debris at a group of soldiers. The redcoats panicked and fired into the crowd, killing five men, who lie in the Old Granary Burying Ground.

State Street at Devonshire Street. T: State (Blue or Orange Line).

Faneuil Hall
Downtown

The "Cradle of Liberty" was a gift to the city from prosperous merchant Peter Faneuil. Built in 1742, the site grew to more than twice the original size in 1805, using a Charles Bulfinch design. Note the statue on the Congress Street side of Samuel Adams (yes, as in the beer), one of the countless orators whose declamations shook the building in the years before the Revolution. Faneuil Hall also played host to advocates of abolition, temperance, and women's suffrage. Under the terms of Faneuil's will, the building remains a public meeting (and sometimes concert) hall, and

On the trail of Charles Bulfinch

On Hanover Street between Prince and Fleet streets — between the Paul Revere House and Old North Church stops on the Freedom Trail — is **St. Stephen's,** the only church still standing in Boston that was designed by the preeminent architect of the Federal style, Charles Bulfinch. The church was Unitarian when it was dedicated in 1804. St. Stephen's became Roman Catholic in 1862 to serve the North End's burgeoning immigrant population. Rose Fitzgerald, mother of President John F. Kennedy, was baptized in this church in 1898. During refurbishment in 1965, it regained its original appearance, with clear glass windows, white walls, and gilded organ pipes.

the ground floor holds retail space. National Park Service rangers give free 20-minute talks every half-hour in the second-floor auditorium and operate a visitor center on the first floor.

The French Huguenot name "Faneuil" more or less rhymes with "Daniel"; *Fan*-yoo-ul is another pronunciation.

Across North Street on Union Street, you see a series of glass towers in a small park; this is the **New England Holocaust Memorial** (☎ 617-457-8755; www.nehm.org). Built in 1995, this memorial is a moving reminder, in the midst of attractions that celebrate freedom, of the consequences of a world without it. The pattern on the glass is 6 million random numbers, one for each Jew who died during the Holocaust.

Dock Square (Congress Street off North Street). ☎ 617-242-5675. T: Government Center (Green or Blue Line) or Haymarket (Orange Line). Admission: Free. Open: Second floor daily 9 a.m.–5 p.m.; ground floor Mon–Sat 10 a.m.–9 p.m., Sun noon to 6 p.m.

Paul Revere House
North End

Remember "Listen, my children, and you shall hear / Of the midnight ride of Paul Revere"? Paul Revere's ride started here, in what's now one of the most enjoyable stops on the Freedom Trail. On April 18, 1775, Revere set out for Lexington and Concord and into the American imagination (courtesy of Henry Wadsworth Longfellow) from his home, which he had bought in 1770. The oldest house in downtown Boston, Revere's home dates to around 1680. The self-guided tour permits a glimpse of 18th-century life and many family heirlooms.

19 North Square (at North Street between Richmond and Prince streets). ☎ 617-523-2338. www.paulreverehouse.org. T: Haymarket (Green or Orange Line). Follow signs to the North End and follow the Freedom Trail. Admission: $3 adults, $2.50 seniors and students, $1 children 5–17, free for children under 5. Open: Daily April 15–Oct 9:30 a.m.–5:15 p.m., Nov–April 14 9:30 a.m.–4:15 p.m. Closed Mon Jan–March, Jan 1, Thanksgiving, and Dec 25.

Old North Church
North End

Formally named Christ Church, this is the oldest church in Boston, dating to 1723. In the original steeple, sexton Robert Newman hung two lanterns on the night of April 18, 1775, alerting Paul Revere to the movement of British troops. The second beacon told Revere the redcoats were crossing the Charles River by boat, not on foot ("One if by land, two if by sea"). Markers and plaques dot the building and gardens; note the bust of George Washington, reputedly the first memorial to the first president. The quirky gift shop and museum (☎ 617-523-4848), in a former chapel, is open daily from 9 a.m. to 5 p.m., and all proceeds go to support the church.

Robert Newman was a great-grandson of George Burroughs, one of the victims of the Salem witch trials of 1692. I found out this fact by studying the plaques and tablets in and around the hideaway garden on the north side of the church (to the left as you face the outside of the front doors). The garden makes a peaceful respite from the throngs on Salem Street.

193 Salem St. (at Hull Street). ☎ *617-523-6676.* www.oldnorth.com. *T: Haymarket (Green or Orange Line); follow signs to the North End and walk 6 blocks on Salem Street. Admission: Free; $3 donation requested. Open: Daily 9 a.m.–5 p.m. Services (Episcopal) Sun 9 a.m. and 11 a.m.*

Copp's Hill Burying Ground
North End

The Mather family of Puritan ministers, Robert Newman, and Prince Hall lie in the second-oldest graveyard (1659) in the city. Hall, a prominent member of the free black community that occupied the hill's north slope in colonial times, fought at Bunker Hill and established the first black Masonic lodge. The highest point in the North End enjoys a great view of the Inner Harbor, the Zakim Bridge, and Charlestown (look for the masts of the USS *Constitution*).

Between Hull, Snowhill, and Charter streets. T: North Station (Green or Orange Line). Follow Causeway Street to North Washington Street, where it becomes Commercial Street. Walk 2 blocks, turn right, and climb the hill. Open: Daily 9 a.m.–5 p.m. (until 3 p.m. in winter).

USS Constitution
Charlestown

In modern terms, "Old Ironsides" retired undefeated. Launched in 1797 as one of the U.S. Navy's six original frigates, USS *Constitution* never lost a battle. The tour guides are active-duty sailors in 1812 dress uniforms, honoring the ship's prominent role in the War of 1812. The frigate earned the nickname during an engagement on August 19, 1812, with the French warship *Guerriere,* whose shots bounced off Old Ironsides' thick oak hull as if it were iron. The ship sailed under its own power in 1997 for the first time since 1881, drawing international attention. Tugs tow the *Constitution* into the harbor every Fourth of July.

Neighborhood watch

Boston and Cambridge are famous for neighborhoods that make good destinations for out-of-towners interested in exploring beyond the usual attractions. I particularly enjoy these three 'hoods (two in Boston, one in Cambridge), but if you're visiting friends who want to explore an area you've never heard of, jump at the chance — it's one of the best ways to get to know a new city.

✔ **Beacon Hill,** west and north of the golden dome of the State House, is one of the city's oldest neighborhoods, a festival of brick and brownstone that looks the way you probably think Boston "should." Wander downhill toward Charles Street, making sure to explore the lovely side streets and tiny parks. One of the oldest black churches in the country, the African Meeting House, is at 8 Smith Court.

Between Beacon Street, Embankment Road, Cambridge Street, and Park Street. T: Charles/MGH (Red Line) or Park Street (Green Line).

✔ **The North End,** traditionally an Italian-American neighborhood, today is more than half newcomers, but the area retains an Italian flavor. You see Italian restaurants, *caffès,* bakeries, pastry shops, and food stores. This detour is easy from the Freedom Trail and worth more than just a quick trip for a pasta dinner. Hanover and Salem streets are the main drags; you can find plenty of action on the side streets, too.

Between Cross Street, Commercial Street, and North Washington Street. T: Haymarket (Green or Orange Line); cross under the elevated highway.

✔ **Harvard Square,** Cambridge's best-known intersection, attracts a kaleidoscopic assortment of students, shoppers, street musicians, and sightseers. This area is a retail playground (see Chapter 12) that's especially lively on weekend afternoons. Stop at the information booth near the main T entrance (☎ **617-497-1630;** open Monday through Saturday 9 a.m. to 5 p.m., Sunday 1 to 5 p.m.), visit Harvard University (see the listing in this chapter), or explore on your own. The area's three main thoroughfares and the connecting side streets make great places for wandering.

Intersection of Mass. Ave., John F. Kennedy Street, and Brattle Street. T: Harvard (Red Line).

The nearby **Constitution Museum** (☎ 617-426-1812; www.uss
constitutionmuseum.org) contains participatory exhibits that illustrate
the history and operation of the ship. Also at the navy yard, National Park
Service rangers (☎ 617-242-5601) staff an information booth and give free
one-hour guided tours of the base.

*Charlestown Navy Yard (off Constitution Road). ☎ 617-242-5670. T: North Station
(Green or Orange Line); follow Causeway Street to North Washington Street, turn
left, and cross the bridge. Total walking time: About 15 minutes. Or T: Aquarium (Blue
Line); take ferry from Long Wharf to Navy Yard and then follow signs. Admission for
tours and museum: Free; museum donations encouraged. Open: Museum daily
May–Oct 9 a.m.–6 p.m.; daily Nov–April 10 a.m.–4 p.m. Constitution tours daily*

10 a.m.–3:30 p.m.; call ahead for open days and hours in winter. Closed Jan 1, Thanksgiving, and Dec 25.

Bunker Hill Monument
Charlestown

One of Boston's best-known landmarks, this 221-foot granite obelisk honors the colonists who died in the Battle of Bunker Hill on June 17, 1775. The victory proved costly for the British; half of their troops died or were injured. The battle led to the British decision to abandon Boston nine months later. A flight of 294 stairs leads to the top — there's no elevator, and the windows are small, but the view affords a look at the harbor, the river, and the Zakim Bridge. The ranger-staffed lodge at the base holds dioramas and exhibits.

Monument Square (at Tremont Street). ☎ *617-242-5644. T: Aquarium (Blue Line); take ferry from Long Wharf to navy yard and then follow the Freedom Trail up the hill. Or T: Community College (Orange Line); cross Rutherford Avenue and walk toward the monument. Or Number 92 or 93 bus along Main Street (foot of the hill) to and from Haymarket. Admission: Free. Open: Monument daily 9 a.m.–4:30 p.m.; visitor center daily 9 a.m.–5 p.m.*

Finding More Cool Things to See and Do

Well-known, high-profile attractions are great — that's why they're so popular, right? But when you get comfortable with Boston, you may feel ready for something more offbeat. The sights and activities in this section don't have the same broad appeal as those described earlier in this chapter, but they're equally fun. In fact, if you're particularly interested, these attractions may even be more fun. In this section, I offer suggestions for keeping the kids (small and large) happy, entertaining travelers with specific interests, and captivating sports fans.

Especially for kids

Nearly every attraction in the Boston area appeals to children, and I'm not just saying that — kids clearly have fun all over town. That doesn't mean everyone loves every destination, however. For example, the little ones feeding the birds at the Public Garden may find the Museum of Science overwhelming, while an older sibling may be more interested in the New England Aquarium. And leading anyone, child or adult, on a forced march along the Freedom Trail is cruel and unusual — especially in the summer.

Make sure that you know what your kids are looking forward to and that they know what to expect in Boston. The Web is a great tool for this research — a virtual visit from home can make a new destination feel more familiar.

The **Boston Tea Party Ship & Museum** (☎ 617-338-1773; www.boston teapartyship.com), long a fixture on the family-sightseeing circuit, closed indefinitely after a devastating fire in 2001. A full-scale replica of one of the three merchant ships used in the pivotal pre-Revolutionary uprising, it was a fun stop on the way to or from the Children's Museum. Check ahead to see whether it has reopened.

Children's Museum
Waterfront/Museum Wharf

Visitors under 10 or so usually have a great time here, and most older travelers admit that they have fun, too. The novelty of raising your voice in a place with *museum* in the name is just the beginning; the exhibits combine recreation and education to good effect. The displays include "Science Playground," where everyday objects such as golf balls and soap bubbles illustrate principles of physics; "Boats Afloat," where kids operate model vessels on a giant water tank; the "Dress-Up Shop," with enough costumes for any aspiring thespian; and the "New Balance Climb," a kids-only two-story maze. A room is reserved for toddlers, and the gift shop is tremendous. Allow at least two hours.

Museum Wharf, 300 Congress St. (at Fort Point Channel). ☎ *617-426-8855.* www.bostonkids.org. *T: South Station (Red Line); walk north on Atlantic Avenue 1 block (past the Federal Reserve Bank), turn right onto Congress Street, follow it 1 long block, and cross the bridge. Admission: $9 adults, $7 children ages 2–15 and seniors, $2 children age 1, free for children under 1; Fri 5–9 p.m. $1 for all. Open: Sept–June Sat–Thurs 10 a.m.–5 p.m., Fri 10 a.m.–9 p.m. Closed Thanksgiving, Dec 25, and until noon Jan 1.*

Especially for teens

Occupying teenagers can be tricky, but keeping the lines of communication open can pay off for everyone. For example, does a campus tour count as fun or as pressure? Talk things out.

Shopping options abound. Two excellent malls — the **Shops at Prudential Center** and **Copley Place** — connect through a skybridge so that you don't need to go outside. The **CambridgeSide Galleria** mall offers almost nothing unusual but is about five minutes on foot from the Museum of Science. For information on these places and other stores, see Chapter 12.

The shopping in **Harvard Square** also tends toward the generic, but with plenty of unconventional items, too. (For more information, see Chapter 12.) And the neighborhood scene, especially in "the Pit," near the main T entrance, is always . . . well, let's just call it eye-opening.

Nightlife may not be the first thing that springs to mind when you're thinking about teen diversions, but a trip to a theme restaurant or the theater can be a great family excursion. Kids love the food and music at the **Hard Rock Cafe,** and the interactive theater of *Shear Madness* and **Blue Man Group.** During the day (kids aren't allowed at night), teens also enjoy the high-tech games at **Jillian's Boston** and bowling at **Kings.** For family-oriented nightlife suggestions, turn to Part V and look for the Kid Friendly icon.

Finally, consider a **campus tour.** The Boston area is home to dozens of schools. Most admissions offices are eager to show you around, and every college-oriented high school student knows where to find a few top choices on the Web. Tours are fun, free, and potentially inspirational for the younger kids in your party. Among the many schools in the Boston area are Bentley College, Boston College, Boston University, Brandeis University, Emerson College, Harvard University, Lesley University, the Massachusetts Institute of Technology (MIT), Northeastern University, Simmons College, Suffolk University, Tufts University, the University of Massachusetts, and Wellesley College.

Especially for sports fans

Perhaps you've heard that the Boston Red Sox won the 2004 World Series. (And if you haven't, I hope you left the space shuttle neater than it was when you got there.) The team's last title before that was in 1918. And the victory party is still raging.

Boston's sports scene offers more than just the Red Sox. Included here are a few other teams and places to round out your sports tour.

Fenway Park
Kenmore Square

The **Red Sox** plays from April until at least early October. Tickets go on sale in December; the highest prices in baseball start at $18 for the bleachers. Just about every seat in the place is narrow, cramped, and delightfully close to the action. If you failed to plan your trip months in advance, not to worry: Check with the ticket office when you arrive in town or visit on the day of the game you want to see. A limited number of standing-room tickets go on sale the day of the game, and ticket holders sometimes return unused ones. Your concierge may be able to lend a hand, too.

Given a choice between a right-field grandstand seat (in sections 1 through 11 or so) and the bleachers, go for the slightly less expensive bleachers and the better view. The most coveted tickets are for "Monster seats," in the new section above the famed left-field wall. They go on sale in batches throughout the season; check the Web site for details.

You can also take a **tour of Fenway Park,** which includes a walk on the warning track. Tours begin on the hour daily from 9 a.m. to 4 p.m. or three hours before game time (whichever is earlier). Tours operate year-round except on holidays and before day games. Admission is $10 for adults, $9 for seniors, $8 for children under 15. Call ☎ **617-236-6666** for more information.

Red Sox ticket office, 4 Yawkey Way (near the corner of Brookline Avenue, in the park). ☎ ***877-REDSOX-9*** *or 617-267-1700.* www.redsox.com. *T: Fenway (Green Line D) or Kenmore (Green Line B, C, or D). Games usually begin at 6 or 7 p.m. on weeknights, 1 or 3 p.m. on weekends.*

TD Banknorth Garden
North Station

The TD Banknorth Garden (formerly called the FleetCenter) is home to two professional teams and a museum. The NBA's **Celtics** (www.boston celtics.com) play from early October to April or May. Prices start as low as $10 for some games. Assuming that the NHL has worked out its labor woes by the time you read this book, the **Bruins** (www.bostonbruins. com) should be back in action. Their tickets sometimes sell out despite being among the most expensive in the league ($37 and up).

Also at the TD Banknorth Garden, you can get a sense of how the Boston area earned its reputation as a sports paradise. The **Sports Museum of New England** (☎ **617-624-1234;** www.sportsmuseum.org) occupies the arena's fifth- and sixth-level concourses. This museum offers a specialized collection, most appealing for devoted fans of regional sports. Admission is $6 for adults; $4 for seniors, students, and children 6 to 17. Hours are daily 11 a.m. to 5 p.m., but they're subject to change during events — always call first.

Visitors may not bring any bags, including backpacks and briefcases, into the arena.

Off Causeway Street at North Station. ☎ ***617-624-1000*** *for general event information.* www.tdbanknorthgarden.com. *T: Green or Orange Line.*

Gillette Stadium
Foxboro

The 2002, 2004, and 2005 Super Bowl champion **New England Patriots** (☎ **800-543-1776;** www.patriots.com) consistently sell out Gillette Stadium. Plan as far ahead as possible. The team plays from August through December or January. If you're lucky enough to land one, tickets start at $49. In warm weather, Gillette Stadium is the home field of Major League Soccer's **New England Revolution** (☎ **877-438-7325;** www.nerevolution.com), as well as a major concert venue.

Route 1. Call the Patriots' number or check the Web site, both listed in the preceding paragraph, for stadium information. Special commuter rail service runs from Boston and Providence before and after games. You may also be able to catch a bus from South Station or the Riverside Green Line T station to the stadium (call ☎ ***800-23-LOGAN*** *for information about the bus).*

College sports are much less expensive than their pro counterparts, and they're loads of fun. Ice hockey is the most hotly contested of the dozens of sports in which local teams compete. Check the papers to see what's up during your visit and then call to check ticket availability. The

Division I schools are **Boston College** (☎ 617-552-3000), **Boston University** (☎ 617-353-3838), **Harvard University** (☎ 617-495-2211), and **Northeastern University** (☎ 617-373-4700).

Especially for art lovers

Art galleries cluster on **Newbury Street** in the Back Bay and Harrison Avenue in the South End and dot many other Boston and Cambridge neighborhoods. If you enjoy seeing workspaces as well as the final product, check the Friday, Saturday, or Sunday *Globe* when you arrive to see whether one of the area's artist-intensive neighborhoods has scheduled "open studios" during your visit. Or just head to Newbury Street; the big names tend to be near the Public Garden end, but the whole street is worth wandering. At your first stop, pick up a copy of the free *Gallery Guide.* When strolling along Newbury Street, remember to look above the first floor, where you're sure to find many more galleries.

Institute of Contemporary Art
Back Bay

This museum has no permanent collection, so the displays are different every time you visit. The rotating exhibits concentrate on 20th- and 21st-century art. The broad-minded curatorial approach doesn't confine the shows to one medium or era, or even to what most people typically consider art. For example, a recent installation focused on classic automobiles.

The ICA has commissioned a new building for a site on the South Boston waterfront, near the federal courthouse on Fan Pier. Check at this location for updates on the construction, including architectural diagrams and models.

955 Boylston St. ☎ *617-266-5152.* www.icaboston.org. *T: Hynes/ICA (Green Line B, C, or D); turn left onto Mass. Ave. and left onto Boylston Street and then go 1 long block. Admission: $7 for adults, $5 for seniors and students, free for children under 12; free to all Thurs after 5 p.m. Open: Tues–Wed and Fri noon to 5 p.m.; Thurs noon to 9 p.m.; Sat–Sun noon to 5 p.m.*

Harvard University Art Museums
Cambridge

Harvard's three art museums house some 160,000 works. The **Fogg Art Museum** consists of 19 rooms, which concentrate on topics that range from 17th-century Dutch landscapes to contemporary sculpture. The **Busch-Reisinger Museum** is the only museum in North America devoted to the art of northern and central Europe — specifically Germany. The **Arthur M. Sackler Museum** houses the university's collections of Asian, ancient, Islamic, and later Indian art.

The "Harvard Hot Ticket" includes admission to the art museums, the natural-history museums (see "For something different," later in this chapter), and the Semitic Museum (which is free anyway). The ticket costs $10

for adults, $8 for seniors and college students, and is good for one year from the date of purchase. Tickets are available at the museums and at the Harvard Collections store in Holyoke Center, 1350 Mass. Ave.

Fogg Art Museum, 32 Quincy St. (near Broadway); Busch-Reisinger Museum, enter through the Fogg; Arthur M. Sackler Museum, 485 Broadway (at Quincy Street). ☎ *617-495-9400.* www.artmuseums.harvard.edu. *T: Harvard (Red Line); cross Harvard Yard diagonally and then cross Quincy Street. Or turn your back on the Coop and follow Mass. Ave. to Quincy Street and then turn left. Admission (covers all three museums): $6.50 for adults, $5 for seniors and students, and free for children under 18; free to all on Sat before noon. Open: Mon–Sat 10 a.m.–5 p.m.; Sun 1–5 p.m. Closed: Major holidays.*

For something different

Mapparium / Mary Baker Eddy Library
Back Bay

One of the most unusual attractions anywhere, the Mapparium is a hollow glass globe 30 feet across. The 608 stained-glass panels show the political divisions of the world as they were from 1932 to 1935, during the globe's construction. Visitors walk through the globe on a bridge below the equator, enjoying the view and the unusual acoustics. The Mapparium is part of the Mary Baker Eddy Library, a research center that includes two floors of multimedia and interactive exhibits.

World Headquarters of the First Church of Christ, Scientist, 200 Mass. Ave. (between Clearway Street and Westland Avenue). ☎ *888-222-3711 or 617-450-7000.* www.mary bakereddy.org. *T: Symphony (Green Line E) or Mass. Ave. (Orange Line). Or Hynes/ICA (Green Line B, C, or D); turn left at exit and walk 4 blocks. Admission (includes library exhibits): Adults $5; seniors, students and children 6–17 $3; children under 6 free. Open: Tues–Fri and some Mon holidays 10 a.m.–9 p.m.; Sat 10 a.m.– 5 p.m.; Sun 11 a.m.–5 p.m. Closed: Jan 1, Thanksgiving, and Dec 25.*

Museum of Afro-American History
Beacon Hill

This museum highlights the history of blacks in Boston and Massachusetts with fascinating displays and interactive exhibits. The complex includes the **African Meeting House,** 8 Smith Court, also known as the "Black Faneuil Hall." This place of worship is the oldest standing black church in the United States (1806).

46 Joy St. ☎ *617-742-1854.* www.afroammuseum.org. *T: Park Street (Red or Green Line); climb the hill, walk around the State House to the left, and follow Joy Street 3½ blocks. Admission: Free; donations encouraged. Open: Memorial Day to Labor Day daily 10 a.m.–4 p.m.; day after Labor Day to day before Memorial Day Mon–Sat 10 a.m.–4 p.m. Closed: Jan 1, Thanksgiving, and Dec 25.*

Harvard Museum of Natural History and Peabody Museum of Archaeology & Ethnology
Cambridge

These museums house world-famous collections of items related to the natural world. The natural-history museum comprises three collections: botanical, zoological (from insects to dinosaurs), and mineralogical. The Glass Flowers exhibit, 3,000 eerily lifelike models of more than 840 plant species, is the best-known display. The Peabody mounts great displays on international people and cultures; the Native American collections are especially noteworthy.

The "Harvard Hot Ticket" includes admission to the natural-history museums, the art museums (see "Especially for art lovers," in this chapter), and the Semitic Museum (which is free anyway). The ticket costs $10 for adults, $8 for seniors and college students, and is good for one year from the date of purchase. The ticket is available at the museums and at the Harvard Collections store in Holyoke Center, 1350 Mass. Ave.

Museum of Natural History, 26 Oxford St. ☎ *617-495-3045.* www.hmnh.harvard. edu. *Peabody Museum, 11 Divinity Ave.* ☎ *617-496-1027.* www.peabody. harvard.edu. *T: Harvard (Red Line); cross Harvard Yard, keeping the John Harvard statue on your right, turn right at the Science Center, and take the first left onto Oxford Street. Admission (covers both museums): $7.50 adults, $6.50 students and seniors, $5 children 3–18, children under 3 free; free to all on Sun before noon and Wed 3– 5 p.m. during the school year. Open: Daily 9 a.m.–5 p.m. Closed: Jan. 1, July 4, Thanksgiving, and Dec. 25.*

For architecture admirers

Sheer variety makes Boston a unique treat for architecture buffs. Some areas boast fairly consistent style — notably Beacon Hill, where Federal-era construction abounds (and draconian zoning keeps things that way), and the Back Bay, which didn't exist until the 1830s and remains a 19th-century showpiece. Elsewhere in Boston and Cambridge, the most enjoyable feature is the juxtaposition of classic and cutting-edge.

Here's a convenient twist: Two of the city's architectural gems face each other across Copley Square.

Boston Public Library
Copley Square

This library is home to a museum-quality art collection — and that's just in the main entrance. The 1895 building, an Italian Renaissance–style design by Charles F. McKim, overflows with gorgeous doors, murals, frescoes, sculptures, and paintings. Pick up a brochure, or take a free **Art and Architecture Tour.** The 30-minute excursions focus on the McKim building, which boasts ornamentation by such late-19th-century giants as John Singer Sargent, Daniel Chester French, and Pierre Puvis de Chavannes.

700 Boylston St. ☎ 617-536-5400. www.bpl.org. *T: Copley (Green Line) or Back Bay (Orange Line). Admission: Free. Open: Mon–Thurs 9 a.m.–9 p.m.; Fri–Sat 9 a.m.– 5 p.m.; Sun (Oct–May only) 1–5 p.m. Tours: Mon 2:30 p.m.; Tues and Wed 6:30 p.m.; Thurs and Sat 11 a.m.; Sun (Sept–May only) 2 p.m.*

Trinity Church
Copley Square

This Romanesque masterwork by H. H. Richardson sits across the square from the Boston Public Library. Completed in 1877, the church rests on a foundation of 4,502 vertical supports called *pilings.* (Remember, most of the Back Bay is landfill.) Brochures and guides can direct you around the building, one of the finest examples of American church architecture. On Fridays, you can enjoy an organ recital beginning at 12:15 p.m.

206 Clarendon St. ☎ 617-536-0944. www.trinitychurchboston.org. *Admission: $5 for sightseeing, free for services. Open: Daily 8 a.m.–6 p.m. Sunday services (Episcopal): 8 a.m., 9 a.m., 11 a.m., 6 p.m.*

For history buffs

The **Paul Revere House** (see "The Freedom Trail," earlier in this chapter) is the foremost historic house in Boston but hardly the only one. Charles Bulfinch, the renowned Federal-era architect, designed two Beacon Hill houses that are open for tours; another residence nearby offers a look at a later era. You must take a tour to visit these house museums. Across the river, you can walk in the footsteps of one of the most famous American poets. A tour is not mandatory but greatly enhances the experience.

Harrison Gray Otis House
Beacon Hill

Charles Bulfinch designed this house in 1796 for a promising lawyer who was later mayor of Boston. The historic furnishings and anecdote-laden tour give a sense of the life of a prosperous family in the young republic.

141 Cambridge St. ☎ 617-227-3956. www.historicnewengland.org. *T: Charles/ MGH (Red Line); follow Cambridge Street away from the river. Or Bowdoin (Blue Line; weekdays only); walk 1 block on Cambridge Street away from Government Center. Tour: $8. Tours: Wed–Sun hourly 11 a.m.–4 p.m.*

Longfellow National Historic Site
Cambridge/Harvard Square

The books and furnishings at Henry Wadsworth Longfellow's longtime home have remained intact since the legendary poet died in 1882. The house was already famous: When the British laid siege to Boston in the winter of 1775 and 1776, General George Washington made camp here. The ranger-led tour tells the story of the lovely house and famous occupants.

105 Brattle St., Cambridge ☎ *617-876-4491.* www.nps.gov/long. *T: Harvard (Red Line); exit toward back of Alewife-bound train and follow Brattle Street 6 blocks. Admission: Free. Tour: $3 for adults, free for children under 17. Open: May–Oct Wed–Sun 10 a.m.–4:30 p.m. Tours: 10:30 a.m., 11:30 a.m., 1 p.m., 2 p.m., 3 p.m., 4 p.m.*

Nichols House Museum
Beacon Hill

The furnishings and fine art at the 1804 house reflect the taste of several generations of the Nichols family. Charles Bulfinch designed the building (and the neighboring one at Number 57), which was a family home before becoming a museum in 1960. The neighborhood's only private-house museum, it's a singular chance to see how the upper crust lived.

55 Mount Vernon St. ☎ *617-227-6993.* www.nicholshousemuseum.org. *T: Park St. (Red or Green Line); climb the hill, walk around the State House to the left, follow Joy Street 1 long block, and turn left. Tour: $5. Tours: Every half-hour May–Oct Tues–Sat noon–4 p.m.; Nov–April Thurs–Sat noon–4 p.m.*

Gibson House Museum
Back Bay

This 1859 house overflows with elaborate decorations that personify the word *Victorian*. To modern eyes, that seems synonymous with "over the top." The only design element more outrageous than the ornamentation is the accessories — including a little pink pagoda for the cat.

137 Beacon St. ☎ *617-267-6338. T: Arlington (Green Line); follow Arlington Street past the Public Garden and turn left on Beacon Street. Tour: $5. Tours: On the hour Wed–Sun 1–3 p.m. Closed: Major holidays.*

For a walk in the park
The **Public Garden** (see listing earlier in this chapter) will probably satisfy most horticultural cravings. Its gorgeous seasonal plantings (which change as soon as specimens start looking tired) complement a variety of trees and shrubs arranged to allow aimless strolling and quiet contemplation. Nature fans can also visit the following attraction.

Arnold Arboretum
Jamaica Plain

Devoted green thumbs may want to set aside half a day for a trip to this botanical garden. Founded in 1872, it's one of the country's oldest parks, with about 15,000 ornamental trees, shrubs, and vines from all over the world on its 265 acres.

125 The Arborway (Jamaica Plain is southwest of downtown Boston). ☎ *617-524-1718.* www.arboretum.harvard.edu. *T: Forest Hills (Orange Line); follow signs to the entrance. Admission: Free. Open: Daily sunrise to sunset. Visitor center open: Weekdays 9 a.m.–4 p.m.; weekends noon to 4 p.m.*

For more Cambridge destinations

The MIT campus isn't just for students. Just a mile or so down Mass. Ave. from Harvard Square, across the Charles River from Beacon Hill and the Back Bay, it's a great place to spend a few hours. To get there, take the bus, subway, or a stroll along the riverbank.

Massachusetts Institute of Technology (MIT)
Cambridge

MIT is the most prestigious technical college in . . . well, anywhere that doesn't have a Cal Tech alum nearby. Science gets top billing, but the techies care about more than just practical matters. Picasso, Alexander Calder, Eero Saarinen, I. M. Pei, and Frank Gehry are among the big names represented in the school's outdoor sculpture collection and architecture. Stop by the Information Center to take a free tour or pick up maps and brochures. The campus of MIT lies a mile or so down Mass. Ave. from Harvard Square, across the Charles River from Beacon Hill and the Back Bay.

MIT Information Center, 77 Mass. Ave. ☎ *617-253-4795.* http://web.mit.edu. *Tours: Weekdays 10 a.m., 2 p.m.*

MIT Museum
Cambridge

This museum shows holography and more conventional works. Exhibits don't always have an MIT connection, but some of the most interesting — for example, an interactive installation on artificial intelligence and a look at the work of pioneering photographer Harold "Doc" Edgerton — come straight from campus.

MIT's contemporary art repository, the **List Visual Arts Center,** 20 Ames St., off Main Street (☎ 617-253-4680; http://web.mit.edu/lvac), is open Tuesday through Sunday from noon to 6 p.m., Friday until 8 p.m. Admission is free.

265 Mass. Ave. ☎ *617-253-4444.* http://web.mit.edu/museum. *T: No. 1 (Dudley-Harvard) bus; exit at first stop across bridge. Or Kendall/MIT (Red Line); follow the campus map at street level. Admission: $5 adults; $2 seniors; $1 students and children under 18. Open: Tues–Fri 10 a.m.–5 p.m.; weekends noon to 5 p.m. Closed: Major holidays.*

Whale watching

The waters off New England are choice whale-migration territory, and Boston is a center of whale watching. The magnificent mammals seek out the feeding grounds of **Stellwagen Bank,** which extend from Gloucester to Provincetown about 27 miles east of Boston. The most common species are the finback and humpback, but you may also see minke whales and rare right whales. The aquatic mammals often perform for spectators by jumping out of the water, and dolphins sometimes join the show. Trained naturalists serve as tour guides, identifying animals and interpreting activities.

The trip to the bank is long. (Children who are accustomed to immediate gratification may not appreciate the journey.) The tedium vanishes in an instant when the first whale appears.

Dress in plenty of layers to fend off the cool sea air, and add sunglasses, a hat, and rubber-soled shoes. Don't forget sunscreen and, of course, a camera. If you tend to suffer from motion sickness, take precautions before you leave the dock.

New England Aquarium whale-watching expeditions (☎ **617-973-5200** for information, 617-973-5206 for tickets; www.newenglandaquarium. org) operate daily from May through mid-October and on weekends in April and late October. On-board hands-on exhibits help pass the time and prepare passengers for spotting duty. The trips take four to five hours; check departure times when you make reservations. Tickets are $29 for adults, $24 for seniors and college students, $23 for youths 12 to 18, and $18 for children 3 to 11. Children must be 3 years old and at least 30 inches tall. Reservations are strongly recommended. The T stop is Aquarium (Blue Line).

If the Aquarium whale watches are booked, try **Boston Harbor Cruises** (☎ **617-227-4321;** www.bostonharborcruises.com) or **Beantown Whale Watch** (☎ **617-542-8000;** www.beantownwhalewatch.com).

Seeing Boston by Guided Tour

The most important question about guided tours is "Why?" If your time is limited, you have trouble getting around, or you haven't a clue what to expect from Boston, a general tour may be right for you. Visitors interested in a particular topic often want a guide who knows the details cold. And if you crave something offbeat, Boston has tours that cover land *and* water.

"Why not?" is an equally good question. Maybe a day trundling off and on a trolley sounds touristy, or you can't bear the cookie-cutter sameness of standard tours. Don't let that turn you off all tours, though — a special-interest walking tour may be perfect. One thing to note: Don't waste money on a tour ticket that covers a whole day if you think one circuit of a trolley is all you need (or can stand). You'll be cheating yourself out of the rich experiences you can enjoy only at ground level.

Boston offers four main types of guided tours: walking, trolley (a bus with a trolley-style body), cruise, and duck.

✔ **Walking tours** place you face to face with the city. Boston abounds with small pleasures — a whiff of ocean air, sunlight through a blown-glass window — and walking tours put you in touch with them. But the tours don't cover everything. Most are brief, and they can be tiring. And most regularly scheduled walking tours don't run in winter.

✔ For an overview, a narrated **trolley tour** can be a reasonable option. You can choose specific attractions on which to focus or take advantage of the all-day pass to visit as many places as you can. Some trolley stops, especially in the North End, lie some distance from the attractions. And piling off a trolley with a little sticker on your shirt (it allows you to reboard) is very much a "typical tourist" thing. But these tours operate year-round.

✔ **Sightseeing cruises** offer sensational scenery and an unusual vantage point. Tours on the Inner Harbor pass the airport (a hit with aviation buffs), include some maritime history, and make pleasant alternatives to walking or driving. But these generally pricey tours aren't comprehensive or long lasting, and they close for the winter.

✔ **Boston Duck Tours,** the only amphibious operation in town, offers a great deal of fun for a fair amount of money. These tours, too, shut down in cold weather.

Walking tours

Check the Thursday *Globe* "Calendar" section when you arrive to see whether any operators are offering special-interest or one-shot tours to coincide with events or anniversaries during your visit.

Free 90-minute Freedom Trail walking tours with **National Park Service** rangers as guides start as often as four times a day during busy periods, once daily in the winter. These tours cover the "heart" of the trail, from the Old South Meeting House to the Old North Church (see "The Freedom Trail," earlier in this chapter). Schedules change seasonally. You don't need reservations, but try to arrive 30 minutes prior to the start of the tour, especially during busy times; groups are no larger than 30. Tours depart from the Visitor Center, 15 State St. (T: State [Orange or Blue Line]; ☎ **617-242-5642;** www.nps.gov/bost), off Washington Street across from the Old State House. Call to check on tour times and schedules.

The best private walking tour provider is the not-for-profit organization **Boston by Foot** (☎ **617-367-2345,** or 617-367-3766 for recorded information; www.bostonbyfoot.com). From May through October, this company offers historical and architectural tours that concentrate on certain neighborhoods and topics. The volunteer guides love the subjects and welcome questions. The 90-minute tours run rain or shine; you don't need reservations. Buy tickets ($10 for adults, $8 for children age 6 to 12) from the guide. Excursions that leave from Faneuil Hall meet at the statue of Samuel Adams on Congress Street. The regularly scheduled tours include the following:

✔ The **"Heart of the Freedom Trail"** tour starts at Faneuil Hall daily at 10 a.m.

✔ The **Beacon Hill** tour starts at the foot of the State House steps on Beacon Street weekdays at 5:30 p.m., Saturday at 10 a.m., and Sunday at 2 p.m.

✔ The **Victorian Back Bay** tour starts at the steps of Trinity Church at 10 a.m. Friday through Sunday and 5:30 p.m. Tuesday and Thursday.

✔ The **North End** tour starts at Faneuil Hall on Friday and Saturday at 2 p.m.

✔ The **"Boston Underground"** tour includes the subway and Big Dig. This tour starts at Faneuil Hall Sunday at 2 p.m.

✔ The **"Literary Landmarks"** tour starts at Borders, 10–24 School St., at Washington Street, at 2 p.m. on Saturday.

✔ The **"Boston by Little Feet"** tour targeting 6- to 12-year-olds (who must be accompanied by an adult) spends 60 minutes ($8 per person, including a map) concentrating on the architecture along the Freedom Trail and on Boston's role in the American Revolution. This tour starts at the statue of Samuel Adams on the Congress Street side of Faneuil Hall on Saturday at 10 a.m., Sunday at 2 p.m., and Monday at 10 a.m. — rain or shine.

Historic New England (☎ 617-227-3956; www.historicnewengland.org) offers a two-hour tour that focuses on life in the upstairs—downstairs world of Beacon Hill in 1800. "Magnificent and Modest" ($10) starts at the Harrison Gray Otis House, 141 Cambridge St. (see "For history buffs," earlier in this chapter), at 11 a.m. on Saturdays and Sundays from May through October. The price includes a tour of the Otis House; reservations are recommended.

The **Boston Park Rangers** (☎ 617-635-7383; www.ci.boston.ma.us/parks) offer free tours of the "Emerald Necklace," pioneering landscape architect Frederick Law Olmsted's loop of green spaces. The tours include Boston Common, the Public Garden, the Commonwealth Avenue Mall, the Muddy River in the Fenway, Olmsted Park, Jamaica Pond, the Arnold Arboretum, and Franklin Park. The full six-hour walk happens only a few times a year; one-hour tours that highlight a location or theme take place year-round. Check ahead for topics and schedules.

The **Boston History Collaborative** (☎ 617-574-5950; www.bostondiscoveries.com), a nonprofit group created to promote historic tourism, coordinates several heritage trails that focus on subjects significant to local history. This group's offerings range from simple (a downloadable self-guided tour route) to elaborate (a 90-minute cruise or 5-hour trolley excursion). Check ahead for information about **Boston by Sea: The Maritime Trail** (www.bostonbysea.org), the **Literary Trail** (www.lit-trail.org), **Boston Family History** (www.bostonfamilyhistory.net), and the **Innovation Trail** (www.innovationodyssey.com).

From October through early May, free volunteer-led tours of **Symphony Hall,** 301 Mass. Ave. (☎ 617-266-1492; www.bso.org), take visitors around the landmark building and relate the Boston Symphony Orchestra's fascinating history. The hour-long tours start on Wednesday at 4:30 p.m., except during the last three weeks of December, and on the first Saturday of each month at 1:30 p.m. Reservations aren't necessary; meet in the lobby at the Mass. Ave. entrance. For information about performances, see Chapter 15.

National Park Service rangers lead free two-hour walking tours of the **Black Heritage Trail,** a 1.6-mile route on Beacon Hill that includes stations of the Underground Railroad, homes of famous citizens, and the first integrated public school. Tours leave from the Visitor Center, 46 Joy St. (☎ 617-742-5415; www.nps.gov/boaf); check ahead for schedules. To explore on your own, pick up a brochure from the visitor center; these brochures include maps and descriptions of the buildings.

The **Boston Women's Heritage Trail** creates walking tours that include homes, churches, and social and political institutions associated with influential women. You can buy a guide at the National Park Service Visitor Center at 15 State St.; you can also check local bookstores and historic sites. For more detailed information, call ☎ 617-522-2872 or visit www.bwht.org.

Trolley tours

These popular tours are an easy way to "see" everything without getting a good sense of what Boston is like. Don't fall into that trap — if you can manage the journey, climb down and look around.

The cutthroat competition among operators makes their offerings virtually indistinguishable. Each has slightly different stops, but all cover the major attractions. The 90- to 120-minute tours usually include a map and all-day reboarding (so that you don't have to do it all at once).

The guide makes or breaks the tour; if you have time, shop around to find one you particularly like before you pay (ask for a tryout). Local news outlets periodically "break" the story that guides are embellishing the facts in narratives (a whole summer of reciting the same stories would probably get to you, too), but most are on the level. And some of the most improbable-sounding stories are actually true. (For example, Trinity Church really is built on wooden pilings, and the story of a woman and her lover buried alive by her husband inspired Edgar Allan Poe's creepy story "The Cask of Amontillado.")

Trolley tickets cost $19 to $24 for adults, $12 or less for kids. Stops usually are at hotels, attractions, and tourist information centers. To start, look for busy waiting areas where you can check out the guides to see whether you click with one. Trolleys line up near the New England Aquarium and near the corner of Boylston Street and Charles Street South, where the Common meets the Public Garden.

Each company has cars painted a different color. Orange-and-green **Old Town Trolleys** (☎ 617-269-7150; www.trolleytours.com) are the most numerous. These tours include "JFK's Boston," which visits sights related to the former president; a brewpub tour; a chocolate-tasting tour; and a seafood tour. Tickets usually cost at least $22 for adults, more if the tour includes refreshments. Call for information, schedules, and reservations. Minuteman Tours' **Boston Trolley Tours** (☎ 617-867-5539; www.historictours.com) are blue, **Freedom Trail Trolleys** (☎ 800-343-1328 or 781-986-6100; www.bostontrolley.com) are red, and **CityView Trolleys** (☎ 617-363-7899; www.cityviewtrolleys.com) are silver. The **Discover Boston Trolley Tours** (☎ 617-742-1440) vehicle is white; tours are available with taped narration translated into Japanese, Spanish, French, German, and Italian.

Sightseeing cruises

Seeing Boston from the water gives you a sense of the city's maritime history — and confirms that (except in winter) the water is cooler than the land. On a sweaty summer day, a breezy cruise makes an enjoyable break from a march along the tourist track. The new perspective will help you remember that the city remains an active port, and the sheer number of sailboats will make you wonder if every office in the city is empty.

The season for narrated cruises runs April through October, with spring and fall offerings usually on weekends only. If you get seasick, check the size of the vessel before you pay; larger boats are more comfortable.

Boston Harbor Cruises, 1 Long Wharf (☎ 877-SEE-WHALE or 617-227-4321; www.bostonharborcruises.com), operates 90-minute historic tours of the Inner and Outer Harbor at 11 a.m., 1 p.m., 3 p.m., and 6 or 7 p.m. (the sunset cruise). Tickets are $18 for adults, $16 for seniors, $13 for children 4 to 12. The 45-minute *Constitution* round-trip cruise takes you around the Inner Harbor and docks at the Charlestown Navy Yard so that you can go ashore and visit "Old Ironsides." Tours start every hour on the half-hour from 10:30 a.m. to 4:30 p.m. and leave the navy yard on the hour from 11 a.m. to 5 p.m. Tickets are $12 for adults, $11 for seniors, and $9 for children. Trips leave from Long Wharf, off Atlantic Avenue between the New England Aquarium and the Marriott.

The **Charles Riverboat Company** (☎ 617-621-3001; www.charles riverboat.com) operates out of the CambridgeSide Galleria mall, on First Street in East Cambridge. From the Charles, you can enjoy a panoramic view of Boston (including the towers of the Back Bay) and Cambridge (the landmark dome indicates that you're approaching MIT). The 55-minute cruises depart five times a day, daily in June, July, and August and on weekends only in April, May, and September. Call for the time of the sunset cruise. Tickets (cash only) are $11 for adults, $9 for seniors, $6 for children 2 to 12.

The cheapest "cruise" is the $1.50 ferry ride from Long Wharf to the Charlestown Navy Yard. The MBTA visitor pass (see Chapter 8) covers the ferry, which makes a great way to finish the Freedom Trail.

Boston Light is North America's oldest lighthouse (1716) and the only lighthouse in the country that's still staffed by the Coast Guard. Excursions to the 102-foot lighthouse include a narrated cruise; 90 minutes to explore the island; and, if you're at least 50 inches tall, a chance to climb the spiral stairs to the top. The 3½-hour tours leave from the Moakley Courthouse at Fan Pier and from the John F. Kennedy Library. From early June to mid-October, trips leave from Fan Pier Saturday at 10 a.m. and 2 p.m. and Sunday at 2 p.m., and from the Kennedy Library Friday at 2 p.m. Between July 4th and Labor Day, additional departures launch from Fan Pier on Sunday at 10 a.m. and from the Kennedy Library Thursday and Friday at 10 a.m. Tickets from Fan Pier cost $25 for adults, $20 for seniors, $15 for children 6 to 12, free for children under 6. From the Kennedy Library (including library admission), they cost $29, $22, and $15, respectively. Only 32 people may take each tour; reservations (☎ **617-223-8666;** www.bostonislands.com) are strongly recommended.

Duck tours

The most unusual excursions in town are 80-minute **Boston Duck Tours** (☎ **800-226-7442** or 617-723-DUCK; www.bostonducktours.com), which operate from April through November. These tours are relatively expensive, but you're paying for a novelty that's well worth the money. The vehicles are reconditioned World War II amphibious landing craft known as "ducks" — and like the real thing, they move easily between land and water. The duck leaves from behind the Prudential Center on Huntington Avenue or from the Museum of Science, cruises around Boston, passes most of the major sights, and then heads to the Charles River dam and right into the water for a turn around the basin.

Tickets, available at the Prudential Center, the Museum of Science, and Faneuil Hall Marketplace, cost $24 for adults, $21 for seniors and students, $14 for children 3 to 11, and $3 for children under 3. Tours run every 30 or 60 minutes from 9 a.m. to 30 minutes before sunset. Reservations are not accepted for groups of 15 or less, and tickets usually sell out, especially on weekends. Try to buy same-day tickets early in the day, or ask about the tickets available starting five days ahead. No tours run from December through March.

Chapter 12

Shopping the Local Stores

●●

In This Chapter

▶ Checking out the big names and other famous labels

▶ Exploring the main shopping areas

▶ Finding the right place for what you want

●●

*B*efore you feel guilty about shopping when there's so much sightseeing to do, consider this: Visitors to Boston consistently list the city's stores as favorite destinations, even ahead of the museums. Retail outlets of every description await you, from unusual boutiques to indistinguishable chain stores. In this chapter, I concentrate on the offbeat destinations, with plenty of attention to big national names and retail-intensive neighborhoods. All over town, you'll also find tons of businesses you recognize from the mall at home.

Unless otherwise noted, see the "Boston Shopping" map in this chapter for the locations of the stores I mention.

Surveying the Scene

The first thing to know is that the 5 percent Massachusetts sales tax doesn't apply to clothing priced below $175 or to food items. (The 5 percent meal tax applies to takeout, though.) If you buy an article of clothing for $175 or more, the tax applies only to the amount over $175. But if you're shipping merchandise to a state where the store has a branch, the sales tax for that state usually applies.

Stores usually open at 9:30 or 10 a.m. and close at around 6 or 7 p.m. A few don't open on Sunday, but most do, from noon to 5 or 6 p.m. Exceptions include shopping malls, which stay open later; art galleries, which typically don't open until 11 a.m. and are closed on Monday; and smaller shops, which often keep odd hours. When in doubt, call ahead.

Checking Out the Big Names

The biggest name in Boston shopping is **Filene's Basement,** 426 Washington St., at Summer Street (☎ 617-542-2011; www.filenes basement.com). Founded in Boston in 1908, "the Basement" (now part of a Midwestern chain) has maintained the cachet accumulated in nearly a century of great deals on men's, women's, and children's clothing and accessories.

The legendary "automatic markdown" policy applies only at this store. After merchandise has been on the racks for four weeks, the price drops by 25 percent. Boards hanging from the ceiling bear the all-important dates; the original sale date is on the back of the price tag. Prices continue to fall until, after eight weeks (and 75 percent off), everything remaining goes to charity. To fit in with the locals, be aggressive, and don't be shy about telling people how much — actually, how little — you paid for that stunning designer outfit. And if you can't make up your mind about something, just buy it. You can always return merchandise, but you can't always come back and find that special something the next day. Yes, this is the voice of experience talking.

The store is open weekdays 9:30 a.m. to 7:30 p.m., Saturday 9 a.m. to 7:30 p.m., and Sunday 11 a.m. to 7 p.m. Hours may vary during special sales. Crowds can be huge at lunch and after work; try to shop in the morning or midafternoon. Take the T to Downtown Crossing (Red or Orange Line); enter directly from the station or through Filene's, the unaffiliated department store upstairs.

Many of Boston's other high-profile retailers are branches, often of chains based in New York. I single out a few in the neighborhood descriptions that appear later in this chapter; for that only-in-Boston feeling, check out the following:

✔ **Shreve, Crump & Low,** 330 Boylston St. (☎ 617-267-9100; www. shrevecrumpandlow.com), is the oldest jewelry store in the country (in business since 1796), selling legendary diamonds, traditional silver baby presents, and even antiques on the second floor. Call it "Shreve's," and remember to check out the estate jewelry.

✔ The **Museum of Fine Arts** (www.mfa.org) operates gift shops at Copley Place (☎ 617-536-8818) and in the South Market Building at Faneuil Hall Marketplace (☎ 617-720-1266), as well as in the museum itself. The well-stocked satellites can't replace the real thing, but they make a fine substitute.

✔ **Newbury Comics** (www.newbury.com) is a Boston-based chain of fantastic music stores that has responded to the online-music boom by beefing up its selections of gifts and comics. Here are three handy locations: 332 Newbury St., Back Bay (☎ 617-236-4930); 1 Washington Mall, Washington Street off State Street, Downtown Crossing (☎ 617-248-9992); and 36 John F. Kennedy St., in the Garage mall, Harvard Square, Cambridge (☎ 617-491-0337).

Boston Shopping

Artful Hand Gallery **5**
Barnes & Noble
 (Downtown Crossing) **18**
Barnes & Noble
 (Prudential Center) **3**
Barnes & Noble
 at Boston University **1**
Black Ink **14**
Borders **20**
Brattle Book Shop **16**
Copley Place **5**
Dairy Fresh Candies **24**
Emerson College Book Store **11**
Faneuil Hall Marketplace **23**
Filene's **19**

Filene's Basement **19**
Gucci **5**
Hermès of Paris **10**
High Gear Jewelry **27**
Koo De Kir **12**
Lord & Taylor **6**
Macy's **17**
Museum of Fine Arts
 (Copley Place) **5**
Museum of Fine Arts
 (Faneuil Hall Marketplace) **23**
Neiman Marcus **5**
Newbury Comics **22**
Northeastern University
 Bookstore **2**

Origins **23**
Paper Source **8**
Restoration Hardware **7**
Saks Fifth Avenue **4**
Salumeria Italiana **26**
Sephora **3**
Shake the Tree Gallery **25**
Shops at Prudential Center **3**
Shreve, Crump & Low **9**
Suffolk University Bookstore **15**
Thomas Pink (Copley Place) **5**
Thomas Pink
 (Downtown Crossing) **21**
Tiffany & Co. **5**
Upstairs Downstairs Antiques **13**

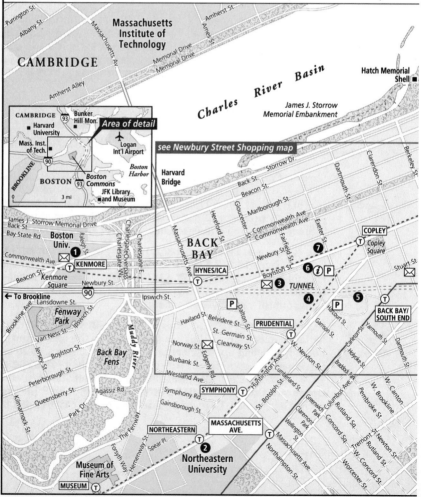

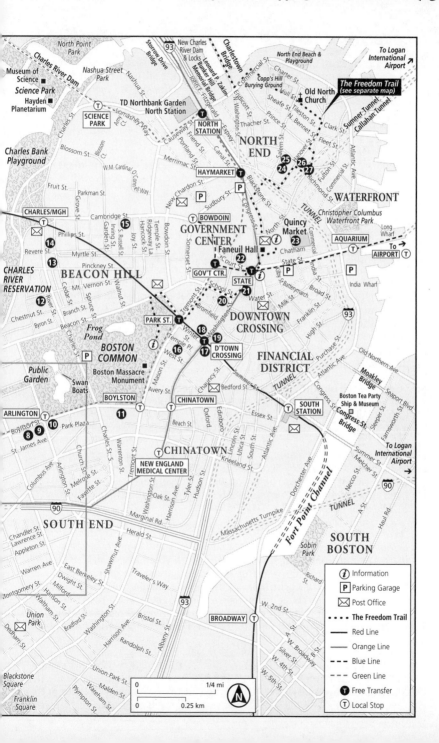

Discovering the Best Shopping Neighborhoods

Here, I zero in on some consumer-friendly areas and single out some favorite stops. By no means does that mean that these areas are the only parts of town worth strolling through or that the shops I mention are the only ones you should visit. Ask at your hotel if you have a specific item in mind or just follow your nose.

The Back Bay

From name-dropping socialites to skateboarders in droopy pants, everyone shops in the Back Bay. The main shopping streets are Newbury and Boylston (T: Arlington or Copley [Green Line]).

For locations of shops on Newbury Street, see the "Newbury Street Shopping" map in this chapter.

Newbury Street is the Rodeo Drive of New England, home of the area's toniest boutiques and art galleries. It's a retail wonderland from Arlington Street — where you find **Chanel,** 15 Arlington St., in the Ritz-Carlton, Boston (☎ 617-859-0055; www.chanel.com), and **Burberry,** 2 Newbury St. (☎ 617-236-1000; www.burberry.com) — to Mass. Ave., where the **Virgin Megastore,** 360 Newbury St. (☎ 617-896-0950; www.virginmega.com), faces **Urban Outfitters,** 361 Newbury St. (☎ 617-236-0088; www.urbanoutfitters.com). You'll see a huge assortment of other famous names, including dozens of upscale fashion brands.

I tend to seek out the smaller retailers that celebrate specialties in an attitude free parallel universe: for exquisite jewelry, **John Lewis, Inc.,** 97 Newbury St. (☎ 617-266-6665; www.johnlewisinc.com); for museum-quality artisan work, the **Society of Arts and Crafts,** 175 Newbury St. (☎ 617-266-1810; www.societyofcrafts.org); and for gothic home accessories (not as far-out as it sounds), **Gargoyles, Grotesques & Chimeras,** 262 Newbury St. (☎ 617-536-2362). Though they're part of chains, two skin-care and bath-product purveyors are well worth a visit: **Lush,** 166 Newbury St. (☎ 617-375-5874; www.lush.com), and **Kiehl's,** 112 Newbury St. (☎ 617-247-1777; www.kiehls.com).

Dozens of art galleries are Newbury Street's other claim to fame. Pick up a copy of the free *Gallery Guide* (at any gallery and many other businesses), or start at Arlington Street and work your way west. Remember that some of the most interesting collections are above ground level. Don't be afraid to ask questions — the people hanging around the gallery, who often include the manager, love to talk about the art. You're sure to find a gallery that matches your taste; my favorite is the **International Poster Gallery,** 205 Newbury St. (☎ 617-375-0076; www.international poster.com).

Boylston Street retail really gets going at Arlington Street, with **Hermès of Paris,** 22 Arlington St. (☎ 617-482-8707; www.hermes.com), and **Shreve, Crump & Low** (see "Checking Out the Big Names," earlier in this

Newbury Street Shopping

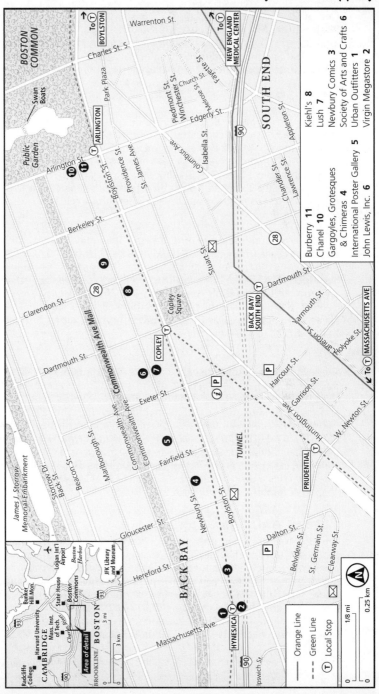

Burberry **11**
Chanel **10**
Gargoyles, Grotesques
  & Chimeras **9**
International Poster Gallery **5**
John Lewis, Inc. **6**

Kiehl's **8**
Lush **7**
Newbury Comics **3**
Society of Arts and Crafts **6**
Urban Outfitters **1**
Virgin Megastore **2**

chapter), and extends past the entrance to the **Shops at Prudential Center** (see later in this section). This street is where you find the Boston branch of **Paper Source**, 338 Boylston St. (☎ 617-536-3444; www.paper-source.com), which carries stationery from formal to whimsical and offers a delightful selection of gifts. Branches of chains here include **Restoration Hardware**, 711 Boylston St. (☎ 617-578-0088; www.restorationhardware.com), and **Lord & Taylor**, 760 Boylston St. (☎ 617-262-6000; www.lordandtaylor.com).

Boylston Street also holds one entrance to the giant consumer wonderland of the **Shops at Prudential Center**, 800 Boylston St. (T: Prudential [Green Line E] or Back Bay [Orange Line]; ☎ 800-SHOP-PRU or 617-267-1002; www.prudentialcenter.com), and **Copley Place**, 100 Huntington Ave. (☎ 617-375-4400; www.shopcopleyplace.com). Skybridges link the malls, which incorporate dozens of national chains that allow you to pretend you've never left home, plus a smattering of unique boutiques.

The "Pru" contains a food court; a **Legal Sea Foods** (☎ 617-266-6800) restaurant (see Chapter 10); a huge **Barnes & Noble** (☎ 617-247-6959; www.barnesandnoble.com); a branch of the cosmetics wonderland **Sephora** (☎ 617-262-4200; www.sephora.com); dozens of other shops; an entrance to **Saks Fifth Avenue** (☎ 617-262-8500; www.saksfifth avenue.com); and various pushcarts that sell souvenirs, crafts, and accessories. The **Greater Boston Convention & Visitors Bureau** (☎ 800-SEE-BOSTON or 617-536-4100; www.bostonusa.com) operates the information booth.

Copley Place is a more upscale complex — **Tiffany & Co.** (☎ 617-353-0222; www.tiffany.com) is one of the first stores you see entering from the Pru. **Neiman Marcus** (☎ 617-536-3660; www.neimanmarcus.com) is the anchor store; its neighbors include such big names as **Gucci** (☎ 617-247-3000; www.gucci.com), London haberdasher **Thomas Pink** (☎ 617-267-0447; www.thomaspink.com), and **Legal Sea Foods** (☎ 617-266-7775). Independent retailers tend not to thrive in this location; a welcome exception is the **Artful Hand Gallery** (☎ 617-262-9601), which carries a discriminating selection of jewelry, wood and glass pieces, ceramics, and sculpture.

Faneuil Hall Marketplace

Boston's top attraction, **Faneuil Hall Marketplace** (T: Government Center [Green or Blue Line]; ☎ 617-338-2323; www.faneuilhallmarketplace. com) draws much of its appeal from abundant consumer enticements. Most street-level shops are chain outlets that you'd see in the mall at home; less common names include a freestanding branch of department-store cosmetics favorite **Origins** (☎ 617-742-7447; www.origins.com). Second-floor shops tend to be quirkier independents, as do the pushcarts that cluster between the North Market Building and Quincy Market.

Craft shows

New England is a hotbed of fine craft creation, and the Boston area affords many opportunities to explore the latest trends in every medium and style you can imagine. Prominent artisans often have exclusive relationships with galleries, so an excellent way to get an overview is to attend a show and sale. The best-known craft exhibitions are prestigious weekend events that benefit nonprofit organizations. **Crafts at the Castle** (☎ **617-523-6400**, ext. 5987; www.artfulgift.com/catc) takes place in late November or early December at the Castle, an exhibition space on Columbus Avenue at Arlington Street, and **CraftBoston** (☎ **617-266-1810**; www.craftboston.org) is in mid-May at the World Trade Center.

Charles Street

Beacon Hill's main street is both a neighborhood hangout and a gift-shop magnet. **Charles Street** (T: Charles/MGH [Red Line]) is also home to some excellent antiques shops and a curiously refined 7-Eleven — thanks to the strict zoning laws that cover the landmark district.

Head for a specific destination, or just stroll up one side of the street and down the other. My favorite gift shops are **Koo De Kir,** 34 Charles St. (☎ **617-723-8111;** www.koodekir.com), and **Black Ink,** 101 Charles St. (☎ **617-723-3883;** www.blackink.com). **Upstairs Downstairs Antiques,** 93 Charles St. (☎ **617-367-1950**), is a good place to start antique hunting.

Downtown Crossing

At the corner of Washington and Summer streets, the busiest stretch of the pedestrian mall at the center of **Downtown Crossing** (T: Downtown Crossing [Red or Orange Line]), two big names face off. **Macy's,** 450 Washington St. (☎ **617-357-3000;** www.macys.com), sits opposite **Filene's,** 426 Washington St. (☎ **617-357-2100;** www.filenes.com), which is above its former corporate sibling **Filene's Basement** (see "Checking Out the Big Names," earlier in this chapter). The shopping here isn't as highfalutin as in the Back Bay or as touristy as at Faneuil Hall Marketplace. Downtown Crossing is where the locals shop.

Washington and Winter streets overflow with discount clothing and shoe stores, souvenir carts, and places for office workers to grab a quick lunch. An exception is the tony British haberdasher **Thomas Pink,** 280 Washington St. (☎ **617-426-7859;** www.thomaspink.com). Another Bostonian necessity is a well-stocked bookstore, and Downtown Crossing has three. **Barnes & Noble,** 395 Washington St. (☎ **617-426-5184;** www.barnesandnoble.com), and **Borders,** 10–24 School St. (☎ **617-557-7188;** www.borders.com), carry a predictably huge range of books. The stock at the **Brattle Book Shop,** 9 West St. (off Washington Street; ☎ **800-447-9595** or 617-542-0210; www.brattlebookshop.com), is an unpredictably huge assortment of used, rare, and out-of-print titles.

Fired up

A good souvenir is something you'd never find anywhere else, and a **Boston Fire Department T-shirt** is a great one. They cost about $15 at most neighborhood fire-houses. The handiest for out-of-towners are Engine 8, Ladder 1, on Hanover Street at Charter Street in the North End (off the Freedom Trail), and Ladder 15, Engine 33, on Boylston Street at Hereford Street in the Back Bay (near the Hynes Convention Center).

The North End

The North End is known for its authentic, delicious pasta dinners. In Chapter 10, I tell you where to find my favorite restaurants in this neighborhood. But if you want to make your own pasta back home, the **North End** (T: Haymarket [Green or Orange Line]) is also the place to stock up.

Italian groceries and fresh meats and cheeses cram the tiny **Salumeria Italiana,** 151 Richmond St. (☎ **617-523-8743;** www.salumeriaitaliana. com). Your sweet tooth can lead you to **Dairy Fresh Candies,** 57 Salem St. (☎ **800-336-5536** or 617-742-2639; www.dairyfreshcandies.com).

The neighborhood has nonfood retailers, too. For unique and unusual gifts, crafts, and jewelry, visit **Shake the Tree Gallery,** 95 Salem St. (☎ **617-742-0484**). The inventive and classic designs at **High Gear Jewelry,** 139 Richmond St. (☎ **617-523-5804**), on the Freedom Trail, are catnip to costume-jewelry fans.

Cambridge

Harvard Square (T: Harvard [Red Line]) grows less individualized by the day, but this area is still worth a trip if you know where to look. Bookstore enthusiasts and T-shirt collectors will be particularly happy. (For locations of stores in this section, see the "Harvard Square Shopping" map in this chapter.)

Agreeable chain stores in the neighborhood include **Urban Outfitters,** 11 John F. Kennedy St. (☎ 617- 864-0070; www.urbanoutfitters.com), and **Barnes & Noble** (which runs the book operation at the **Harvard Coop,** 1400 Mass. Ave. [☎ **617-499-2000;** www.thecoop.com]).

"The Square" is great for window-shopping, and the best displays are at **Calliope,** 33 Brattle St. (☎ **617-876-4149**), a terrific children's clothing and toy store. **Colonial Drug,** 49 Brattle St. (☎ **617-864-2222**), a family business that specializes in hard-to-find fragrances, is 1 block away. A spinoff of the Beacon Hill favorite, **Black Ink,** 5 Brattle St. (☎ **617-497-1221**), is one of the best places in Harvard Square for that I'll-know-it-when-I-see-it perfect gift.

Harvard Square Shopping

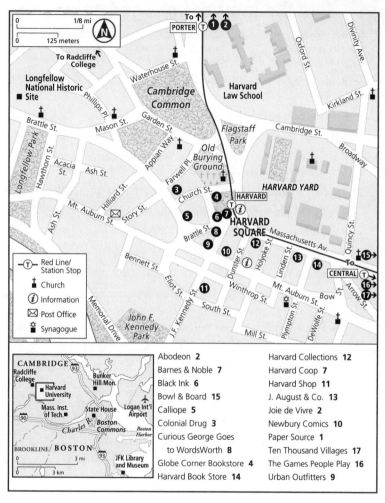

Abodeon **2**
Barnes & Noble **7**
Black Ink **6**
Bowl & Board **15**
Calliope **5**
Colonial Drug **3**
Curious George Goes
  to WordsWorth **8**
Globe Corner Bookstore **4**
Harvard Book Store **14**

Harvard Collections **12**
Harvard Coop **7**
Harvard Shop **11**
J. August & Co. **13**
Joie de Vivre **2**
Newbury Comics **10**
Paper Source **1**
Ten Thousand Villages **17**
The Games People Play **16**
Urban Outfitters **9**

If something at one of the Harvard museums catches your eye, visit
Harvard Collections, in Holyoke Center, 1350 Mass. Ave. (☎ 617-496-
0700), for pieces copied from or inspired by objects in the university's
vast stores of art and artifacts — excellent, unusual souvenirs.

Now, how about those bookstores? One of the area's best general-interest
stores is here: the **Harvard Book Store,** 1256 Mass. Ave. (☎ 800-542-
READ outside the 617 area code or 617-661-1515; www.harvard.com).
The basement overflows with discounted and used books.

Join the crowd: College bookstores

Anything big enough to hold a college logo is for sale somewhere, and Boston offers a breathtaking variety. The big name is Harvard, but savvy sightseers may prefer something less predictable. If that's you, check out the following:

- ✔ **Barnes & Noble at Boston University,** 660 Beacon St., Kenmore Square (☎ 617-267-8484)

- ✔ **Emerson College Book Store,** 80 Boylston St., Theater District (☎ 617-728-7700)

- ✔ **MIT Coop,** 3 Cambridge Center, Kendall Square (☎ 617-499-3200)

- ✔ **Northeastern University Bookstore,** 360 Huntington Ave., Fenway (between Symphony Hall and the Museum of Fine Arts; ☎ 617-373-2286)

- ✔ **Suffolk University Bookstore,** 148 Cambridge St., Beacon Hill (☎ 617-227-4085)

For Harvard paraphernalia, try the following, all in Harvard Square:

- ✔ **Harvard Coop,** 1400 Mass. Ave. (☎ 617-499-2000)

- ✔ **Harvard Shop,** 52 John F. Kennedy St. (☎ 617-864-3000)

- ✔ **J. August & Co.,** 1320 Mass. Ave. (☎ 617-864-6650)

Two worthwhile special-interest bookstores are **Curious George Goes to WordsWorth,** 1 John F. Kennedy St. (☎ 617-498-0062; www.wordsworth.com), an excellent children's store, and the **Globe Corner Bookstore,** 28 Church St. (☎ 617-497-6277; www.globecorner.com), where you'll find travel books, maps, narratives, and atlases.

Harvard Square also makes a good starting point for a shopping stroll. **Mass. Ave.** runs north to **Porter Square** (T: Porter [Red Line]) through boutique country and southeast toward funkier **Central Square** (T: Central [Red Line]). Heading toward Porter, be sure to leave time for a stop at **Abodeon,** 1713 Mass. Ave. (☎ 617-497-0137), a quirky home-furnishings store; **Joie de Vivre,** 1792 Mass. Ave. (☎ 617-864-8188), a superb gift shop with a great kaleidoscope collection; and a branch of **Paper Source,** 1810 Mass. Ave. (☎ 617-497-1077; www.paper-source.com), with its funky gifts and gorgeous handmade papers. On the way to Central Square, you pass **Bowl & Board,** 1063 Mass. Ave. (☎ 617-661-0350), which specializes in upscale home accessories, and **The Games People Play,** 1100 Mass. Ave. (☎ 800-696-0711 or 617-492-0711), which carries tons of board games, as well as puzzles, chess sets, and more. Just outside Central Square, **Ten Thousand Villages,** 694 Mass. Ave. (☎ 617-876-2414), is part of a nonprofit craft-and-gift-shop chain; a friend of mine fondly calls it "the Third World tchotchke emporium."

In **East Cambridge,** the **CambridgeSide Galleria,** 100 CambridgeSide Place (☎ 617-621-8666; www.shopcambridgeside.com), is a three-level mall that would be at home in any suburb in the country. It holds more than 100 specialty stores, including a huge **J. Crew** store (☎ 617-225-2739; www.jcrew.com), a branch of **Borders** (☎ 617-679-0887; www.borders.com), several restaurants, and a food court. Part of the appeal is how astonishingly generic this place is; it may be just the bargaining chip you need to lure your teenagers to the nearby Museum of Science. T: Lechmere (Green Line) and then walk two blocks. Or Kendall/MIT (Red Line) and then the free shuttle bus, which runs every 10 to 20 minutes Monday through Saturday from 10 a.m. to 9:30 p.m. and Sunday from 11 a.m. to 7 p.m.

Index of Stores by Merchandise

Antiques
Upstairs Downstairs Antiques (Beacon Hill)

Art and Posters
International Poster Gallery (Back Bay)

Books
Barnes & Noble (Downtown Crossing)
Borders (Downtown Crossing, Cambridge)
Brattle Book Shop (Downtown Crossing)
Curious George Goes to WordsWorth (Cambridge)
Globe Corner Bookstore (Cambridge)
Harvard Book Store (Cambridge)
Harvard Coop (Cambridge)

Clothing and Accessories
Ann Taylor (Faneuil Hall Marketplace)
Armani (Back Bay)
Burberry (Back Bay)
Brooks Brothers (Back Bay, Faneuil Hall Marketplace)
Chanel (Back Bay)
Coach (Back Bay, Faneuil Hall Marketplace)
Gucci (Back Bay)
Hermès of Paris (Back Bay)
J. Crew (Cambridge)
Thomas Pink (Back Bay, Downtown Crossing)

Urban Outfitters (Back Bay, Cambridge)

Cosmetics and Perfume
Colonial Drug (Cambridge)
Kiehl's (Back Bay)
Lush (Back Bay)
Sephora (Back Bay)

Crafts
Artful Hand Gallery (Back Bay)
Society of Arts and Crafts (Back Bay)

Department Stores
Filene's (Downtown Crossing)
Lord & Taylor (Back Bay)
Macy's (Downtown Crossing)
Neiman Marcus (Back Bay)
Saks Fifth Avenue (Back Bay)

Discount Clothing
Filene's Basement (Downtown Crossing)

Food and Candy
Dairy Fresh Candies (North End)
Salumeria Italiana (North End)

Gifts and Toys
Black Ink (Beacon Hill, Cambridge)
Calliope (Cambridge)
The Games People Play (Cambridge)

Joie de Vivre (Cambridge)
Koo De Kir (Beacon Hill)
Museum of Fine Arts gift shops (Back Bay, Faneuil Hall Marketplace)
Paper Source (Back Bay, Cambridge)
Shake the Tree Gallery (North End)
Urban Outfitters (Back Bay, Cambridge)

Home Accessories

Abodeon (Cambridge)
Bowl & Board (Cambridge)
Gargoyles, Grotesques & Chimeras (Back Bay)
Restoration Hardware (Back Bay)

Jewelry

High Gear Jewelry (North End)
John Lewis, Inc. (Back Bay)
Shreve, Crump & Low (Back Bay)
Tiffany & Co. (Back Bay)

Malls

CambridgeSide Galleria (Cambridge)
Copley Place (Back Bay)
Shops at Prudential Center (Back Bay)

Music

Newbury Comics (Back Bay, Downtown Crossing, Cambridge)
Virgin Megastore (Back Bay)

Chapter 13

Following an Itinerary: Seven Great Options

*F*rom the moment you land in a new destination, you can almost hear the clock ticking. An unfamiliar place offers so much for you to see, and you never seem to have enough time to explore all the possibilities.

So consider two things: First, Boston is a compact place; you can get a good sense of the city in a short time. Second, you can't master *any* destination of appreciable size in just a few days.

Do what you want with the time you have. Be realistic — for the record, scheduling more than three major destinations in a day is trying to do too much — and remember to schedule some just-sitting-around time. In this chapter, I suggest outlines for trips of certain durations or focuses; feel free to mix and match as you see fit.

Boston in One Day

Two itineraries leap to mind if you can spend only one day in Boston: You can concentrate on one attraction or neighborhood (such as the Museum of Fine Arts, Harvard Square, Newbury Street, or the Museum of Science) without the smallest pang about not doing more, or you can try to sample enough of the city to get a sense that you've actually been here, not just *seen* everything. Here, I offer suggestions for the latter. This itinerary works in a loop — you can start at the beginning in the morning or pick things up in the middle and go from there.

On top of the world

The **Prudential Center Skywalk,** 800 Boylston St. (☎ 617-859-0648), offers a 360-degree view of Boston and far beyond. From the enclosed observation deck on the 50th floor of the Prudential Tower, you can see for miles, even (when it's clear) as far as the mountains of southern New Hampshire to the north and the beaches of Cape Cod to the south. Away from the windows, interactive audiovisual exhibits chronicle the city's history. Call before visiting, because the space sometimes closes for private events. Hours are 10 a.m. to 10 p.m. daily. Admission is $7 for adults, $4 for seniors and children 4 to 10; adults must show a photo ID to enter the Prudential Tower. T: Green Line E to Prudential, or B, C, or D to Hynes/ICA.

Start with an hour or less at **Filene's Basement** (see Chapter 12). Be there when it opens at 9:30 a.m., or earlier if the store is offering a special sale — check the newspapers when you arrive. Then follow the **Freedom Trail** from **Boston Common** to **Faneuil Hall Marketplace** or take a 90-minute National Park Service ranger tour (see Chapter 11). Have lunch at the marketplace (see Day 1 in the next itinerary, "Boston in Three Days") as you evaluate your options for what to do after lunch. Pick one of these four: Finish the Freedom Trail, take a **sightseeing cruise** (see Chapter 11), explore the **New England Aquarium** (see Chapter 11), or head to the **Children's Museum** (see Chapter 11). In the late afternoon, make your way to the Back Bay and enjoy the view from the **Prudential Center Skywalk.** Sunset is the perfect time to visit; let your appetite and the time of year determine whether you eat dinner before or after. If you can't leave town without a lobster, three branches of **Legal Sea Foods** (see Chapter 10) are close by. If trekking to the Back Bay doesn't appeal, have dinner at the waterfront Legal's, and wander over to the **North End** for dessert at a *caffè* (see Chapter 10).

Boston in Three Days

Day 1: In the morning, follow at least part of the **Freedom Trail** (see Chapter 11). The trail officially starts at Boston Common, but you can start in Charlestown, somewhere in the middle, or at the National Park Service Visitor Center with a ranger tour (see Chapter 10). The trail takes at least two hours. On the first section, consider a shopping detour to **Filene's Basement** (see Chapter 12), especially if you can get there before the lunch rush. Break for coffee, snacks, or lunch at **Faneuil Hall Marketplace,** where takeout counters and sit-down restaurants satisfy nearly every taste. **Durgin-Park** (see Chapter 10) is a good choice for the latter. If the weather is fine, take a picnic — stock up in the Quincy Market food court — across Atlantic Avenue to the end of Long Wharf (past the Marriott) or to Christopher Columbus Waterfront Park.

In the afternoon, push on to the **North End.** Between the Paul Revere House and the Old North Church, pause on **Hanover Street** for espresso or cappuccino and a pastry at a *caffè* (see Chapter 10). If you opt to finish the trail — and I'm *not* saying you have to — return downtown on the MBTA **ferry** to Long Wharf from the Charlestown Navy Yard. When you arrive at Long Wharf, look for a branch of **Legal Sea Foods** across the street from the ferry dock; you can grab some dinner here (but first, you may decide to visit your hotel to rest and wash up — the people at the next table certainly will appreciate it). If all this activity sounds exhausting, pick a restaurant near your hotel instead. If you're still up for more, make evening plans that include a trip to the **Prudential Center Skywalk** or back to Faneuil Hall Marketplace before or after dinner.

Day 2: This is museum day. Be there when the doors open at the **Museum of Fine Arts (MFA)** at 10 a.m., or the **Museum of Science** at 9 a.m., and plan to stay at least through midday — both museums offer decent options for lunch. If art is your interest, consider spending part of the afternoon at the **Isabella Stewart Gardner Museum,** up the street from the MFA. From the Museum of Science, a strenuous but rewarding walk leads to the **Bunker Hill Monument** (the last stop on the Freedom Trail, in case you didn't get there on Day 1). The walk takes about 30 minutes, and most of it is uphill.

If none of that appeals to you, start the day at the **John F. Kennedy Library and Museum** or the **Children's Museum.**

Any of these options can land you in the Back Bay by midafternoon, the perfect time for a **Duck Tour,** a **Swan Boat** ride, or just some downtime in the **Public Garden.** Collect yourself and do a little **shopping** on Newbury or Boylston Street (see Chapter 12). Freshen up and head to the **North End** for a hearty Italian dinner. Follow with dessert and people-watching in a Hanover Street *caffè* (especially if you didn't indulge on Day 1). Or plan a visit to a bar or club — maybe the **Comedy Connection, Cheers,** or the **Black Rose,** all at Faneuil Hall Marketplace (see Chapter 16).

Check the forecast when you arrive; inclement weather may mean scheduling your museum-visiting day to coincide with nasty outdoor conditions.

Day 3: Now you're off to **Cambridge.** This area can occupy a whole day or just half. (If it's the latter, use the extra time to further explore one of the options in the Day 1 or 2 itineraries earlier in this section.) Start with breakfast in the heart of **Harvard Square** — continental at **Au Bon Pain,** 1360 Mass. Ave. (☎ 617-497-9797), or full at the **Greenhouse Coffee Shop,** 3 Brattle St. (☎ 617-354-3184). Then tour the Harvard campus (see Chapter 11), visit one or more of the **university museums** (see Chapter 11), or do some **shopping** (see Chapter 12). Stroll along picturesque Brattle Street to the **Longfellow National Historic Site** (see Chapter 11). For lunch, follow the students to **Mr. Bartley's Burger Cottage** (see

Day 1 and Day 2 in Boston

Black Rose **14**
Boston Common **10**
Boston Harbor Cruises
   (sightseeing cruises) **18**
Bunker Hill Monument **7**
Charlestown Navy Yard
   (MBTA ferry to Long Wharf) **9**
Cheers **14**
Children's Museum **19**
Comedy Connection **14**
Duck Tours **3,8**
Durgin-Park **13**
Faneuil Hall **12**
Filene's Basement **11**
Hanover Street **16**

Isabella Stewart Gardner
   Museum **1**
John F. Kennedy Library
   and Museum **20**
Legal Sea Foods
   (Prudential Center) **4**
Legal Sea Foods (Waterfront) **18**
Museum of Fine Arts (MFA) **2**
Museum of Science **8**
New England Aquarium **17**
North End **15**
Prudential Center Skywalk **4**
Public Garden **5**
Swan Boats **6**

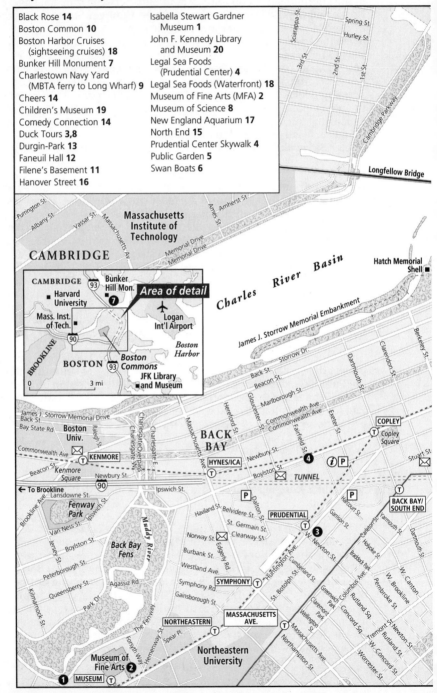

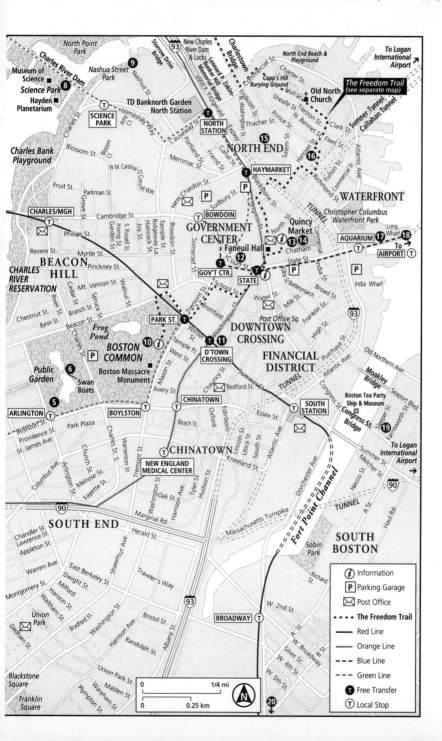

Day 3 in Cambridge

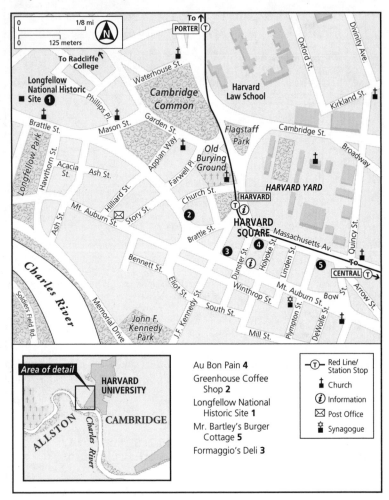

Au Bon Pain **4**

Greenhouse Coffee Shop **2**

Longfellow National Historic Site **1**

Mr. Bartley's Burger Cottage **5**

Formaggio's Deli **3**

- —Ⓣ— Red Line/ Station Stop
- ✝ Church
- ⓘ Information
- ✉ Post Office
- ⚯ Synagogue

Chapter 10), or picnic by the river on something tasty from **Formaggio's Deli** (see Chapter 10). In the afternoon, continue to explore or shop in Cambridge, or head back to Boston. Spend this time hitting **Filene's Basement,** if you haven't yet (or even if you have). For the evening, consider activities that don't strain your budget, starting with dinner at one of Boston's neighborhood restaurants (see Chapter 10). Follow with a student play or performance, or a free concert or film. If you're up for another big night out, consider a **Boston Symphony Orchestra** performance or a pre- or post-Broadway **play** (see Chapter 15).

Boston in Five Days

If you have five days in Boston, follow the itinerary in the preceding section for the first three days and then continue with the following:

Day 4: Road trip! Turn to Chapter 14, and pick a town or two where you can spend the day. Explore **Lexington, Concord, Salem, Marblehead, Gloucester, Rockport, Plymouth,** or some sensible combination thereof. You don't need to rent a car for this trip, but you may want to; at busy times, book the car when you reserve your flight and hotel. Have dinner at your day-trip destination, or return to Boston or Cambridge. Afterward, you can hear jazz at the **Regattabar** in Cambridge or **Scullers** in Boston, or barely hear yourself think at a **club** in Cambridge, Somerville, or Boston (see Chapter 16).

Suggested evening itineraries

If you're traveling as a family, you may be setting up your evening itineraries based on the TV listings. If not — or if you had the foresight to book a sitter — here are some suggestions. See Chapter 10 for detailed restaurant reviews and Chapters 15 and 16 for comprehensive nightlife listings. You can find all the following restaurants and nightlife venues in those sections of this book.

✔ Dinner in the North End, and coffee and dessert at an Italian cafe. Afterward, a show at the Comedy Connection at Faneuil Hall or the Improv Asylum, and a drink at the *Cheers* bar in Quincy Market.

✔ Dinner at Legal Sea Foods in the Prudential Center, followed by a visit to the 50th-floor Prudential Center Skywalk or a drink in the lounge at Top of the Hub on the 52nd floor.

✔ Summer only: Assemble a picnic, and head to the Hatch Shell for music or a movie or to Boston Common for a play or concert.

✔ Winter only: A Boston Symphony Orchestra or Boston Ballet performance and then a late supper at Brasserie Jo or dessert at Finale.

✔ Dinner at the State Street Legal Sea Foods and then a stroll to the plaza at the end of Long Wharf. Hit the food court at Faneuil Hall Marketplace for dessert.

✔ Dinner at Bob the Chef's Jazz Cafe and music at Wally's Café or a Huntington Theatre Company performance.

✔ Dinner at Rialto and music at the Regattabar or Sculler's Jazz Club.

✔ Shopping at the Coop, the Harvard Book Store, and then dinner at Mr. Bartley's Burger Cottage.

✔ Dinner at the Green Street Grill, ice cream at Toscanini's, and music at The Middle East or T.T. the Bear's Place.

✔ Dinner at The Blue Room or Oleana and then music at the Cantab Lounge.

Day 5: Today, you tie up loose ends that would have left you saying, "If only we'd had time for (fill in the blank)." Leaf through Chapters 10 and 11 to refresh your memory about places that sounded good — a **historic house?** The **New England Aquarium?** The **Freedom Trail** stops you skipped? A special-interest **walking tour?** One of the **museums** you couldn't fit in on Day 2? Yet another **restaurant?** In the evening, check out a **sporting event,** one of the earlier nightlife suggestions, or your room (you need to pack, right?).

Boston with Kids

Here's an outline of a single kid-centric day in Boston. This itinerary is designed for warm weather; at colder times of the year, you may want to concentrate on indoor destinations such as museums and, if you must, malls. This plan is flexible enough to allow lingering at some stops and trimming (or even eliminating) others, and the schedule cries out to be personalized.

Order extra unbuttered toast at breakfast, or hang on to that extra half bagel; you'll need it later.

Start with a **Boston Duck Tour** (see Chapter 11) from the Prudential Center, which Bostonians call the Pru. Buy tickets in advance or when the booth opens (no later than 9 a.m.). If you face a wait before your tour, wander around the shopping plaza or check out the **Christian Science Center reflecting pool,** across the street from the back of the Pru.

Smile and say "Boston"

Many travelers are going digital these days when it comes to taking vacation photographs. Not only are digital cameras left relatively unscathed by airport X-rays, but also, with digital equipment, you don't need to lug armloads of film with you as you travel. In fact, nowadays you don't even need to carry your laptop to download the day's images to make room for more. With a **media storage card,** sold by all major camera dealers, you can store hundreds of images in your camera. These "memory" cards come in different configurations — from memory sticks to flash cards to secure digital cards — and different storage capacities (the more megabytes of memory, the more images a card can hold) and range in price from $30 to over $200. (**Note:** Each camera model works with a specific type of card, so you need to determine which storage card is compatible with your camera.) When you get home, you can print the images on your own color printer, or take the storage card to a camera store, drugstore, or chain retailer. Or have the images developed online with a service like **Snapfish** (www.snapfish.com) for something like 25¢ a shot.

Later, use the Boylston Street exit at the front of the Pru, turn right, and walk 3 blocks to Copley Square. The square contains a fountain; benches; and *The Tortoise and Hare at Copley Square,* a two-piece sculpture by Nancy Schön. Where's that camera?

Continue on Boylston Street 2 more blocks, and you come to the **Public Garden.** The **Swan Boats** make a good low-tech break. The vessels share the lagoon with live swans, ducks, and geese that want the rest of your breakfast. *Make Way for Ducklings,* another enchanting work by Nancy Schön, is near the corner of Beacon and Charles streets (diagonally across from where you enter the Garden).

Kids with liberal TV privileges may want to head across the street for lunch at **Cheers Beacon Hill,** formerly the Bull & Finch Pub (see Chapter 16) and the inspiration for the classic sitcom. Solid pub fare (including fine burgers) and a children's menu may make up for the fact that the real thing looks nothing like the set of the show. Alternatively, walk 2 blocks back on Boylston Street, turn left, and walk 2½ blocks to the **Hard Rock Cafe** (see Chapter 16).

In the afternoon, pick a museum or other learning experience: the **Children's Museum** for the younger set, the **Museum of Science** or the **New England Aquarium** for older kids.

For dinner, let the children name the restaurant — perhaps the Hard Rock Cafe, if you had lunch elsewhere; a **North End** pasta place; or the multiple options at **Faneuil Hall Marketplace.** Finally, if this plan doesn't blow anyone's bedtime, spend the evening taking in a live performance of *Shear Madness* or **Blue Man Group** (see Chapter 15).

Boston for Art Lovers

Would-be artists and would-be art collectors flock to Boston for inspiration of all sorts in museums and galleries. From the dazzling Impressionist paintings at the Museum of Fine Arts to work by promising artists and craftspeople in cutting-edge galleries, the city abounds with aesthetic treats. (Unless otherwise noted, see the map in Chapter 11 for most of these locations.)

Check ahead for special museum shows. Short-term exhibits often require separate tickets, sometimes good only at a specific time.

For high-profile traveling exhibitions, many large hotels arrange packages that include museum tickets. Start investigating as soon as you hear about the show. You may not save money, but the tickets usually are valid at any time — an invaluable perk if your schedule is uncertain.

Boston with Kids

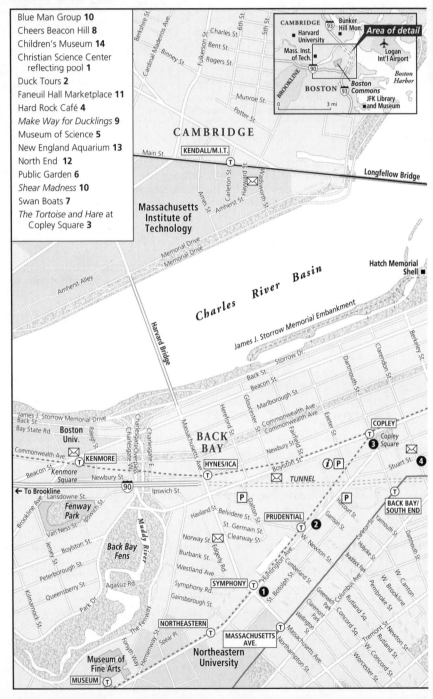

Blue Man Group **10**
Cheers Beacon Hill **8**
Children's Museum **14**
Christian Science Center
 reflecting pool **1**
Duck Tours **2**
Faneuil Hall Marketplace **11**
Hard Rock Café **4**
Make Way for Ducklings **9**
Museum of Science **5**
New England Aquarium **13**
North End **12**
Public Garden **6**
Shear Madness **10**
Swan Boats **7**
The Tortoise and Hare at
 Copley Square **3**

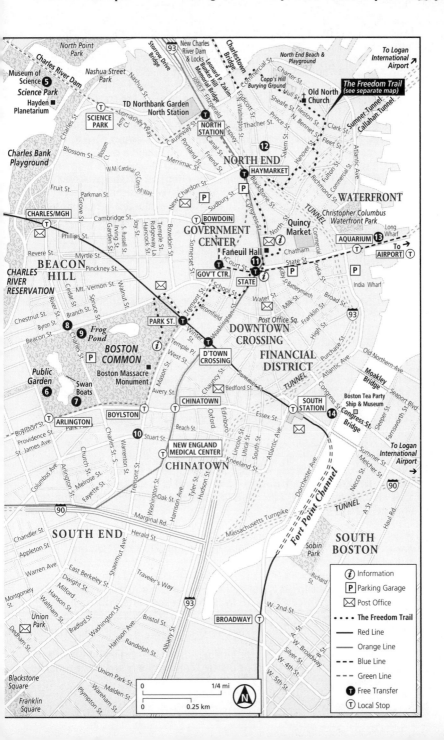

Stop one is the **Museum of Fine Arts (MFA),** which opens at 10 a.m. Take a free tour at 10:30 a.m., or help yourself to a floor plan and wander. I could cheerfully spend a day here, but you may not have that kind of time. Go in with some sense of what you want to see; the Web site (www.mfa.org) is a great planning tool. When you've had your fill, move on (2 blocks or so) to the **Isabella Stewart Gardner Museum.** Have lunch in the MFA's cafeteria, cafe, or restaurant (you may need a reservation) or in the Gardner's cafe. Then hop on the Green Line and head for the Copley or Arlington stop. One block away is **Newbury Street,** home to more art galleries than you can possibly see in half a day — or even a whole day. If time allows, plan for an hour or so at one of the **historic houses** nearby (see Chapter 11) before or after you hit the galleries. Wind down with afternoon tea (see Chapter 10) or a drink in the elegant confines of the **Four Seasons** or the **Ritz-Carlton, Boston** (see Chapter 16). If you've kept your spending under control at the art galleries, you may want to have a little caviar with your tea.

Boston for Sports Fans

Boston enjoys a well-deserved reputation as a great sports town and regularly ranks high on lists of physically fit cities. Whether as a spectator or a participant, you can make yourself an honorary Bostonian with relatively little effort.

Start by slapping on a Red Sox cap. Then head out to the team's home field, **Fenway Park,** which offers tours year-round — a good fallback if you can't land tickets to a game. Tickets were tough to get even before the Sox won the World Series in 2004 for the first time since 1918 (maybe you heard a little something about this victory). See Chapter 11.

Now lace up your walking or **running shoes** (or inline skates, if you have them with you). In all but the nastiest weather, Bostonians flock to the Esplanade, between Storrow Drive and the Charles River on the edge of Beacon Hill and the Back Bay, to exercise and take in the river views. This area is equally well known as the home of the Hatch Shell amphitheater; see Chapter 15.

When snow piles up or the wind howls off the river, the Esplanade turns positively arctic. The Frog Pond skating rink (☎ 617-635-2120; www. cityofboston.gov/parks/frogpond_winter.asp) on Boston Common is an excellent alternative. It's an open rink with an ice-making system and a clubhouse. Admission is $3 for adults and free for children under 14; skate rental costs $7 for adults, $5 for kids. Weekend afternoons are the most popular and crowded time to skate; try to go in the morning or on a weekday.

Before or after you go jogging (or skating), head to the **TD Banknorth Garden** (formerly called the FleetCenter) to visit the **Sports Museum of New England** (see Chapter 11).

Depending on the time of year and time of day, you'll probably be able to fit a **game** into this itinerary. If you can't buy (or afford) tickets to the Red Sox, Patriots, Celtics, or Bruins, consider a college event. *The Boston Globe* publishes daily schedules; you can also check individual schools' Web sites before you hit town. Men's hockey is the marquee event for Boston College, Boston University, Harvard, and Northeastern University, but you might find anything from a nationally ranked lacrosse game to a Saturday-morning crew race. (The finish line is on Memorial Drive, across the street from the Hyatt Regency Cambridge.)

Boston for Day-Tripping Historians

Make Boston your home base while you explore American history in roughly chronological order. Take as little as three days or as long as a week to meet the Pilgrims, trace the steps of the revolution-minded Minutemen, and explore the spoils of the China trade. A car makes this itinerary more manageable than relying on public transit, but buses and trains will take you nearly everywhere. Unless otherwise indicated, turn to Chapter 14 for details of the destinations in this itinerary.

The Pilgrims kicked things off in **Plymouth,** and you will, too. "American's Hometown" can be a half-day jaunt, if you visit only attractions that sound especially appealing (starting with Plymouth Rock), or an all-day destination, if you study every artifact (starting with Plymouth Rock) and immerse yourselves in the experience of Plimoth Plantation.

From the 17th century, move on to the 18th. A day split between **Boston** and **Cambridge** — with special attention to the colonial and Revolutionary destinations on the Freedom Trail and to the Longfellow National Historic Site (see Chapter 11), where George Washington once lived — fits well here, but you can also head straight to **Lexington.** Visit the Village Green and at least one of the Historical Society's well-preserved houses. Continue to **Concord,** a fascinating town that abounds with sites associated with both the Revolution and the 19th-century intellectual glory days known as the "flowering of New England."

Nathaniel Hawthorne spent the final years of his life in Concord, but he made his reputation in **Salem,** which attained such prosperity in the years following the Revolution that many traders in the Far East believed it was an independent country. The **North Shore** and **Cape Ann** make up the final leg of this itinerary. Let your interests dictate how you organize your time. Salem's Peabody Essex Museum offers a good overview of the area. You probably already know something about the 1792 witch trials; less familiar but equally interesting is the Federal-era China trade; magnificent residential architecture all over the North Shore originated during this period. The area also encompasses the prosperous yachting community that centers on **Marblehead,** as well as the commercial fishing port

Boston for Historians

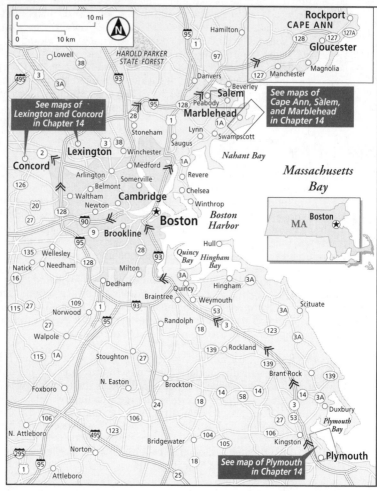

of **Gloucester.** Both Gloucester and **Rockport** have been popular destinations for artists since the 19th century. Both the Rocky Neck section of Gloucester and downtown Rockport retain their artsy associations, to the delight of 21st-century visitors like you.

Chapter 14

Going Beyond Boston: Four Day Trips

· ·

In This Chapter

▶ Remembering the Revolutionary War in Lexington and Concord

▶ Meeting sorceresses and sailors in Salem and Marblehead

▶ Enjoying seafood and scenery in Gloucester and Rockport

▶ Imagining the Pilgrims in Plymouth

· ·

*P*art of Boston's appeal is its proximity to other fascinating destinations. Lexington, Concord, Salem, Marblehead, Gloucester, Rockport, and Plymouth lie within an hour or so of downtown, and they all make enjoyable day trips. (For the locations of the towns in relation to Boston, see the map on the inside back cover of this book.) Each boasts abundant historic associations and excellent sightseeing, with enough shopping and dining opportunities to keep everyone happy.

In this chapter, I suggest ways to combine visits to some of the nearby municipalities. I start with general pointers and then offer specific tips on getting there and making the most of your day by planning what to see and where to eat.

General Pointers

Rental cars and overnight stays are two items that can inflate the cost of your day trip. If your visit to the Boston area is relatively short, I suggest you skip the room but consider the car — packing up and moving for the second time in just a few days is more disruptive than convenient, but having wheels increases your flexibility and touring range. That said, remember that reliable public transportation serves each of the towns in this chapter; if you don't want to deal with a car, you don't need to. (For information about the commuter rail and buses, contact the **T** at ☎ **800-392-6100** outside Massachusetts or 617-222-3200; www.mbta.com.)

If you want to plan an overnight stay, the Chamber of Commerce or other tourism authorities in each town will eagerly advise you. One good option is a bed-and-breakfast; see Chapter 9 for names and numbers of agencies that can book one for you.

Summer and fall weekends are the day-trip version of rush hour. In pleasant weather, gridlock is a problem. If you can, try to schedule your trip for a weekday, preferably in the spring or fall, when car and pedestrian traffic are more manageable and the weather is relatively predictable. Some businesses and attractions close for the winter, but if you visit then, the open ones will be practically empty.

Finally, if you don't want to worry about details, consider a guided half- or full-day bus trip. For a good selection and fair prices, contact Gray Line's **Brush Hill Tours,** 435 High St., Randolph, MA 02368 (☎ **800-343-1328** or 781-986-6100; www.grayline.com).

Where to find out more

Information offices can assist walk-in visitors. To receive information in advance (a good way to involve kids in the planning), contact the following:

- ✔ **Massachusetts:** Massachusetts Office of Travel & Tourism, 10 Park Plaza, Suite 4510, Boston, MA 02116 (☎ **800-227-6277** or 617-973-8500; www.massvacation.com)

- ✔ **Lexington and Concord:** Lexington Chamber of Commerce, 1875 Massachusetts Ave., Lexington, MA 02421 (☎ **781-862-2480**; www.lexingtonchamber.org); Concord Chamber of Commerce, 100 Main St., Suite 310-2, Concord, MA 01742 (☎ **978-369-3120**; www.concordmachamber.org); and Greater Merrimack Valley Convention & Visitors Bureau, 9 Central St., Suite 201, Lowell, MA 01852 (☎ **800-443-3332** or 978-459-6150; www.merrimackvalley.org)

- ✔ **Salem and Marblehead:** Destination Salem, 63 Wharf St., Salem, MA 01970 (☎ **877-SALEM-MA** or 978-744-3663; www.salem.org); Marblehead Chamber of Commerce, 62 Pleasant St., Marblehead, MA 01945 (☎ **781-631-2868**; www.marbleheadchamber.org); and North of Boston Convention & Visitors Bureau, 17 Peabody Sq., Peabody, MA 01960 (☎ **800-742-5306** or 978-977-7760; www.northofboston.org)

- ✔ **Gloucester and Rockport:** Gloucester Tourism Commission, 22 Poplar St., Gloucester, MA 01930 (☎ **800-649-6839** or 978-281-8865; www.gloucesterma.com); Rockport Chamber of Commerce and Board of Trade, 22 Broadway, Rockport MA 01966 (☎ **978-546-6575**; www.rockportusa.com); and Cape Ann Chamber of Commerce, 33 Commercial St., Gloucester, MA 01930 (☎ **800-321-0133** or 978-283-1601; www.capeannvacations.com)

- ✔ **Plymouth:** Destination Plymouth, 170 Water St., Suite 10C, Plymouth, MA 02360 (☎ **800-USA-1620** or 508-747-7533; www.visit-plymouth.com), and Plymouth County Convention & Visitors Bureau, 32 Court St., Plymouth, MA 02360 (☎ **508-747-0100**; www.seeplymouth.com)

Lexington and Concord

The Revolutionary War started in these prosperous suburbs, which were then country villages. With an assist from a Henry Wadsworth Longfellow poem, the events of April 1775 vaulted Lexington and Concord into immortality. On your day trip, you'll understand why.

A visit to both towns makes a reasonable one-day excursion. Lexington is a half-day trip; if Concord appeals to you, you can spend the whole day there. Some attractions close for the winter and reopen after Patriots' Day, the third Monday of April.

 Hit the Boston Public Library (Chapter 11) or the Old North Church gift shop (Chapter 11), and track down Longfellow's poem "Paul Revere's Ride," a classic but historically dubious account of Revere's journey on April 18 and 19, 1775. You'll hear about the poem all over Lexington and Concord, and you may already know a little. (The first lines are "Listen, my children, and you shall hear / Of the midnight ride of Paul Revere.")

Getting to Lexington

To drive from Boston (9 miles) or Cambridge (6 miles), take Soldiers Field Road or Memorial Drive west to Route 2. Exit at Route 4/225, and follow signs into the center of town. From Route 128 (I-95), use Exit 31A and proceed into town. Parking is available on Mass. Ave., and a public metered lot is near the corner of Mass. Ave. and Waltham Street. The National Heritage Museum and Minute Man National Historical Park have free parking lots.

Public transportation is more complicated. Start by riding the Red Line to the last stop, Alewife. From there, bus routes number 62 (Bedford) and 76 (Hanscom) serve Lexington. The buses run Monday through Saturday, hourly during the day, and every 30 minutes during rush hours. They don't operate on Sunday. The bus trip takes about 25 minutes and costs 90¢ one-way.

Taking a tour of Lexington and Concord

The **Liberty Ride** (☎ 781-862-1450; www.libertyride.us) is a narrated tour that connects the attractions in Lexington and Concord, including Minute Man National Historical Park. At press time, the service ran July through Columbus Day only. The fare is $20 for adults, $10 for students 5 to 17, and free for children under 5. That's steep if you have a car, but worth the money if you're using public transportation — and your ticket gets you discounts at businesses around both towns.

Seeing the sights in Lexington

Pick up maps and other information at the **Chamber of Commerce Visitor Center,** 1875 Mass. Ave. (☎ 781-862-2480). The center is open mid-April through October daily from 9 a.m. to 5 p.m. and November through mid-April daily from 10 a.m. to 4 p.m. Displays include a diorama that illustrates the battle.

The visitor center is on the **Village Green** or Battle Green, site of the Revolution's first skirmish. The monuments and memorials include the Minuteman Statue (1900) of the militia commander, Captain John Parker, who instructed his troops, "Don't fire unless fired upon, but if they mean to have a war, let it begin here!" It takes about an hour to check out the center displays and outdoor sights on the Battle Green.

The Lexington Historical Society (www.lexingtonhistory.org) operates the town's most compelling attraction, the **Buckman Tavern,** 1 Bedford St. (☎ 781-862-1703). The tavern is the only remaining building that stood on the Green on April 19, 1775. Costumed guides lead an outstanding tour that describes the building's history, the battle, and details of colonial life. Even if time is short, don't miss this one.

Tours of the society's other two properties are well worth your time but are short of can't-miss experiences. The **Hancock-Clarke House,** 36 Hancock St. (☎ 781-861-0928), one-third of a mile from the Green, houses the Historical Society's museum of the Revolution. The 1690 **Munroe Tavern,** 1332 Mass. Ave. (☎ 781-862-1703), is about a mile from the Green in the other direction. During the battle, the tavern fell into British hands and became the headquarters and, later, field hospital.

To see the houses, you must take a guided tour, which lasts 30 to 45 minutes per house. The Buckman Tavern is open from April through mid-November Monday through Saturday from 10 a.m. to 5 p.m. and Sunday from noon to 5 p.m. The Hancock-Clarke House and the Munroe Tavern are open over the third weekend in April (for Patriots' Day) and from Memorial Day weekend through late October Monday through Saturday 11:30 a.m. to 4:30 p.m. and Sunday 1 to 4:30 p.m. Admission for adults is $5 per house, $8 for two, and $12 for all three; for seniors, $7 for two houses and $11 for three; for children 6 to 16, $3 per house, $5 for two houses, and $7 for three. Group tours run by appointment only.

The other major attraction in Lexington is the **National Heritage Museum,** 33 Marrett Rd. (Route 2A), at Mass. Ave. (☎ 781-861-6559; www.monh.org), which takes a fun approach, illustrating history with cultural artifacts. It's anything but a stuffy old museum — the curators wisely remember that pop culture is culture, too. In recent years, subjects of the temporary exhibits have included the Beatles and Elvis Presley, circus posters, mail-order catalogs, jigsaw puzzles, George Washington, and Frank Lloyd Wright, to name a few. For another look at the Revolution, visit the permanent installation on the Battle of Lexington. For a tasty lunch, visit the Courtyard Café. The Scottish Rite of Freemasonry sponsors the museum. Admission is free; the museum is open Monday through Saturday from 10 a.m. to 5 p.m. and Sunday from noon to 5 p.m.

Lexington

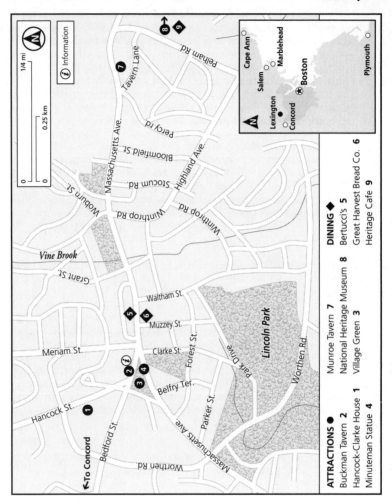

Dining in Lexington

The center of town, near the intersection of Mass. Ave. and Waltham Street, offers a number of choices. For a muffin or scone to start the day, Lexington has a branch of **Great Harvest Bread Co.,** 1736 Mass. Ave. (☎ **781-861-9990**). For lunch, you may want to hold out until Concord. If you can't, the **Courtyard Café** at the National Heritage Museum (☎ **781-861-6558,** ext. 4143) is a popular spot for soups, salads, and sandwiches. Or try **Bertucci's,** 1777 Mass. Ave. (☎ **781-860-9000**), for pizza and pasta.

Seeing the sights en route from Lexington to Concord

Minute Man National Historical Park (www.nps.gov/mima) spreads over 900 acres in Lexington, Concord, and Lincoln. The park encompasses the scene of the first Revolutionary War battle and a 4-mile piece of the road that the vanquished British troops used to retreat from Concord to Boston. Artwork and artifacts illustrate the displays at visitor centers in Lexington and Concord, either of which makes an excellent starting point. Visiting the park takes as little as half an hour (to see Concord's North Bridge) or as long as several hours, if you include stops at both visitor centers and maybe a ranger-led program.

The park is open daily year-round. Admission is free; charges for special tours may apply. In Lexington, the **Minute Man Visitor Center** is off Route 2A, ½ mile west of I-95 (Massachusetts Route 128) Exit 33B (☎ **781-862-7753**). The center is open daily from 9 a.m. to 5 p.m. (until 4 p.m. in winter). Concord's **North Bridge Visitor Center,** 174 Liberty St., off Monument Street (☎ **978-369-6993**), overlooks the Concord River and the bridge. The center is open daily from 9 a.m. to 5 p.m. (until 4 p.m. in winter).

Walden Pond State Reservation, Route 126, Concord (☎ **978-369-3254;** www.state.ma.us/dem/parks/wldn.htm), preserves the site of the cabin where Henry David Thoreau lived from 1845 to 1847. Besides being a literary pilgrimage site, this spot is popular with visitors who hike around the pond, picnic, swim, and fish. In fine weather, call before heading over to make sure that the parking lot has space available (there's no additional parking). Parking costs $5 year-round.

To get to Walden Pond from Lexington, take Mass. Ave. west to Route 2A, bear left onto Route 2, and turn left onto Route 126. From Concord, take Walden Street (Route 126) south, away from Concord Center; cross Route 2; and look for signs pointing to the parking lot.

Getting to Concord

To drive from Lexington, take Mass. Ave. west, across Route 128, and pick up Route 2A. Pass through Lincoln and bear right onto Lexington Road in Concord. Follow HISTORIC CONCORD signs into the center of town. If you miss the turnoff, continue about ½ mile, and take the next right onto Cambridge Turnpike, which runs into the center of town. To go straight to Walden Pond, take what's now Route 2/2A another mile or so, and turn left onto Route 126. From Boston (18 miles) and Cambridge (15 miles), take Soldiers Field Road or Memorial Drive west to Route 2. In Lincoln, stay in the right lane. Where the road makes a sharp left, go straight onto Cambridge Turnpike. Parking is available throughout town and at the attractions.

By public transportation, the commuter rail takes about 45 minutes from North Station in Boston, with a stop at Porter Square in Cambridge. The one-way fare is $5. (The only transportation between Lexington and

Concord is the seasonal Liberty Ride tour.) The station is about three-quarters of a mile from the town center. The attractions are accessible on foot but not all that close together; in hot or cold weather, make appropriate preparations (hats, water, sunscreen, and such).

If you want to fit in, pronounce it *conquered* (not *con*-cored).

Taking a tour of Concord

The **Chamber of Commerce** (☎ **978-369-3120**; www.concordmachamber.org) offers 90-minute tours from mid-April through October on Friday, Saturday, Sunday, and Monday holidays, and other days by appointment. These tours start at the information booth on Heywood Street, 1 block southeast of Monument Square. Also check to see whether Park Service rangers from the **North Bridge Visitor Center** (☎ **978-369-6993**; www.nps.gov/mima) are leading tours during your visit.

For information about a tour of Concord and Lexington, see the listing for the Liberty Ride, earlier in this section.

Seeing the sights in Concord

The monuments and descriptions around and in the North Bridge Visitor Center give a good sense of Concord's best-known event: the Battle of Concord. The town is equally famous for literary associations, and indications of that abound, too. Visit **Sleepy Hollow Cemetery,** off Route 62 west (☎ **978-318-3233**; www.concordnet.org), and climb to Author's Ridge. In this area, you find the graves of Ralph Waldo Emerson, Nathaniel Hawthorne, Henry David Thoreau, and Louisa May Alcott and her father, Bronson Alcott, among others. The cemetery is open daily from 7 a.m. to dusk and doesn't allow buses; call ahead for wheelchair access.

Concord Museum

The Concord Museum offers a fascinating, comprehensive look at the town's storied history. The best features of the galleries aren't the abundant objects and artifacts, although they're impressive; the best features are the accompanying descriptions and interpretations that place the exhibits in context. For example, you can see one of the lanterns that signaled Paul Revere from the steeple of the Old North Church. This display includes just enough explanatory text to show why that's a big deal. To help orient the kids, pick up a family activity pack near the entrance.

Lexington Road and Cambridge Turnpike. ☎ *978-369-9609 (recorded info) or 978-369-9763.* www.concordmuseum.org. *Follow Lexington Road out of Concord Center and bear right at museum onto Cambridge Turnpike; entrance is on the left. Parking: In lot or on road. Admission: $8 adults, $7 seniors and students, $5 children under 16. Open: June–Aug daily 9 a.m.–5 p.m.; April–May and Sept–Dec Mon–Sat 9 a.m.–5 p.m., Sun noon to 5 p.m.; Jan–March Mon–Sat 11 a.m.–4 p.m., Sun 1–4 p.m.*

Concord

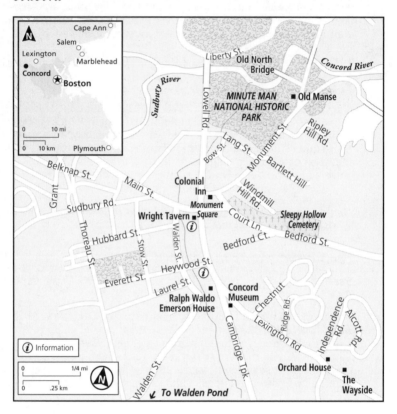

The Old Manse

The Reverend William Emerson, Ralph Waldo Emerson's grandfather, built this house in 1770 and watched the Battle of Concord from the yard. For almost 170 years, the house was home to his widow, her second husband, their descendants, and (briefly) newlyweds Nathaniel and Sophia Peabody Hawthorne. The tour traces the history of the house and its occupants, using a rich trove of family memorabilia.

269 Monument St. (at North Bridge). ☎ *978-369-3909.* www.thetrustees.org. *From Concord Center, follow Monument Street until you see North Bridge parking lot on the right; the Old Manse is on the left. Guided tours: $7.50 adults, $6.50 seniors and students, $5 children 6–12, $22 families. Open: Mid-April–Oct Mon–Sat 10 a.m.– 5 p.m.; Sun and holidays noon to 5 p.m. Last tour at 4:30 p.m. Closed Nov–mid-April.*

Orchard House

If you are or were a preadolescent girl, this stop may be one of the best parts of your trip. Louisa May Alcott lived and wrote at Orchard House, the setting for her best-known book, *Little Women* (1868). If you loved the book, don't leave town without seeing the house; if you don't understand what the fuss is about, this attraction may not be the best use of your time. The tour offers an intriguing look at 19th-century family life, overflowing with anecdotes and heirlooms.

399 Lexington Rd. ☎ 978-369-4118. www.louisamayalcott.org. *Follow Lexington Road out of Concord Center past Concord Museum; the house is on the left. Parking: In lot; overflow parking lot is across the street. Guided tours: $8 adults, $7 seniors and students, $5 children 6–17, $20 families (up to 2 adults and 4 children). Open: April–Oct Mon–Sat 10 a.m.–4:30 p.m., Sun 1–4:30 p.m.; Nov–March Mon–Fri 11 a.m.–3 p.m., Sat 10 a.m.–4:30 p.m., Sun 1–4:30 p.m. Closed Jan 1–15.*

Ralph Waldo Emerson House

Emerson is a household name in Concord, where he remains such a towering presence that guides here still call him "Mr. Emerson." The philosopher, essayist, and poet lived in this house from 1835 until he died, in 1882. The tour highlights Emerson's domestic life and the house's over-the-top Victorian decor.

28 Cambridge Turnpike. ☎ 978-369-2236. Take Cambridge Turnpike out of Concord Center; just before Concord Museum, house is on the right. Guided tours: $7 adults, $5 seniors and students; call to arrange group tours. Open: Mid-April–Oct Thurs–Sat 10 a.m.–4:30 p.m.; Sun 1–4:30 p.m. Closed Nov–mid-April.

The Wayside

Nathaniel Hawthorne lived at the Wayside from 1852 until his death in 1864. The Alcott family lived here, too, as did Harriett Lothrop, who wrote the *Five Little Peppers* books under the pen name Margaret Sidney. This house is part of Minute Man National Historical Park; rangers lead the interesting tours, which explore the patchwork architecture and the lives and careers of the house's famous residents.

455 Lexington Rd. ☎ 978-369-6975. www.nps.gov/mima/wayside. *Follow Lexington Road past Concord Museum and Orchard House; the Wayside is on the left. Guided tours: $4 adults; free for children under 17. Open: May–Oct Thurs–Tues 10:30 a.m.–4:30 p.m. Closed Nov–April.*

Dining in Concord

Concord's Colonial Inn, 48 Monument Sq. (☎ 978-369-2372; www.concordscolonialinn.com), is a traditional — the main building dates to 1716 — establishment with a fine restaurant and two friendly lounges. The food is certainly tasty, but you're really here to soak up the atmosphere. The inn serves afternoon tea from Wednesday through Sunday. Call to make a reservation.

In an off-the-tourist-track location, **Nashoba Brook Bakery & Cafe,** 152 Commonwealth Ave., West Concord (☎ 978-318-1999; www.slowrise.com), is a delightful soup–salad–sandwich place that also serves fantastic breads and desserts made in-house. From Concord

Center, take Main Street west, cross Route 2, and proceed to the traffic light in front of the West Concord train station, bear right, and go 3 blocks. Park on the street or in one of the handful of spots in the lot, or continue on Commonwealth Avenue as it bears right and cross the bridge to reach the overflow parking lot on Winthrop Street. The cafe is open Monday through Friday from 6 a.m. to 6:30 p.m., weekends from 8 a.m. to 5 p.m.

For picnic fixings, visit the **Cheese Shop,** 25–31 Walden St. (☎ **978-369-5778**), near the town center.

Salem and Marblehead

The North Shore played a prominent role in the Revolution and attained great prosperity by dominating the China trade in the early Federal era, but we both know that's not why you flipped to this page. When you read "Salem," you thought, "Witches!"

The witch trials of 1692 left an indelible mark on Salem, which good-naturedly welcomes the association — while never forgetting that 20 people died in the unfounded hysteria. When you discover this pleasant city, you may want to hang around and find out about its rich maritime history, too. Salem shares that legacy with the affluent, picturesque town of Marblehead, which (Newport be hanged) is the self-proclaimed "Yachting Capital of America."

Much like Lexington and Concord, Salem and Marblehead together make a full day trip. You can also easily spend an entire day in either place.

Getting to Salem

To drive from Boston (17 miles), take the Callahan or Ted Williams Tunnel to Route 1A north past the airport and into downtown Salem. Be careful in Lynn, where the road turns left and immediately right. Or take I-93 or Route 1 to Route 128 and then Route 114 into Salem. From Marblehead, follow Route 114 (Pleasant Street) west. Plenty of on-street parking is available, and a municipal garage is across from the National Park Service Visitor Center.

Bus route Number 450 runs from Haymarket (Green or Orange Line), and commuter trains operate from North Station (Green or Orange Line). The bus takes an hour; the train, 30 to 35 minutes. The one-way fare is $3.45 for the bus, $3.75 for the train.

Taking a tour of Salem

The **Salem Trolley** (☎ 978-744-5469) operates daily from 10 a.m. to 5 p.m. from April through October and on weekends in March and November. Tickets ($10 adults, $9 seniors, $5 children 5 to 14) are good all day, and you can get off and on as much as you like at any of the 15 stops. The driver narrates a one-hour tour while making a loop around town; the first stop is at the Essex Street side of the National Park Service Visitor Center on New Liberty Street.

Seeing the sights in Salem

The **National Park Service Visitor Center,** 2 New Liberty St. (☎ **978-740-1650;** www.nps.gov/sama), distributes brochures and pamphlets, including one that describes a walking tour of the historic district. The center is open daily from 9 a.m. to 5 p.m. Architecture buffs will want to see **Chestnut Street,** a gorgeously preserved example of colonial style; the whole street is a registered National Historic Landmark.

The House of the Seven Gables

Nathaniel Hawthorne visited this house as a child, and legends about the building and its inhabitants inspired Hawthorne's 1851 novel of the same name. If you haven't read the book (or even if you have), watch the audio-visual program that tells the story before you start the tour. The six rooms of period furniture in the main house include pieces mentioned in the book and a steep secret staircase. Costumed guides lead the tour (sometimes playing to the kids in the audience) and can answer just about any question about the novel, buildings, and artifacts.

54 Turner St. ☎ *978-744-0991.* www.7gables.org. *From downtown, follow Derby St. east 3 blocks past Derby Wharf. Guided tours: $11 adults, $9.90 seniors, $7.15 children 5–12, free for children under 5. Open: July–Oct daily 10 a.m.–7 p.m.; Nov–June daily 10 a.m.–5 p.m. Closed first 3 weeks of Jan.*

Peabody Essex Museum

The focus of this fascinating museum is evolving, from the history of Salem to the history of the world — seen through the prism of a historic New England seaport. The foundation of the collection is two centuries' worth of objects and artifacts Salem residents considered worth preserving, including nationally and internationally acclaimed art and architecture. The museum expanded both its vision and its physical presence in 2003, when it opened a huge new wing and an unusual exhibit — an entire 18th-century Chinese house, Yin Yu Tang.

The Peabody Museum began as a repository for the spoils of the China trade; the Essex Institute was the county historical society. The sprawling collections now encompass everything from toys to animal specimens to East Asian and Native American art. Visitors can tour a historic house or gallery or take a self-guided tour using a pamphlet from about a dozen available on various topics. The museum restaurant (☎ **978-745-9500,** ext. 3118) serves lunch daily and afternoon tea on Tuesday, Saturday, and Sunday.

East India Square. ☎ *866-745-1876 or 978-745-9500.* www.pem.org. *Take Hawthorne Boulevard to Essex Street, following signs for Visitor Center, and enter on Essex or New Liberty Street. Admission: To museum $13 adults, $11 seniors, $9 students with ID, free for children under 17; to Yin Yu Tang (available only with museum admission) $4. Open: Daily 10 a.m.–5 p.m.*

Salem

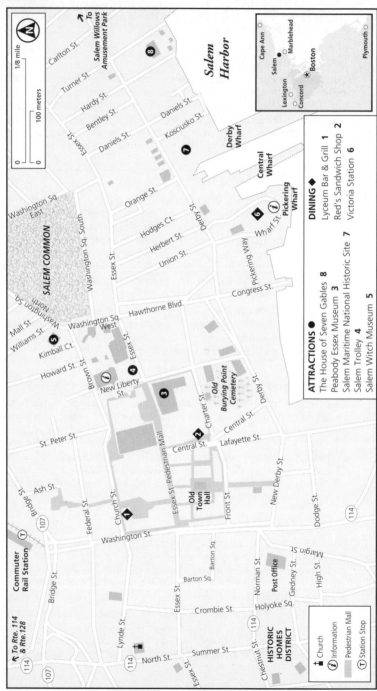

ATTRACTIONS ●
The House of Seven Gables **8**
Peabody Essex Museum **3**
Salem Maritime National Historic Site **7**
Salem Trolley **4**
Salem Witch Museum **5**

DINING ◆
Lyceum Bar & Grill **1**
Red's Sandwich Shop **2**
Victoria Station **6**

✝ Church
ⓘ Information
Pedestrian Mall
Ⓣ Station Stop

HISTORIC HOMES DISTRICT

Salem Maritime National Historic Site

The waterfront linked Salem to the world for many years before beginning to decay in the early 1800s. On this harborfront land, National Park Service buildings and displays recall the port's heyday. The most recent addition to the site is in the water alongside the orientation center: a full-size replica of a 1797 East Indiaman merchant vessel. The excellent ranger-led tour includes the three-masted 171-footer *Friendship.*

174 Derby St. ☎ 978-740-1660. www.nps.gov/sama. Take Derby Street east, just past Pickering Wharf; the orientation center is on the right. Admission: Free; guided tours: $5 adults, $3 seniors and children 6–15. Open: Daily 9 a.m.–5 p.m.

Salem Witch Museum

The Salem Witch Museum is so memorable that I'm fighting the urge to call the place "haunting" (oh, well). The informative and frightening museum's three-dimensional audiovisual presentation uses life-sized figures to illustrate the witchcraft trials and the accompanying hysteria. That sounds a little corny, but the 30-minute narration does a good job of explaining the historical context and consequences. (One "man" dies when others pile rocks onto a board on his chest — you may need to remind small children that he's not real.)

The "witch" on the traffic island across from the Witch Museum is Roger Conant, who founded Salem in 1626. Nice outfit, Roger.

19½ Washington Square. ☎ 978-744-1692. www.salemwitchmuseum.com. Follow Hawthorne Boulevard to the northwest corner of Salem Common. Admission: $7 adults, $6 seniors, $4.50 children 6–14. Open: July–Aug daily 10 a.m.–7 p.m.; Sept–June daily 10 a.m.–5 p.m.; check ahead for extended Oct hours.

Dining in Salem

The **Lyceum Bar & Grill,** 43 Church St. (at Washington St.; ☎ 978-745-7665; www.lyceumsalem.com), is one of the best restaurants north of Boston. The bar and grill serves creative American fare at lunch on weekdays, dinner daily, and Sunday brunch. For any meal, make a reservation. For a quick bite, try **Red's Sandwich Shop,** 15 Central St. (☎ 978-745-3527). The fare's cheap, good, and served fast; cash only. **Victoria Station,** Pickering Wharf, at the corner of Derby and Congress streets (☎ 978-744-7644), is part of a chain that serves American cuisine and offers a terrific view of the marina.

Getting to Marblehead

To drive from Boston (15 miles), take the Callahan or Ted Williams Tunnel and follow Route 1A past the airport north through Revere and Lynn. Bear right where you see signs for Swampscott and Marblehead. Follow Lynn Shore Drive into Swampscott, bear left onto Route 129, and follow it to Marblehead. Or take I-93 or Route 1 to Route 128, and then

Route 114 through Salem into Marblehead. From Salem, take Route 114 east. Parking is limited — grab the first spot you see, and be sure you know your time limit.

Bus route Number 441/442 runs from Haymarket (Green or Orange Line) in Boston to downtown Marblehead. During rush periods on weekdays, the Number 448/449 connects Marblehead to Downtown Crossing (Red or Orange Line). The 441 and 448 buses detour to Vinnin Square shopping center in Swampscott; otherwise, the routes are the same. The trip takes about an hour and costs $3.45 one-way.

Seeing the sights in Marblehead

The **Marblehead Chamber of Commerce** operates an information booth on Pleasant Street near Spring Street. The booth is open weekends from late May through October, 10 a.m. to 6 p.m. (When it's closed, visit the office at 62 Pleasant St., just up the hill.) You can pick up pamphlets and a map, but the town is ideal for wandering, especially around "Old Town," the historic district. Be sure to visit Crocker Park or Fort Sewall, on the harbor at opposite ends of Front Street; the view from either place is amazing.

Marblehead is a top-notch shopping destination. Shops, boutiques, and galleries dot Washington and Front streets, with another prime area on Atlantic Avenue.

Abbot Hall

The Selectmen's Meeting Room houses Archibald M. Willard's painting *The Spirit of '76*. That title may not ring a bell, but the painting will when you see the widely imitated drummer, drummer boy, and fife player. Cases in the halls contain objects and artifacts from the collections of the Marblehead Museum & Historical Society; a stop here takes five or ten minutes at most.

Washington Square. ☎ *781-631-0528. From the historic district, follow Washington Street up the hill toward the clock tower. Admission: Free. Open: Nov–April Mon, Tues, Thurs 8 a.m.–5 p.m., Wed 7:30 a.m.–7:30 p.m., Fri 8 a.m.–1 p.m.; May–Oct Mon, Tues, Thurs 8 a.m.–5 p.m., Wed 7:30 a.m.–7:30 p.m., Fri 8 a.m.–5 p.m., Sat 9 a.m.–6 p.m., Sun 11 a.m.–6 p.m.*

Jeremiah Lee Mansion

For a house with an apparently obscure claim to fame, the 1768 Lee Mansion is surprisingly appealing. The original hand-painted wallpaper is the headliner, and the house is an excellent example of pre-Revolutionary Georgian architecture. The Marblehead Museum & Historical Society's informative guides bring the history to life with stories about the home and its renovations. The visitor center across the street at 170 Washington St. (free admission) contains two galleries and is open June to mid-October Tuesday through Saturday 10 a.m. to 4 p.m.; November to May Tuesday to Friday 10 a.m. to 4 p.m.

Marblehead

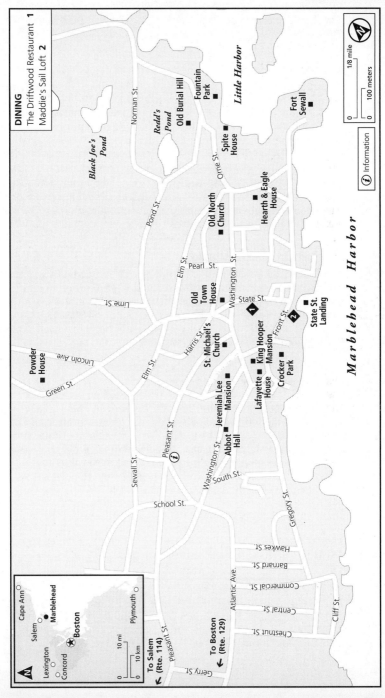

DINING
The Driftwood Restaurant **1**
Maddie's Sail Loft **2**

Black Joe's Pond

Norman St.

Redd's Pond

Old Burial Hill

Fountain Park

Little Harbor

Pond St.

Spite House

Orne St.

Fort Sewall

Hearth & Eagle House

Old North Church

Elm St.

Pearl St.

Washington St.

Lime St.

Old Town House

State St.

State St. Landing

Marblehead Harbor

Harris St.

St. Michael's Church

King Hooper Mansion

Lafayette House

Crocker Park

Front St.

Powder House

Lincoln Ave.

Green St.

Elm St.

Jeremiah Lee Mansion

Abbot Hall

Washington St.

Pleasant St.

Sewall St.

South St.

School St.

Gregory St.

Hawkes St.

Barnard St.

Commercial St.

Atlantic Ave.

Central St.

Cliff St.

Chestnut St.

Gerry St.

To Boston (Rte. 129)

To Salem (Rte. 114)

Pleasant St.

Cape Ann

Marblehead

Salem

Lexington

Concord

Boston

Plymouth

10 mi

10 km

(i) Information

0   1/8 mile

0   100 meters

161 Washington St. ☎ 781-631-1069. Follow Washington Street uphill toward Abbot Hall; the mansion is on the right. Guided tours: $5 adults, $4.50 seniors and students. Open: June–mid-Oct Mon–Sat 10 a.m.–4 p.m. Closed mid-Oct–May.

King Hooper Mansion

Robert Hooper was a shipping magnate who earned his nickname by treating his sailors well. His 1728 mansion, which gained a Georgian addition in 1747, now contains period furnishings. Though these pieces aren't original to the home, the furnishings give a sense of upper-crust life in the 18th century. The building houses the Marblehead Arts Association, which stages monthly exhibits and operates the gift shop, which sells members' work.

8 Hooper St. ☎ 781-631-2608. www.marbleheadarts.org. *Look for the colorful sign off Washington Street at the foot of the hill near the Lee Mansion. Guided tours: Free; donations requested for tour. Open: Tues–Sat 10 a.m.–4 p.m.; Sun 1–5 p.m. Call ahead; no tours during private parties.*

Dining in Marblehead

The **Driftwood Restaurant,** 63 Front St. (☎ 781-631-1145), a diner-style neighborhood hangout, serves excellent fresh seafood at lunch, and breakfast all day (until 5 p.m. in the summer, 2 p.m. in the winter). The casual **Maddie's Sail Loft,** 15 State St. (☎ 781-631-9824), enjoys a well-deserved reputation for fresh seafood and strong drinks. It serves lunch daily, dinner Monday through Saturday.

Gloucester and Rockport

Gloucester, Rockport, Essex, and Manchester-by-the-Sea make up Cape Ann, a dizzyingly beautiful peninsula that gained international attention with the 2000 release of the movie *The Perfect Storm*. Gloucester is a city in transition, a sightseeing and whale-watching center that's also one of the few commercial fishing ports remaining in New England. The fading industry traces its roots even further back than the city's first European settlement in 1623. Rockport, at the tip of the cape, is nearly as old but has a less hardscrabble history. Rockport enjoys a reputation as a summer community overflowing with gift shops and galleries.

The contrast of Gloucester and Rockport makes for an enjoyable one-day trip; exploring either can also fill a day.

Getting to Gloucester

To drive from Boston (33 miles), take I-93 or Route 1 to Route 128, which ends in Gloucester. Exit 14 puts you on Route 133, a longer but prettier approach to downtown than exits 11 and 9. Plenty of on-street parking is available, and a free lot is on the causeway to Rocky Neck.

Gloucester and Rockport

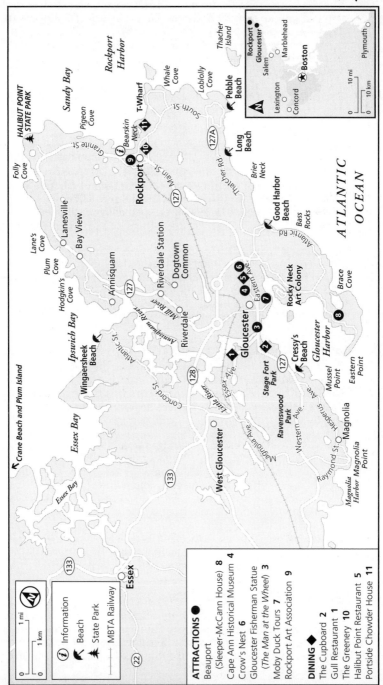

Rockport Harbor

Sandy Bay

Thacher Island

Whale Cove

Loblolly Cove

Pebble Beach

HALIBUT POINT STATE PARK

Pigeon Cove

T-Wharf

Bearskin Neck

South St

127A

Long Beach

i 10

9 Rockport

Brier Neck

ATLANTIC OCEAN

Folly Cove

Granite St

Main St

127

Thacher Rd

Good Harbor Beach

Bass Rocks

Atlantic Rd

Lane's Cove

Lanesville

Bay View

Riverdale Station

Dogtown Common

Plum Cove

Hodgkin's Cove

Annisquam

127

Riverdale

Mill River

4 5 6
Eastern Ave
4 5 6
7 Rocky Neck Art Colony

Brace Cove

8

Ipswich Bay

Atlantic St.

Wingaersheek Beach

Annisquam River

Gloucester

3

Cressy's Beach

Gloucester Harbor

Eastern Point

Crane Beach and Plum Island

Essex Bay

128

Little River

Essex Ave.

2

1 Stage Fort Park

127

Mussel Point

Hesperus Ave.

Magnolia

Concord St.

Magnolia Ave.

Ravenswood Park

Western Ave.

Raymond St.

Magnolia Point

West Gloucester

133

Essex Bay

133

Essex

22

Inset map

Rockport
Gloucester
Marblehead
Salem
Boston
Lexington
Concord
Plymouth

N

0 10 mi
0 10 km

Legend

i Information
Beach
State Park
MBTA Railway

N

0 1 mi
0 1 km

The commuter rail runs from North Station in Boston to Gloucester. The trip takes about an hour and costs $5.50 one-way. The **Cape Ann Transportation Authority,** or CATA (☎ **978-283-7916;** www.canntran. com), runs buses on Cape Ann (from the Gloucester station to the waterfront, for example) and operates special routes during the summer; call for schedules.

Remember that *Gloucester* rhymes with *roster;* it's pronounced *glos-ter.*

Taking a tour of Gloucester

Pick up a *Gloucester Maritime Trail* brochure, which describes four excellent self-guided tours. You can find this brochure at the **Visitors Welcoming Center** (☎ **800-649-6839** or 978-281-8865), open summer only at Stage Fort Park, off Route 127 near the intersection with Route 133; or the **Cape Ann Chamber of Commerce,** 33 Commercial St. (☎ **800-321-0133** or 978-283-1601), open daily in summer and weekdays in winter.

Moby Duck Tours (☎ **978-281-3825;** www.mobyduck.com) are 55-minute sightseeing excursions that travel on land before plunging into the water. The amphibious vehicles leave from Harbor Loop downtown. Tickets (cash only) cost $16 for adults, $14 for seniors, and $10 for children under 12. Tours run daily from Memorial Day through Labor Day and on weekends in September.

Seeing the sights in Gloucester

On Stacy Boulevard just west of downtown, the statue that symbolizes the city testifies to the danger of the seafaring life. More than 10,000 fishermen lost their lives in Gloucester's first three centuries; Leonard Craske's bronze Gloucester Fisherman, *The Man at the Wheel,* memorializes them.

To reach East Gloucester, follow signs from downtown or use Exit 9 from Route 128. On East Main Street, follow signs to the Rocky Neck Art Colony, the oldest continuously operating art colony in the country. Park in the lot on the tiny causeway and follow the crowds to Rocky Neck Avenue and its studios, galleries, and restaurants. Most galleries are open daily in the summer from 10 a.m. to 10 p.m.

Just east of downtown is the **Crow's Nest,** 334 Main St. (☎ **978-281-2965**), the fishermen's bar that gained fame through the book and movie of *The Perfect Storm.* The bar is a local hangout.

Beauport (Sleeper-McCann House)

Henry Davis Sleeper decorated this "fantasy house" to illustrate literary and historical themes, which you can learn about during the fascinating house tour. Sleeper, an interior designer, drew on huge collections of American and European art and antiques to create the home from 1907 to

1934. The entertaining tour visits more than two dozen of the 40 rooms. Note that the house, operated by Historic New England, is not open on summer weekends.

75 Eastern Point Blvd. ☎ *978-283-0800.* www.historicnewengland.org. *Follow East Main Street south to Eastern Point Boulevard (a private road), drive ½ mile to house, and park on the left. Guided tours: $10 adults, $9 seniors, $5 students and children 6–12. Open: Tours on the hour June–Sept 14 Mon–Fri 10 a.m.–4 p.m.; Sept 15–Oct 15 daily 10 a.m.–4 p.m. Closed summer weekends and Oct 16–May.*

Cape Ann Historical Museum

Cape Ann's history and artists dominate the displays at this lovely museum. The American Luminist painter Fitz Hugh Lane, a Gloucester native, has a gorgeous gallery. Other spaces hold contemporary works, and the maritime and fisheries galleries contain fascinating exhibits, models, photographs, and even entire boats (you won't believe how small some of them are).

27 Pleasant St. ☎ *978-283-0455. Follow Main Street west through downtown and turn right onto Pleasant Street; the museum is 1 block up on the right. Parking: Metered street parking or in pay lot across street. Admission: $6.50 adults, $6 seniors, $5 students, free for children under 6. Open: March–Jan Tues–Sat 10 a.m.–5 p.m. Closed Feb.*

Dining in Gloucester and nearby Essex

The **Gull Restaurant,** 75 Essex Ave. (Route 133), at the Cape Ann Marina (☎ 978-281-6060), serves sandwiches at lunch and large portions of ocean-fresh seafood in a picturesque location overlooking the Annisquam River. The Gull is closed from November to late April; a good year-round alternative is **Halibut Point Restaurant,** 289 Main St. (☎ 978-281-1900), a downtown tavern that serves terrific burgers in addition to tasty seafood. Another option: Follow the locals to the Stage Fort Park snack bar, the **Cupboard** (☎ 978-281-1908), for fried seafood and blue-plate specials.

Going to or leaving Cape Ann on Route 128, turn away from Gloucester on Route 133 and head west to Essex. This beautiful little town is both a center of great antiques shopping and an important culinary landmark: the birthplace of the fried clam. According to legend, that's **Woodman's of Essex,** 121 Main St. (☎ 800-649-1773 or 978-768-6451; www.woodmans.com). Woodman's draws locals and out-of-towners for lobster, steamers, onion rings, and — oh, yeah — fried clams. This dining spot is mobbed year-round, but the line moves quickly. An ATM is on the premises; no credit cards are accepted.

Getting to Rockport

By car from Boston (40 miles), take I-93 or Route 1 to Route 128. Just before Route 128 ends, follow signs to Route 127, and go north into Rockport. Or continue to the end (Exit 9), turn left onto Bass Avenue, and go about ½ mile to Route 127A north, which runs into the center of town. From Gloucester, follow Main Street to Eastern Avenue (Route 127) or Bass Avenue. Route 127A is more scenic but longer than Route 127. In downtown Rockport, circle once to look for parking and then try the back streets. Or use the parking lot on Upper Main Street (Route 127) on weekends. Parking is free; the shuttle bus to downtown costs $1.

The commuter rail runs from North Station in Boston to Rockport. The 60- to 70-minute trip costs $6 one-way. The station is off Upper Main Street, less than a mile from the center of town.

The **Cape Ann Transportation Authority,** or CATA (☎ **978-283-7916;** www.canntran.com), runs buses from town to town on Cape Ann.

Seeing the sights in Rockport

Pick up the pamphlet *Rockport: A Walking Guide* from the **Rockport Chamber of Commerce and Board of Trade,** 22 Broadway (☎ **888-726-3922** or 978-546-6575; www.rockportusa.com). The office is open daily in summer and weekdays in winter; the chamber operates an information booth from mid-May to mid-October about a mile from downtown on Upper Main Street (Route 127), just before the WELCOME TO ROCKPORT sign.

Rockport boasts no must-see attractions, but there's more to the town than knickknack shopping. The knickknack shopping *is* excellent, though. Wander around downtown, making sure to detour onto Bearskin Neck, which has more gift shops than some whole cities. (And an interesting name — read the plaque at the entrance to the street to learn the story.) Walk all the way to the end of the neck for a spectacular water view. All over downtown, shops sell jewelry, gifts, toys, clothing, novelties, handmade crafts, paintings, and sculpture.

Opposite Bearskin Neck on the town wharf, you'll see a red wooden fish warehouse called **Motif No. 1.** The warehouse exerts a mysterious totemic power over Rockport residents — or is a testament to the fact that *anything* can become a tourist attraction. Motif No. 1 is famous for being famous. No, I don't know what the big deal is.

More than two dozen art galleries display the works of local and nationally known artists. In addition, the **Rockport Art Association,** 12 Main St. (☎ **978-546-6604;** www.rockportusa.com/raa), sponsors major exhibitions and special shows throughout the year. The association is open in the summer Monday through Saturday mid-morning to late afternoon, Sunday noon to late afternoon; in the winter, it keeps the same hours but closes on Monday.

To get a sense of the power of the sea, take Route 127 north of town to the tip of Cape Ann. **Halibut Point State Park** (☎ **978-546-2997;** www.state.ma.us/dem/parks/halb.htm) has a staffed visitor center, walking trails, tidal pools, and water-filled quarries — but no swimming. This park is great place to wander around and admire the scenery. On a clear day, you can see Maine.

Where to watch whales

Whale-watching is even more popular in Gloucester than in Boston (turn to Chapter 11 for a full description of whale-watching). Prices run about $30 for adults, less for seniors and children; most tour companies will match any competitor's offer, including guaranteed sightings, AAA discounts, or coupons. Downtown, you'll find **Cape Ann Whale Watch** (☎ **800-877-5110** or 978-283-5110; www.caww.com), **Capt. Bill's Whale Watch** (☎ **800-33-WHALE** or 978-283-6995; www.captainbillswhalewatch.com), and **Seven Seas Whale Watch** (☎ **888-238-1776** or 978-283-1776; www.7seas-whalewatch.com). At the Cape Ann Marina, off Route 133, is **Yankee Whale Watch** (☎ **800-WHALING** or 508-283-0313; www.yankeefleet.com).

Dining in Rockport

Woodman's of Essex (see "Dining in Gloucester and nearby Essex," earlier in this chapter) will serve you a drink, but as of press time, Rockport is a dry town. I suggest a picnic, if the day is not too windy. Head to Halibut Point (see "Seeing the sights in Rockport"), the end of Bearskin Neck, or another agreeable spot. Stop for provisions at the **Greenery,** 15 Dock Sq. (☎ **978-546-9593**), or the **Portside Chowder House,** Tuna Wharf, off Bearskin Neck (☎ **978-546-7045**), and then sit back and admire the scenery.

Plymouth

The Pilgrims reside in national memory, wearing tall black hats and buckled shoes. A visit to this town may cause elementary-school flashbacks, but the trip may also leave you with a new sense of the difficulties those early settlers overcame. Best of all, you get a *real* sense — the attractions that are replicas are faithful reproductions, but many are genuine 17th-century relics.

Plymouth is a reasonable day trip that's especially popular with children. The town also makes a good stop between Boston and Cape Cod.

Getting there

By car from Boston (40 miles), follow I-93 south about 9 miles and bear left onto Route 3. Take Route 3 to Exit 6A (Route 44 east) and then follow signs to the historic attractions. Or continue on Route 3 to the Regional Information Complex at Exit 5 for maps, brochures, and information. To go directly to Plimoth Plantation, use Exit 4. The trip from Boston takes 45 to 60 minutes if you avoid rush hour. The downtown area is compact, so park where you can. The waterfront meters are particularly convenient.

The commuter rail serves Plymouth (at peak commuting times, service is to nearby Kingston) from Boston's South Station during the day on weekdays and all day on weekends; the trip takes one hour, and the one-way fare is $6. **Plymouth & Brockton buses** (☎ 617-773-9401 or 508-746-0378; www.p-b.com) leave from South Station and take about the same time. The bus is more expensive than the commuter rail ($10 one-way, $18 round-trip) but runs more often. The **Plymouth Area Link** bus (☎ 506-222-6106; www.gatra.org/pal.htm) connects the train stations with downtown and other destinations. The fare is $1.

Taking a tour

A narrated tour with **Plymouth Rock Trolley** (☎ 800-698-5636 or 508-747-3419; www.plymouthrocktrolley.com) includes unlimited on-and-off privileges. The trolley operates daily from Memorial Day to October and on weekends through Thanksgiving. Trolleys serve marked stops downtown every 20 minutes and stop at the plantation every hour in the summer. Tickets cost $10 for adults, $9 for seniors and AAA members, and $8 for children 3 to 12.

To get a Pilgrim's perspective, take a 90-minute **Colonial Lantern Tour** (☎ 800-698-5636 or 508-747-4161; www.lanterntours.com). Participants carry pierced-tin lanterns as they walk around the original settlement under the direction of a knowledgeable guide. Tours run nightly from April through Thanksgiving. The standard history tour begins at 7:30 p.m. The "Ghostly Haunts and Legends" tour starts at 9 p.m. Call for reservations and meeting places. Tickets are $15 for adults, $12 for children 5 to 12, free for children under 5.

Narrated cruises run from April or May through November. One-hour **Splashdown Amphibious Tours** (☎ 800-225-4000 or 508-747-7658; www.ducktoursplymouth.com) take you around town on land and water. The trips leave from Harbor Place, on Water Street near the Governor Bradford motor inn. These tours cost $17 for adults, $11 for children 3 to 12, and $3 for children under 3.

Seeing the sights

The **Visitor Center,** 130 Water Street (across from the town pier; ☎ 508-747-7525), distributes information on Plymouth's attractions. The center is open seasonally (spring through Thanksgiving); in the winter, stop at the Regional Information Complex at Exit 5 off Route 3 before heading into town.

The sight to see is (ask the kids) **Plymouth Rock,** which history tells us was the landing place of the *Mayflower* passengers. Originally 15 feet long and 3 feet wide, the rock is now much smaller, having been moved (and broken) several times. It sits at tide level on the waterfront not far from the visitor center; signs at nearly every intersection in town point the way. Yes, it's just a rock, but the descriptions are absorbing, and a solemn sense of history surrounds the enclosure.

Plymouth

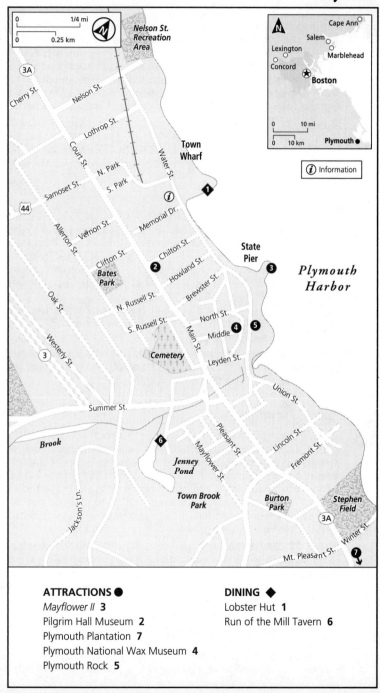

ATTRACTIONS ●

Mayflower II **3**
Pilgrim Hall Museum **2**
Plymouth Plantation **7**
Plymouth National Wax Museum **4**
Plymouth Rock **5**

DINING ◆

Lobster Hut **1**
Run of the Mill Tavern **6**

Mayflower II

A stone's throw from Plymouth Rock, *Mayflower II* is a full-scale reproduction of the type of vessel that brought the Pilgrims from England to Plymouth in 1620. Full scale is a mere 106½ feet — you may want to remind the kids that it's not a scaled-down model. Costumed guides provide first-person narratives about the voyage and the vessel, and displays illustrate the Pilgrims' experiences and the history of the ship, which was built in England from 1955 to 1957. Plan to spend at least an hour here.

State Pier. ☎ *508-746-1622.* www.plimoth.org. *Admission: $8 adults, $7 seniors, $6 children 6–12, free for children under 6. Admission for Plimoth Plantation (good for 2 consecutive days) and Mayflower II: $22 adults, $20 seniors, $14 children 6–12, $72 families, free for children under 6. Open: April–Nov daily 9 a.m.–5 p.m. Closed Dec–March.*

Pilgrim Hall Museum

This museum illustrates the daily lives of Plymouth's first white residents with unbeatable props: original possessions of the Pilgrims and their descendants. Displays include one of early settler Myles Standish's swords; an uncomfortable chair that belonged to the Pilgrims' original leader, William Brewster (you can sit on a modern-day model, not on the original); and Governor Bradford's Bible. The intriguing temporary exhibits focus on one topic per year — recent subjects have included the treatment of children and the development of medicine. Allow at least an hour.

75 Court St. ☎ *508-746-1620.* www.pilgrimhall.org. *From Plymouth Rock, walk north on Water Street and up the hill on Chilton Street. Admission: $6 adults, $5 seniors and AAA members, $3 children 5–17, $16 families, free for children under 5. Open: Feb–Dec daily 9:30 a.m.–4:30 p.m. Closed Jan.*

Plimoth Plantation

Allow at least half a day to experience this recreation of the 1627 Pilgrim village. The "settlers" are actors who assume the personalities of members of the original community; if you chat them up, the actors will pretend not to know anything contemporary, which many kids enjoy. The settlers also take part in typical activities, using only the tools and cookware available at the time; you may be able to join the cast in activities such as harvesting or witnessing a trial. Wear comfortable shoes, because you'll be walking all over, and the plantation isn't paved.

Route 3. ☎ *508-746-1622.* www.plimoth.org. *From Route 3, take Exit 4, "Plimoth Plantation Highway." Admission (good for 2 consecutive days): $20 adults, $18 seniors, $12 children 6–12, free for children under 6. Admission for both Plimoth Plantation and Mayflower II: $22 adults, $20 seniors and students, $14 children 6–12, $72 families, free for children under 6. Open: April–Nov daily 9 a.m.–5 p.m. Closed Dec–March.*

Plymouth National Wax Museum

This museum illustrates the Pilgrim story in vivid detail that makes the experience informative and memorable. If time is tight and kids are along, this is the stop to make (after the Rock, of course). The galleries hold more than 180 life-sized figures, arranged in striking dramatic scenes, with soundtracks narrating the stories. The scenes include the Pilgrims' move to Holland; the harrowing trip to the New World; the first Thanksgiving; and the tale of Myles Standish, Priscilla Mullins, and John Alden, which you may remember from the Longfellow poem you studied in third-grade social studies. Allow 60 to 90 minutes.

16 Carver St. ☎ 508-746-6468. From Plymouth Rock, turn around and walk up the hill or the steps. Admission: $7 adults, $6.50 seniors, $2.75 ages 5–12, free for children under 5. Open: March–May and Nov daily 9 a.m.–5 p.m.; June and Sept–Oct daily 9 a.m.–7 p.m.; July–Aug daily 9 a.m.–9 p.m. Closed Dec–Feb.

Dining in Plymouth

On Town Wharf, off Water Street, the **Lobster Hut** (☎ 508-746-2270) is a self-service seafood restaurant with a sensational harbor view. Try the soups and the excellent "rolls" (hot dog buns with your choice of seafood filling). You can order beer and wine, but only with a meal. The **Run of the Mill Tavern** (☎ 508-830-1262) is near the water wheel at Jenney Grist Mill Village, in Town Brook Park off Summer Street. The tavern doesn't overlook the ocean, but it serves tasty bar fare and seafood in an attractive setting; the clam chowder is great.

Part V

Living It Up after Dark: Boston Nightlife

The 5th Wave   By Rich Tennant

"For tonight's modern reinterpretation of Carmen, those in the front row are kindly requested to wear raincoats."

In this part . . .

Boston offers patrons of the performing arts an abundance of options: an internationally renowned symphony orchestra, the beloved Boston Pops, a top-notch ballet company, theater a step away from Broadway, and student performances of every imaginable type. This part outlines your choices and steers you toward sources that can provide you with more information.

You may notice that I'm not rushing to tout the nightlife options. They're nowhere near as encyclopedic as the cultural options, though some can be just as entertaining. This city loves bars and embraces clubs that schedule everything from comedy to folk to jazz to rock. True, the post-midnight scene is sketchy, but that's not to say that you can't howl at the moon into the wee hours. Just don't expect to have a lot of company.

Chapter 15

Applauding the Cultural Scene

In This Chapter

▶ Finding out what's playing and how to get (discounted?!) tickets
▶ Listening to live music — classical and popular
▶ Enjoying an evening of theater, ballet, or film

*M*aybe you make your nightlife plans months ahead and don't worry again. Perhaps you prefer to wait until after dinner before deciding what to do next. Boston ably accommodates both strategies. In this chapter, I help you lay the groundwork and then direct you toward the resources you need to keep up on the classical and popular music scenes, as well as the theater and film worlds.

For the locations of the venues I recommend, see the maps in this chapter. (The bars and clubs that I describe in Chapter 16 also appear on the maps in this chapter.)

Getting the Inside Scoop

The cultural scene in the Boston area is one of the liveliest in the country. True, it's not New York or Los Angeles — but what is? Your choices may be limited, but you still have more options than you could ever take advantage of. And Boston's compact size means nearly everything worth seeing is easy to reach. From world-class classical musicians in a legendary concert hall to a mime on a grimy sidewalk, people express themselves through their art all over town. Many of those artists are college students, whose performances are generally both cheap and enjoyable.

The main destination for pre- and post-Broadway shows is the Theater District, which centers on the intersection of Tremont and Stuart streets, on the edge of Chinatown. Other major arts destinations: Symphony Hall is at the corner of Mass. Ave. and Huntington Avenue, a block from the Boston University Theatre; Harvard Square is in Cambridge; and the TD Banknorth Garden (formerly called the FleetCenter) sits above Boston's North Station.

If you take a cab or (heaven help you) drive to a show or performance, allow plenty of time, which you'll spend sitting in traffic and trying to park. The best way to get practically everywhere is to take the T or walk (or both). To reach the Theater District, go to Boylston or Arlington (Green Line), or New England Medical Center or Chinatown (Orange Line). South Station (Red Line) is about 15 minutes away on foot. Symphony Hall has a T stop: Symphony (Green Line E). Or get off at Hynes/ICA (Green Line B, C, or D) and then walk ten minutes on Mass. Ave. The TD Banknorth Garden is at North Station (Green or Orange Line). Harvard Square has a stop on the Red Line.

Just as you don't need to dress up for dinner at most restaurants in Boston, you don't need a suit and tie for the theater or a concert. You won't be out of place in something dressy, but for most events, anything clean and neat is fine. If you insist on wearing jeans to the symphony, theater, or ballet, I doubt I can stop you. But I will suggest that a big evening out feels a lot splashier if you're dressed for the occasion.

Whatever you wear, finish primping early. If you're not in your seat when the curtain goes up, you'll have to wait for a break in the action, and that may take a while.

If your plans for the evening include a meal, see the sidebar "Dining before or after a show" (later in this chapter) for suggestions.

Finding Out What's Playing and Getting Tickets

To take a broad look at the performing arts events Boston has to offer, check a general resource such as *The Boston Globe*'s Web site (www. boston.com). Major pop and rock performers play at the **TD Banknorth Garden**, which was formerly called the FleetCenter (☎ **617-624-1000;** www.tdbanknorthgarden.com). Most smaller venues and performing arts companies operate Web sites that list upcoming shows. Also visit your favorite performer's or group's Web site to check schedules.

 A hotel package that includes tickets to a show can be a terrific convenience. The ticket price may not reflect great savings, but knowing for sure that you have seats for *The Nutcracker* will save a lot of worrying.

Some companies and venues sell tickets by phone or on the Web; many use an agency. The major Boston agencies are

- ✔ **Ticketmaster** (☎ **617-931-2000;** www.ticketmaster.com)
- ✔ **Next Ticketing** (☎ **617-423-NEXT** or 617-423-6398; www.next ticketing.com)
- ✔ **Tele-charge** (☎ **800-447-7400;** www.telecharge.com)

Before you finalize your ticket order, be sure to ask for the total price, which will include a service charge and possibly other fees. The service charge can be hefty, and it applies per ticket, not per order. If there's even a tiny chance that your plans may change, double-check the refund policy before you hand over your credit-card number.

 Major events appear months (sometimes years) in advance on venues' Web sites; check ahead to see whether your favorite group, company, or artist is scheduled to play Boston. Knowing this information in advance may influence your travel plans.

If you haven't made plans in advance, the "Calendar" section of the Thursday *The Boston Globe,* the "Edge" section of the Friday *Boston Herald,* and the Sunday arts sections of both papers overflow with possibilities. Other good resources are the weekly *Boston Phoenix* and biweekly *Improper Bostonian* — available free from newspaper boxes all over town.

When you find something appealing, call the box office to see whether the event is sold out. If something jumps out at you, and you're looking for a deal, check at a **BosTix** booth (☎ 617-482-2849; www.bostix. org). BosTix booths are at Faneuil Hall Marketplace (on the south side of Faneuil Hall) and in Copley Square (at the corner of Boylston and Dartmouth streets). They sell same-day theater and concert tickets for half price, subject to availability. No credit cards, refunds, or exchanges are allowed. Check the board or the Web site for the day's offerings. BosTix also sells full-price advance tickets and offers discounts on theater, music, and dance events. Half-price tickets go on sale at 11 a.m. The booths are open Tuesday through Saturday 10 a.m. to 6 p.m. and Sunday 11 a.m. to 4 p.m. The Copley Square booth is open Monday 10 a.m. to 6 p.m.

If a show sounds great but is sold out, ask for help from your concierge, who may have ticket connections. Finally — this is a long shot, but worth a try — visit the box office in person. Patrons sometimes return tickets (good ones, too), and some venues block seats before configuring the performance space and then release the extras.

Dining before or after a show

Most restaurants in and near the Theater District can accommodate the beat-the-clock dining style of patrons with an 8 o'clock curtain to catch, but you must remember to alert (and, if necessary, remind) the staff. Two of my favorite destinations are **Buddha's Delight,** 5 Beach St. (☎ 617-451-2395), for vegetarian Vietnamese and Asian food, and **Finale,** 1 Columbus Ave. (☎ 617-423-3184), which specializes in desserts. There's a **Legal Sea Foods** nearby at 36 Park Sq., between Columbus Avenue and Stuart Street (☎ 617-426-4444). Harvard Square has a branch of Finale at 30 Dunster St. (☎ 617-441-9797), about five minutes from most Harvard University performance spaces, including the American Repertory Theatre. Turn to Chapter 10 for restaurant reviews.

Raising the Curtain on the Performing Arts

Before plunging into specifics of venues and companies, I want to recommend two eclectic series. The first is summer only, outdoors, and free. From early June to early September, the **Hatch Shell** amphitheater (T: Charles/MGH [Red Line] or Arlington [Green Line]; ☎ **617-727-5215**) on the Esplanade, located on the Boston side of the Charles River, between Storrow Drive and the water, books music and dance performances and films. (If you've seen the Boston Pops' Fourth of July concert on TV, you've seen the Hatch Shell.) Seating is on the grass or on a blanket, if you have one. Check ahead for schedules.

The other top series coordinates performances by international stars of classical music, dance, theater, jazz, and world music. The **Bank of America Celebrity Series,** 20 Park Plaza, Boston, MA 02116 (☎ **617-482-2595,** or 617-482-6661 for Celebrity Charge; www.celebrityseries.org), takes place at venues throughout the Boston area. Tickets are available to individual performances or in packages to three or more events.

Classical music

The **Boston Symphony Orchestra (BSO)** and the **Boston Pops** perform at **Symphony Hall,** 301 Mass. Ave. (at Huntington Avenue; T: Symphony [Green Line E]). The hall, known around the world for its perfect acoustics, turned 100 in 2000; when the main tenants are away, the hall books other companies and artists. The BSO is in residence from September to April, and the Pops from May to early July and for three weeks of holiday shows in December. Symphony tickets start at $25 and top out around $90; seeing the Pops will set you back $17 to $70. Call ☎ **617-266-1492** or 617-CONCERT for program information, or 617-266-1200 for tickets, or check www.bso.org.

The Pops also schedule a week of *free* outdoor performances, including the renowned Fourth of July concert, in early summer at the Hatch Shell.

Visit the box office two hours before a BSO or Pops show time, when returns from subscribers go on sale (at full price). A limited number of symphony "rush" tickets (one per person, same day only) go on sale for $8 at 9 a.m. Friday and 5 p.m. on Tuesday and Thursday. Wednesday-evening and Thursday-morning rehearsals are sometimes open to the public; call to see whether rehearsal tickets ($15) are available.

The highly regarded **Handel & Haydn Society** (☎ **617-266-3605;** www.handelandhaydn.org) schedules "historically informed" concerts, often with a choir, year-round. The ensemble uses period instruments and techniques in interpreting baroque and classical music.

Students and faculty members at three prestigious institutions perform frequently during the academic year; admission is usually free or cheap.

Most area colleges schedule student performances, but these are the big three:

- ✔ **Berklee College of Music** (☎ 617-747-2261; www.berklee.edu)
- ✔ **New England Conservatory of Music** (☎ 617-585-1122; www.newenglandconservatory.edu)
- ✔ **Longy School of Music** (☎ 617-876-0956; www.longy.edu)

Pop and rock music

The **TD Banknorth Garden** (formerly known as the FleetCenter), off Causeway Street (T: North Station [Orange or Green Line]; ☎ 617-624-1000; www.tdbanknorthgarden.com), is the major arena for touring groups and artists. Built in 1995, the TD Banknorth Garden is a top-of-the-line facility, but the seating is at a pretty shallow angle; bring binoculars.

The **Bank of America Pavilion,** off Seaport Blvd., South Boston (T: South Station [Red Line]; ☎ 617-374-9000; www.fleetbostonpavilion.com), is a huge white tent open only in the summer. The pavilion books pop, jazz, folk, country, and some rock and rap artists. The airy outdoor setting makes this spot especially enjoyable. The venue is at least a 30-minute walk from the T station; call ahead for shuttle-bus and water-transportation information.

Turn to Chapter 16 for listings of smaller places to hear live rock and pop, as well as for jazz, folk, and blues clubs.

Theater

Pre-Broadway tryouts still play Boston, as do touring national companies of shows that do well in New York. It's not unusual for shows to be up at every major professional stage. Two noted repertory companies and dozens of colleges also contribute to the buzz.

Most Broadway shows play in the Theater District at the following locations:

- ✔ **Colonial Theatre,** 106 Boylston St. (☎ 617-426-9366)
- ✔ **Opera House,** 539 Washington St. (☎ 617-880-2400)
- ✔ **Shubert Theatre,** 265 Tremont St. (☎ 617-482-9393)
- ✔ **Wang Theatre,** 270 Tremont St. (☎ 617-482-9393)
- ✔ **Wilbur Theater,** 246 Tremont St. (☎ 617-423-4008)

Two university spaces are home to professional troupes. The **Huntington Theatre Company** plays at the Boston University Theatre, 264 Huntington Ave. (T: Symphony [Green Line E]; ☎ 617-266-0800; www.huntington.org). The **American Repertory Theatre** (ART, pronounced A-R-T, not *art*)

Boston Performing Arts and Nightlife

Anchovies **10**
The Atrium **37**
Avalon **3**
Axis **2**
Bank of America Pavilion **42**
The Bar at the Ritz **31**
Berklee College of Music **12**
The Big Easy **28**
The Black Rose **38**
Blue Man Group **22**
BosTix (Copley Square) **14**
BosTix
  (Faneuil Hall Marketplace) **38**
Boston Center for the Arts **19**
Boston Pops **7**
Boston Symphony Orchestra **7**
Boston University Theatre **8**
The Bristol **29**

Buzz **26**
Charles Playhouse **22**
Cheers Beacon Hill **32**
Cheers Faneuil Hall
  Marketplace **38**
Club Café **17**
Colonial Theatre **27**
Comedy Connection
  at Faneuil Hall **38**
DeLux Café **18**
TD Banknorth Garden **36**
Fritz **20**
Hard Rock Cafe **16**
Hatch Shell **33**
Hill Tavern **35**
Huntington Theatre Company **8**
Jacques **21**
Jillian's Boston **5**

Kings **11**
Mr. Dooley's Boston Tavern **39**
New England Conservatory
  of Music **6**
The Oak Bar **15**
Opera House **40**
Paradise Rock Club **1**
Parish Café and Bar **30**
Radius **41**
Ramrod **5**
Sevens Ale House **34**
Shear Madness **22**
Shubert Theatre **23**
Symphony Hall **7**
Top of the Hub **13**
Wally's Café **9**
Wang Theatre **25**
Wilbur Theater **24**

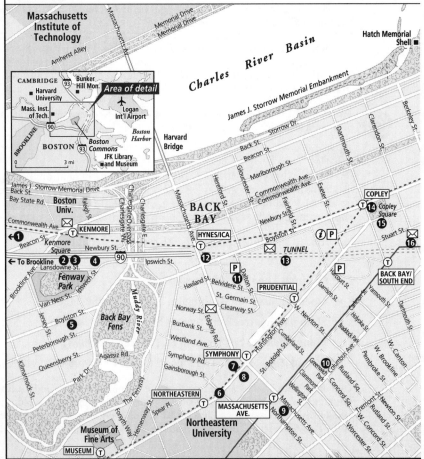

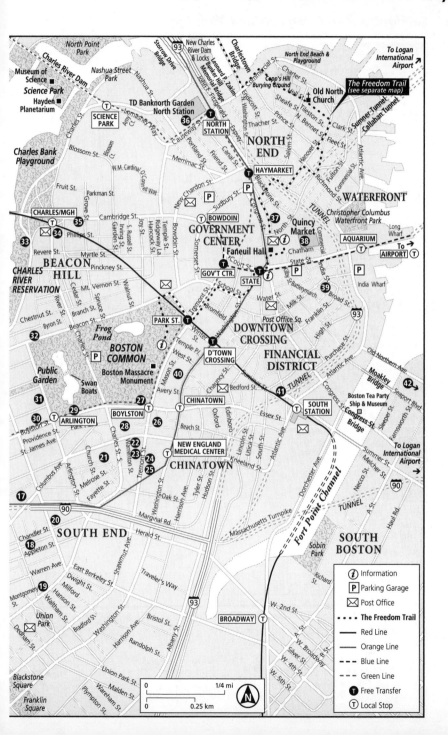

Cambridge Performing Arts and Nightlife

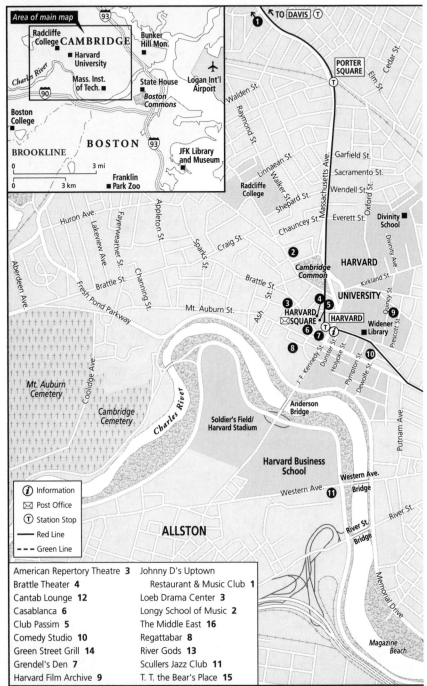

Area of main map

CAMBRIDGE

Radcliffe College
Bunker Hill Mon.
Harvard University
Mass. Inst. of Tech.
State House
Logan Int'l Airport
Boston Commons

Boston College

BROOKLINE

BOSTON

JFK Library and Museum

Franklin Park Zoo

0   3 mi
0   3 km

Charles River

93

90

TO DAVIS

PORTER SQUARE

Radcliffe College

Garfield St.
Sacramento St.
Wendell St.
Everett St.
Divinity School

Huron Ave.
Lakeview Ave.
Fayerweather St.
Appleton St.
Sparks St.
Craig St.
Chauncey St.
HARVARD

Cambridge Common

Aberdeen Ave.
Brattle St.
Channing St.
Brattle St.
Ash St.
Kirkland St.
UNIVERSITY

Fresh Pond Parkway
Mt. Auburn St.
HARVARD SQUARE
HARVARD
Widener Library
Quincy St.
Prescott St.

Mt. Auburn Cemetery

Coolidge Ave.
Cambridge Cemetery
Charles River

J. F. Kennedy St.
Dunster St.
Holyoke St.
Plympton St.
Dewolfe St.

Anderson Bridge

Soldier's Field/ Harvard Stadium

Harvard Business School
Western Ave.
Bridge

Putnam Ave.

ALLSTON

Western Ave.
River St.
River St. Bridge

Memorial Drive

Magazine Beach

(i) Information
⊠ Post Office
(T) Station Stop
— Red Line
- - - Green Line

American Repertory Theatre **3**	Johnny D's Uptown
Brattle Theater **4**	Restaurant & Music Club **1**
Cantab Lounge **12**	Loeb Drama Center **3**
Casablanca **6**	Longy School of Music **2**
Club Passim **5**	The Middle East **16**
Comedy Studio **10**	Regattabar **8**
Green Street Grill **14**	River Gods **13**
Grendel's Den **7**	Scullers Jazz Club **11**
Harvard Film Archive **9**	T. T. the Bear's Place **15**

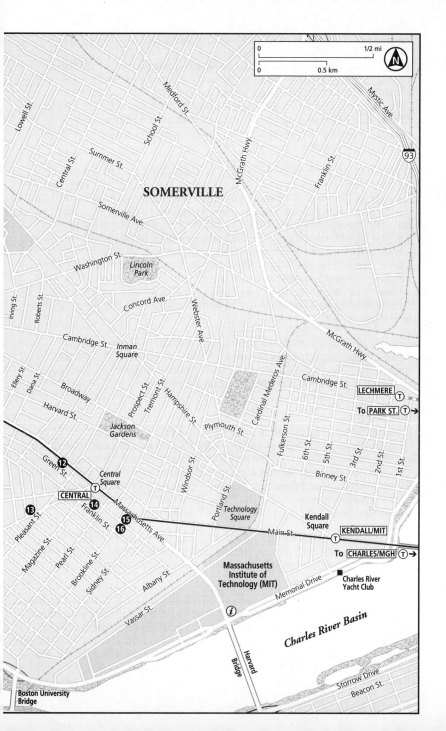

performs at Harvard University's Loeb Drama Center, 64 Brattle St., Cambridge (T: Harvard [Red Line]; ☎ 617-547-8300; www.amrep.org).

The Huntington and the ART tend to be more adventurous than their Theater District counterparts; for something even more audacious, head to the South End. The **Boston Center for the Arts,** 539 Tremont St. (between Berkeley and Clarendon streets; T: Back Bay [Orange Line]; ☎ 617-426-2787; www.bcaonline.org), boasts five performance spaces, including two gorgeous new theaters, and an apparent willingness to try just about anything.

Children old enough to be interested in the theater can enjoy a good introduction at either of two long-running shows: Blue Man Group and *Shear Madness.* How old should your child be to attend these shows? I'd say 10 or so — this is a lot of money to spend on someone who may not last until the curtain falls — but that's your call. **Blue Man Group** (www.blueman.com) consists of three cobalt-colored performance artists and a rock band. The show incorporates goofy props (including food), music, and willing spectators who become participants — one even gets painted. ***Shear Madness*** (www.shearmadness.com) is a "comic murder mystery" set in a hair salon. The audience helps solve the crime; the details have been different at every performance since the show opened in Boston in 1980.

Both shows run (on different stages) at the Charles Playhouse, 74 Warrenton St., off Stuart Street, in the Theater District. Tickets for Blue Man Group cost $43 and $53; *Shear Madness* tickets run $34. Buy tickets at the box office or through Ticketmaster.

Dance

If you've heard of **Boston Ballet** (☎ 617-695-6955; www.bostonballet.org), that's probably because of *The Nutcracker* — an excellent reason, but not the only one. The company presents classic and modern works from October through May. Tickets run $38 to $95; students should check ahead for information about discounted "rush" (same-day) tickets. Performances of the regular repertory are at the Wang Theatre, 270 Tremont St.; *The Nutcracker* runs at the Opera House, 539 Washington St.

Built as a movie palace in the 1920s, the Wang presents certain difficulties for the ballet audience — namely, awkward sight lines and the sensation that you're about to fall out of the balcony. Pack your opera glasses.

Film

Free Friday Flicks (☎ 617-727-5215; www.wbz.com) projects films on a large screen in the amphitheater at the Hatch Shell on the Esplanade (T: Charles/MGH [Red Line] or Arlington [Green Line]). These are family movies, with a tendency to lean toward the last couple of Disney releases rather than the classics. However, the season is long — a couple of gems usually sneak in.

Classic movies and new independent releases turn up at a number of theaters. Film buffs can check out the **Brattle Theater,** 40 Brattle St., Cambridge (T: Harvard [Red Line]; ☎ 617-876-6387; www.brattlefilm. org); the **Coolidge Corner Theater,** 290 Harvard St., Brookline (T: Coolidge Corner [Green Line C]; ☎ 617-734-2500; www.coolidge.org); and the **Harvard Film Archive,** 24 Quincy St., Cambridge (T: Harvard [Red Line]; ☎ 617-495-4700; www.harvardfilmarchive.org).

Chapter 16

Hitting the Clubs and Bars

● ●

In This Chapter

▶ Visiting Boston's bars and lounges

▶ Listening to live music in small venues

▶ Dancing and laughing your way through the clubs

▶ Exploring the gay and lesbian scenes

● ●

*E*ven if you know nothing about Boston except what you saw on the TV show *Cheers,* you already know something important: The neighborhood bar is a big deal. Spending time in a local watering hole is a great way to get to know any new city, and Boston is no exception. Many nightspots schedule live music; if you'd rather shake your booty than bend your elbow, you'll find a number of places to do that, too. In this chapter, I guide you toward the most congenial spots to visit.

For locations of recommended nightspots, see the maps in Chapter 15.

The Basics

The state drinking age is 21; you must have a valid driver's license or passport. Have an ID ready if you look younger than 35 or so, especially near college campuses.

When a club advertises a "21-plus" show, that means that only patrons 21 or older may enter; "18-plus" means 18-, 19-, and 20-year-olds may enter but can't drink alcohol.

 By law, bars close at 1 a.m. or earlier, clubs at 2 a.m. Most clubs open between 7 and 10 p.m., but bars generally open by noon. From Sunday to Thursday, the T shuts down by 1 a.m. systemwide, with the last car from some stations running shortly after 12:30 a.m. Be ready to spring for cab fare. On Friday and Saturday until 2:30 a.m., Night Owl bus service runs on some regular bus routes and on special routes that parallel the subway lines. The fare is $1.50 in coins.

Unless otherwise noted, the establishments in this chapter don't impose a cover charge; of course, that's subject to change, depending on the entertainment on a particular night. Hours are also subject to change, too, depending on who's playing, who's booking, and whether a show is all-ages or 21-plus. If you need specifics, always call ahead.

The information in this section is the most volatile in the book. I steer you toward some reliable places and neighborhoods, but I can't promise that what's hot tonight will even be there next month. Dance clubs that usually book DJs sometimes feature live music; live-music clubs rarely restrict themselves to one genre. Check the "Calendar" section of the Thursday *Globe*, the *Phoenix*, the *Improper Bostonian*, or the "Edge" section of the Friday *Herald* when you're making plans.

Hanging Out: Boston's Best-Known Bars

You've probably already heard of these talked-about spots; they're celebrated for good reason.

- ✔ **Cheers** is the most famous tavern in town. The long-running sitcom remains so popular that the owners of the original bar, which looked nothing like the set of the TV show, opened a bar that looks exactly like the set. That bar is in Faneuil Hall Marketplace, on the south side of Quincy Market (T: Government Center [Green or Blue Line] or State [Orange Line]; ☎ 617-227-0150; www.cheersboston.com). Cheers is open daily from 11 a.m. to 2 a.m. (food service until 11:45 p.m.).

- ✔ The original **Cheers,** formerly the Bull & Finch Pub, is at 84 Beacon St., Beacon Hill (T: Arlington [Green Line]; ☎ 617-227-9605). Somewhat improbably, this location retains a loyal neighborhood clientele, but most patrons are out-of-towners looking for souvenirs and snapshots. The exterior sign is the one you remember from all those late-night reruns. This popular spot is open daily from 11 a.m. to 1 a.m.; your friend can snap a picture of you in front of the sign anytime.

- ✔ The **Hard Rock Cafe,** 131 Clarendon St. (T: Back Bay [Orange Line] or Copley [Green Line]; ☎ 617-424-ROCK; www.hardrock.com), is another fun tourist magnet. The Hard Rock is a huge, noisy space lavishly adorned with rock 'n' roll memorabilia. The food is better than average, and the downstairs room sometimes schedules live music. And guess what? You can buy a souvenir. The Hard Rock is open daily from 11 a.m. to 1 a.m.

Where Everybody Knows Your Name: Neighborhood Bars

This list barely skims the surface and comes with a suggestion: If your wanderings take you past an agreeable-looking establishment, pop in.

✔ In Cambridge (T: Harvard [Red Line]), try **Casablanca,** 40 Brattle St. (☎ **617-876-0999**), and **Grendel's Den,** 89 Winthrop St. (☎ **617-491-1160**). A colorful mix of patrons makes for superior eavesdropping.

✔ In Central Square (T: Central [Red Line]), the **Green Street Grill,** 280 Green St. (☎ **617-876-1655;** www.greenstreetgrill.com), has an amazing blues and jazz jukebox. Live music plays on weekends (with a cover charge, usually less than $10), and excellent food is available every night. A few blocks away, **River Gods,** 125 River St. (☎ **617-576-1881**), is a fun, funky Irish bar that serves good food.

✔ In Beacon Hill (T: Charles/MGH [Red Line]) in Boston — which caters to the postcollegiate set — check out the clean-cut types swilling beer at the **Sevens Ale House,** 77 Charles St. (☎ **617-523-9074**), and the **Hill Tavern,** 228 Cambridge St. (☎ **617-742-6192**).

✔ **Radius,** 8 High St. (T: South Station [Red Line]; ☎ **617-426-1234**), attracts a chic Financial District crowd (no, that's not a contradiction). The restaurant is the headliner here, but the sleek bar is almost as much of a see-and-be-seen spot.

✔ In the Back Bay (T: Arlington [Green Line]), the **Parish Café and Bar,** 361 Boylston St. (☎ **617-247-4777**), offers indoor and outdoor seating. Another after-work hot spot, this place is also a popular lunch stop because of a terrific sandwich menu.

✔ In the South End (T: Back Bay/South End [Orange Line]), two friendly, cramped spots pack in the locals: **Anchovies,** 433 Columbus Ave. (☎ **617-266-5066**), and the **DeLux Cafe,** 100 Chandler St. (☎ **617-338-5258**).

My Goodness, My Guinness: Irish Bars

In one of North America's most Irish cities, Irish bars occupy an honored place. Ponder which came first — the bartending job or the brogue — while you sip a Guinness.

✔ **Mr. Dooley's Boston Tavern,** 77 Broad St. (T: State [Orange or Blue Line]; ☎ **617-338-5656**), a popular Financial District spot, is my favorite. World-class bartenders, hearty food, music, and imported draught beer in an authentic atmosphere — what more could you want? There's a $3 to $5 cover charge on weekend nights.

✔ **The Black Rose,** 160 State St. (at Faneuil Hall Marketplace; T: State [Orange or Blue Line]; ☎ **617-742-2286;** www.irishconnection.com/blackrose), is considerably larger and rowdier. The Black Rose's live entertainment delights huge crowds who often sing along. The location makes this bar popular with tourists, but you'll find plenty of clued-in locals, too. You'll pay a cover of $3 to $5 at night.

Shaken, Not Stirred: Boston's Best Lounges

When you're feeling James Bond–ish, head up to **Top of the Hub,**
800 Boylston St. (T: Prudential [Green Line E]; ☎ 617-536-1775), on the
52nd floor of the Prudential Tower. The lounge is an atmospheric place
to begin or end a big evening out. Sunset offers the best view, but any
nonfoggy time is good. Top of the Hub schedules music and dancing
nightly; dress is casual but neat. The lounge is open Sunday through
Wednesday until 1 a.m., and Thursday through Saturday until 2 a.m.

Other top-shelf martini shakers reside in elegant, expensive hotel bars,
which stay open into the early morning. (Don't think of them as pricier
than a regular bar; think of them as cheaper than booking a room.) Dress
up a little.

  ✔ **The Bar at the Ritz,** in the Ritz-Carlton, 15 Arlington St. (T: Arlington
    [Green Line]; ☎ 617-536-5700), was famous long before *Cheers* was
    even a pilot episode. The Ritz retains the crown with a combination
    of Brahmin atmosphere and killer martinis.

Out on the town with the kids

Maybe there's a better way to look cool in front of your kids than taking them to a
trendy nightlife destination (in the afternoon, but still). I just can't think what it is.

Jillian's Boston, 145 Ipswich St. (at Lansdowne Street; T: Kenmore [Green Line B, C,
or D] or Fenway [Green Line D]; ☎ 617-437-0300; www.jilliansboston.com), is
a 70,000-square-foot complex at the end of the Lansdowne Street nightclub strip. You
can shoot pool on one of the 52 tables, take a virtual-reality movie "ride," or play Texas
hold-'em (for fun, not money). You can tackle a classic or contemporary game in the
250-game video midway, play darts or table tennis, or just watch your kids have a ball.
Jillian's is open Monday through Saturday 11 a.m. to 2 a.m. and Sunday noon to 2 a.m.
The complex admits those under 18, who must be with an adult, before 8 p.m. Adults
who return later can take full advantage of the dance club, five bars, and restaurant.
Valet parking is available Wednesday through Sunday after 6 p.m., except during Red
Sox games.

You can also bowl at Jillian's, but the hottest bowling alley around is **Kings**, 10 Scotia
St. (☎ 617-266-BOWL; www.backbaykings.com). The 25,000-square-foot complex
in a former movie theater has 20 bowling lanes (four of them private) and an eight-
table billiards room. Also here are a retro-cool bar, the DeVille Lounge, and a branch
of the Cambridge restaurant Jasper White's Summer Shack. Scotia Street is off Dalton
Street, across from the Hynes Convention Center. Kings is open Monday through
Wednesday 5 p.m. to 2 a.m., Thursday through Sunday 11:30 a.m. to 2 a.m.; patrons
must be 21 after 6 p.m.

- ✔ **The Bristol,** in the Four Seasons Hotel, 200 Boylston St. (T: Arlington [Green Line]; ☎ **617-351-2000**), is a refined destination for cocktails, luscious American food, afternoon tea, and (on weekend nights) the decadent Viennese Dessert Buffet. The Bristol schedules live piano music every night.

- ✔ The **Oak Bar** at the Fairmont Copley Plaza Hotel, 138 St. James Ave. (T: Copley [Green Line]; ☎ **617-267-5300**), is the clubbiest place in town. Wood paneling, a raw bar, and nightly live entertainment set the scene. Proper dress is required. The Oak Bar is open daily at 4:30 p.m.

- ✔ **The Atrium** lounge in the lobby of the **Millennium Bostonian Hotel,** 40 North St. (at Faneuil Hall Marketplace; T: Government Center [Green or Blue Line] or Haymarket [Orange Line]; ☎ **617-523-3600**), has less of a hideaway feel than many hotel bars. The wraparound windows afford a great view of the marketplace.

Shaking Your Groove Thing: The Best Dance Clubs

Boston's most popular nightlife destination is Kenmore Square, specifically **Lansdowne Street,** off Brookline Avenue outside the square, across the street from Fenway Park. A close second is **Boylston Place,** an alley (known cleverly as "The Alley") off Boylston Street near Tremont Street.

- ✔ The city's best dance club, **Avalon,** 15 Lansdowne St. (T: Kenmore [Green Line B, C, or D]; ☎ **617-262-2424**), is probably reinventing some aspect of itself as you read this book. This multilevel space near Kenmore Square often hosts concerts, but the consistent reason to come here is "Avaland," the Friday night dance party. Management imports high-profile DJs and turns house dancers loose. The cover is usually $5 to $15 but more for special events. Avalon is open Thursday through Sunday 10 p.m. to 2 a.m. The dress code forbids jeans and athletic wear, and requires jackets and shirts with collars for men.

- ✔ Under the same management, **Axis,** 13 Lansdowne St. (T: Kenmore [Green Line B, C, or D]; ☎ **617-262-2437**), boasts a younger (collegiate and postcollegiate), looser crowd. Deafening rock, house, and techno music keep the leather-clad crowds moving. The cover charge is around $7 to $11. Axis is open Tuesday through Sunday 10 p.m. to 2 a.m.

- ✔ The Alley constantly evolves to stay within the attention span of its recent-college-graduate core clientele; if that's you, you're sure to find a congenial landing spot. At the moment, a good place to start the night is the **Big Easy,** 1 Boylston Place (T: Boylston [Green Line]; ☎ **617-351-7000;** www.bigeasyboston.com), a two-level space that schedules top-notch local DJs.

Turning Up the Volume: The Best Rock Clubs

Cambridge's **Central Square** (T: Central [Red Line]) draws enthusiastic crowds that go for music-making over scene-making. Many shows are 18-plus, with room for 30-pluses who can keep their fogeyish musings to themselves. (But *boy*, these places are loud.)

- ✔ The **Middle East,** 472–480 Mass. Ave. (☎ **617-864-EAST;** www.mideastclub.com), is the best rock club in the area. Enthusiastic crowds pack its four performance spaces for rock of all stripes every night. The cover ranges from $7 to $15.

- ✔ **T. T. the Bear's Place,** 10 Brookline St. (☎ **617-492-0082,** or concert line 617-492-BEAR; www.ttthebears.com), runs the musical gamut with eclectic bookings. This place is a little crowded; expect to get to know your neighbors. The cover runs from $3 to $15 but usually under $10.

Across the river in Boston, you find a somewhat more sophisticated clientele at the **Paradise Rock Club,** 967 Commonwealth Ave. (T: Green Line B to Pleasant Street; ☎ **617-562-8804,** or 617-423-NEXT for tickets). This club is one of the best-known live-music venues in the area — the medium size allows artists who aren't ready to tour solo to headline. This club is also famous for tangling with the Boston Licensing Board over the question of underage patrons; you *must* have an ID. Tickets run $10 to $30.

Focusing On the Music: The Best Jazz, Folk, and Blues Clubs

The local jazz, folk, and blues clubs in Boston are some of the best in the country — an enjoyable dilemma for devotees, a great opportunity for novices. You simply can't go wrong at any of the places listed here.

- ✔ The **Regattabar** is in the Charles Hotel, 1 Bennett St., Harvard Square (T: Harvard [Red Line]; ☎ **617-661-5000,** or 617-876-7777 for Concertix; www.regattabarjazz.com). Crowds in the large space sometimes get a little distracted (and chatty). Tickets run $12 to $36. The Regattabar is open Tuesday through Saturday and some Sundays. Check the Web site for show times.

- ✔ **Scullers Jazz Club** is in the Doubletree Guest Suites hotel, 400 Soldiers Field Rd. (☎ **617-562-4111;** www.scullersjazz.com). The room overlooks the Charles. The difficulty of getting to the hotel, which is not near the T, means the crowd includes fewer casual fans — a plus if your favorite artist is playing. Ask about dinner packages, which include preferred seating. Show tickets cost $12 to $50. Check the Web site for show times.

✔ Near a nondescript corner in the South End is a club that's as famous with touring musicians as it is unknown to many locals. **Wally's Cafe,** 427 Mass. Ave. (T: Massachusetts Ave. [Orange Line] or Symphony [Green Line E]; ☎ 617-424-1408; www.wallyscafe. com), a legend since shortly after it opened in 1947, schedules live jazz nightly at 9. Management doesn't charge a cover but does impose a one-drink minimum.

✔ If folk is your thing, you probably already know about **Club Passim,** 47 Palmer St. (T: Harvard [Red Line]; ☎ 617-492-7679), one of the few remaining legends in Harvard Square. It lives up to its international reputation as a folk-music proving ground. The coffeehouse (which does not serve alcohol) has been around for more than 30 years; your favorite folk artist has almost certainly played here. The cover charge is usually $5 to $12 or so; for big names, it may top $20. Open daily 11 a.m. to 11 p.m.

✔ **Johnny D's Uptown Restaurant & Music Club,** 17 Holland St., Somerville (T: Davis [Red Line]; ☎ 617-776-2004, or concert line 617-776-9667; www.johnnyds.com), schedules a wild assortment of musical genres and styles. No matter what your taste, the schedule is worth checking out. If your taste runs to food, Johnny D's has that, too. Cover $2 to $16, usually $10 or less. Open daily 11:30 a.m. to 1 a.m. Somerville is just north of Cambridge.

✔ Central Square's **Cantab Lounge,** 738 Mass. Ave. (T: Central [Red line]; ☎ 617-354-2685; www.cantablounge.com), is a neighborhood bar that happens to book great music — usually R&B or rock, sometimes jazz. The crowd is a cross section of the funky neighborhood, and the cover charge seldom tops $8. Open Sunday through Wednesday until 1 a.m. and Thursday through Saturday until 2 a.m. The kitchen is open 5 to 11 p.m. Monday through Saturday; it's closed Sunday.

Laughing the Night Away: Comedy Clubs

Get ready to clutch your sides and smile until your cheeks hurt at these spots.

✔ The **Comedy Connection at Faneuil Hall,** on the upper level of Quincy Market (T: Government Center [Green or Blue Line] or Haymarket [Orange Line]; ☎ 617-248-9700; www.comedy connectionboston.com), is the best comedy club around. Promising locals and big-name visitors have packed the spacious room since 1978. Tickets run from $8 (for unknowns) to more than $30 (for sitcom stars and the like).

✔ You'll find fewer famous names but more potential in Cambridge at the **Comedy Studio,** in the Hong Kong restaurant, 1236 Mass. Ave. (T: Harvard [Red Line]; ☎ 617-661-6507; www.thecomedystudio. com). This place is good for improv, inspired sparring with the audience, and sketch comedy.

Stepping Out: Gay and Lesbian Scene

Some dance clubs (see earlier in this chapter for locations and telephone numbers) schedule a weekly gay night. The largest and best known is Sunday at **Avalon;** at neighboring **Axis,** Monday is gay night. **Buzz,** 67 Stuart St. (T: Boylston [Green Line]; ☎ **617-267-8969;** www.buzzboston. com), morphs into a red-hot scene for men on Saturday at 10 p.m. For women, the can't-miss night is Sunday at Jamaica Plain's **Milky Way Lounge,** 401 Centre St. (T: Stony Brook [Orange Line]; ☎ **617-524-3720**), which features a wide variety of live entertainment.

For up-to-date entertainment listings, check *Bay Windows* (www.bay windows.com) and the *Phoenix* (www.bostonphoenix.com).

The following are some reliable hangouts:

- ✔ **Club Café,** 209 Columbus Ave., South End (T: Arlington [Green Line] or Back Bay [Orange Line]; ☎ **617-536-0966**), is a lively spot, but not so noisy as to restrict conversation. Club Café attracts men and women with live music and video entertainment. Thursday is see-and-be-seen night. The club is open daily until 1 a.m.

- ✔ **Jacques,** 79 Broadway, in Bay Village, next to the Theater District (T: Arlington [Green Line]; ☎ **617-426-8902**), is Boston's only drag venue. Jacques attracts a mixed (gay and straight) clientele with live music and performance art, too. The club is open daily until midnight.

- ✔ The **Ramrod,** 1254 Boylston St. (T: Hynes/ICA or Kenmore [Green Line B, C, or D]; ☎ **617-266-2986**), is a leather bar on weekends and a dance club all week; the bar opens at noon, and you can play pool every night after 7.

- ✔ **Fritz,** in the Chandler Inn Hotel, 26 Chandler St. (at Berkeley Street; T: Back Bay [Orange Line]; ☎ **617-482-4428**), will make you feel right at home: It's a neighborhood sports bar that's open daily until 1 a.m.

Part VI
The Part of Tens

The 5th Wave   By Rich Tennant

"This is a very old and historical part of Boston, so be careful on the cobblestone escalator."

In this part . . .

People love top-ten lists — just ask Moses. The lists in this part aren't exactly biblical prophecy, but they do offer some insider information. If you want to explore Boston like a Bostonian, Chapter 17 offers the top ten ways to avoid looking like a tourist. If you want to splurge on dinner one night, read Chapter 18 so that you can afford it; I tell you about the top ten free (or almost free) things to do in Boston. And whatever comes your way — snow, rain, heat, or cold — Chapter 19 prepares you for it with the top ten guaranteed good times in bad weather.

Chapter 17

The Top Ten Ways Not to Look Like a Tourist

In This Chapter

▶ Dressing like a local
▶ Keeping in step
▶ Talking the talk

Sometimes one of the best ways to acquaint yourself with a new city is to seek directions and advice from the locals. Other times, you may just want to blend in and do as Bostonians do. This chapter offers suggestions for fitting in without becoming so assimilated that people are asking *you* for directions. But if they do, maybe you can help — by now, you probably know where the maps are in this book!

Always Dress in Layers

Even on the steamiest summer day, a midafternoon change in wind direction (or a stop at an enthusiastically air-conditioned store) can mean a sharp drop in temperature. You'll be glad to pull on a long-sleeved T-shirt or light sweater. And a spring or fall day that starts with a foggy morning can become toasty after the haze burns off — not a good time to have nothing on under your sweatshirt.

Keep Moving

Bostonians reputedly walk and talk faster than any other Americans — even New Yorkers. While sightseeing, step to the curb to check your map, count heads, or admire the architecture. Remember that the neighborhoods that attract hordes of tourists are also places where regular people live and work. When you block locals' paths while you get your bearings, you're forcing the home team off the sidewalks and into the paths of (scary sound effect) Boston traffic.

Stay in Touch with the Freedom Trail

Distinguished by red paint or red brick smack in the middle of the side-walk, the Freedom Trail won't steer you wrong. If you lose track of where you are, follow the trail to an intersection or landmark. You don't need to keep to the trail religiously; in fact, I strongly suggest a bit of wandering. One observation to note: If you're standing right on the trail as you tangle with your map, you'll look like a big ol' tourist.

Don't Exclaim "That Must Be the Old North Church!"

As you follow the Freedom Trail away from the Paul Revere House, you come to a house of worship on Hanover Street. This building is St. Stephen's, the last remaining Boston church designed by legendary architect Charles Bulfinch. The Old North Church is across the street, a block beyond the Paul Revere statue that faces St. Stephen's.

Be in Your Party Clothes Early

Bars close at 1 a.m. or earlier, clubs wrap things up at 2 a.m., and the line between "fashionably late" and "shut out" is all too thin. If the only admirers of your hot new outfit are the other people at the 24-hour pancake house, don't say I didn't warn you.

Bring Cab Fare

Should you manage to scout out some late-night action, don't expect to jump on the T when you're through. On Sunday through Thursday nights, the T closes by 1 a.m. (Every station posts the time of the last train in either direction.) On Friday and Saturday, there's Night Owl bus service, but it doesn't go everywhere, and it shuts down at 2:30 a.m. After that, you're at the mercy of friends and cabbies.

Watch What You Say about Baseball

In cities that take sports less seriously, you can start a casual conversation with "How 'bout those (insert the name of the local nine)?" But Boston no longer has casual fans. Unless you're ready to hear the gory details of where your cabbie — or cardiologist or manicurist or friend's grandmother — was during every nail-biting moment of the Red Sox's march to the 2004 World Series title, break the ice with a quip about the weather.

Likewise, Chowder

This issue is less contentious than it once was but still divisive. The dispute concerns a certain red ingredient found in the clam chowder in a big city some 200 miles south of the right-thinking people of Boston. You can sidestep the issue by ordering the version Legal Sea Foods attributes to Rhode Island (*never* Manhattan), but few other restaurants north of Connecticut will accommodate your heretical preference. In short, New England clam chowder does not contain tomatoes. Deal with it.

Pack the Right Shoes

Especially if you visit downtown, think twice before strapping on sandals. The Big Dig acted as a sort of gravel farm, and the closer you get to the aftermath, the likelier you are to wind up with something uncomfortable in your shoe. Stick to closed footwear. And if you believe wearing socks with your sandals is an acceptable alternative, I'm sorry, but I'm going to have to pretend that we've never met.

Save the "I Pahked My Cah" Jokes

Everybody has an accent, even you — you just can't hear your own. The Boston accent isn't exactly poetic, but making fun of someone who speaks with one is both provincial and rude. That doesn't mean you can't enjoy the accent, though. Use your curious ear for discreet eavesdropping (the T is great for this pastime), and you'll soon be so wrapped up in a discussion of how your fellow passenger's "ahnt" had the wrong "idear" that you may miss your stop.

Chapter 18

The Top Ten Free (or Almost Free) Activities

. . . .

In This Chapter

▶ Finding free — or practically free — cultural events

▶ Touring Boston on the cheap

▶ Locating the best people-watching spots

. . . .

*W*hether your budget resembles an impoverished student's or a blueblood heiress's, a few extra bucks are always welcome. In this chapter, I point you toward activities that can help create financial wiggle room. For general information on all things budgetary, turn to Chapter 4.

Music Outdoors

In warm weather, musicians take to the streets and outdoor venues in droves. The free performances range from impromptu jam sessions to huge concerts that promote local radio stations. One congenial series brings jazz to Christopher Columbus Park, on the waterfront across the street from Faneuil Hall Marketplace, at 6:30 p.m. on summer Fridays. City Hall Plaza and the Hatch Shell on the Charles River Esplanade book larger events. Check around (in the papers or at the front desk) when you arrive — you'll definitely find something that appeals to you.

Music Indoors

Colleges and churches take up the slack when cold weather drives tunesmiths indoors. Students and instructors at local universities as well as prestigious conservatories perform throughout the school year.

The big academic names are **Berklee College** (www.berklee.edu), the **New England Conservatory** (www.newenglandconservatory.edu), and **Cambridge's Longy School** (www.longy.edu), but there's no telling what you may find while in Boston. Churches schedule secular performances as well as religious works; the best-known series runs year-round at historic **Trinity Church,** in Copley Square, Fridays at 12:15 p.m.

Check listings in the *Globe* "Calendar" section (www.boston.com/ae/events) or the *Phoenix* (www.bostonphoenix.com) before or when you arrive for more information about the Boston area's abundant free and cheap activities.

National Park Service Tours

At the Park Service sites that dot eastern Massachusetts, free or inexpensive tours help interpret the historic and cultural attractions. Check the Web site (www.nps.gov) or drop into the **Boston National Historic Park Visitor Center,** 15 State St. (☎ **617-242-5642**), for more information.

Movies

The **Free Friday Flicks** (www.wbz.com) film series brings family movies to the Esplanade every summer. The kid-friendly picture will probably be something that's available on video, but the experience — under the stars, ruffled by a breeze off the river — makes this series feel like more than just another movie.

The **Boston Public Library** (www.bpl.org) schedules free movies year-round at the main branch, in Copley Square, and often at the neighborhood branches. Check ahead; you may stumble upon a gem.

Theater

Theater is another area with a substantial college component, and the usual potential and pitfalls of amateur stagecraft. Again, local listings can point you in the right direction. For the less adventurous (or more discriminating, if you prefer), professionals perform free on Boston Common in July and early August with the **Commonwealth Shakespeare Company** (www.commonwealthshakespeare.org). The top-notch troupe mounts one production per season.

Museums

Your low-budget options are few but fun.

 ✔ **Free:** The USS *Constitution* Museum, the Institute of Contemporary Art on Thursday from 5 to 9 p.m., the Harvard University Art Museums until noon Saturday, and the Harvard natural-history museums until noon on Sunday year-round and Wednesday from 3 to 5 p.m. during the school year.

✔ **Cheap:** The Children's Museum charges $1 per person on Friday from 5 to 9 p.m., and most Freedom Trail sites that do charge admission don't charge too much — the Bostonian Society's museum in Old City Hall is $5 for adults; the Paul Revere House is $3. The Museum of Fine Arts schedules pay-what-you-wish hours on Wednesday from 4 to 9:45 p.m. but "suggests" that adults "donate" $15. If you're just interested in shopping (and believe me, you're not alone), remember that every museum will let you into the gift shop without paying an admission fee.

People Watching

For the price of a cup of coffee or a drink, you can camp out and enjoy a passing parade just about anywhere. Three favorite destinations: sidewalk tables and window seats on Newbury Street in the Back Bay, the Hanover Street *caffès* in the North End, and the outdoor tables at the Au Bon Pain in Harvard Square.

Haymarket

Haymarket could fall under "People Watching," but this is such an unusual experience that it deserves special attention. This open-air market consists of stalls piled high with fruits, veggies, and sometimes fish. Located on Blackstone and North streets, near Faneuil Hall Marketplace and the North End, the market operates only on Friday and Saturday. If you're on the Freedom Trail, slow down and have your camera ready — the gregarious vendors, fanatical bargain-hunters, and colorful produce make a perfect photo op.

Street Fairs

You can find alfresco diversions, from fashion shows to pony rides, all over town on weekends throughout the summer and fall. The North End, the Back Bay, and Harvard Square stage notable multiple-block parties; check the newspapers or ask at your hotel's front desk for details of festivities during your visit.

Hydrotherapy

Check out a map of Boston and Cambridge, both of which abound with waterfront property. Pack a lunch, a camera, or just a craving for a little downtime, and head toward the harbor or the river to kick back. Maritime traffic constantly crisscrosses the harbor, which lies within view of Logan Airport's flight patterns. Recreational craft on the Charles River include graceful sailboats and college crew shells.

You can find excellent spots for a water break in downtown Boston along Long Wharf (follow State Street to the end) and off Commercial Street at Fleet Street and at Hull Street, in Charlestown near the harbor ferry dock, and in the Back Bay on the Charles River Esplanade. The Cambridge side of the river is essentially one long park, with particularly enjoyable spots near Harvard and Kendall squares.

Another great experience involving water and not too much money is the ferry between Long Wharf, near the New England Aquarium, and the Charlestown Navy Yard. The $1.50 one-way fare includes a million-dollar view of the harbor.

Chapter 19

The Top Ten Things to Do in Bad Weather

- -

In This Chapter

▶ Cooling off in the heat of the moment

▶ Taking shelter from the storm

▶ Warming up — baby, it's cold outside

- -

*T*he most familiar cliché about New England weather — "If you don't like it, wait ten minutes" — is often true. But what if the forecast calls for nonstop sweltering heat or continuous bone-chilling cold? In this chapter, I share some coping strategies for the days when peeling off or piling on clothes just isn't getting the job done.

Soak Up Some Culture

Climate control keeps museum artifacts in tip-top condition; a happy side effect is comfortable patrons. In particularly daunting weather, make a day of it. The **Museum of Fine Arts (MFA)** is the size of a small town, with multiple dining options, excellent shopping, and even a movie theater. The art's pretty great, too. Take a tour; enjoy a meal; immerse yourself in a particularly appealing gallery; and before you know it, the guards will be shooing you out. Wednesday, when the museum is open for nearly 12 hours, is the best day to seek refuge from bad weather. See Chapter 11.

Find a Secret (Indoor) Garden

The MFA (see preceding section) can be a bit overwhelming. A stone's throw away, the **Isabella Stewart Gardner Museum** is home to a less encyclopedic collection in an even more beautiful building. The pictur-esque interior courtyard overflows with a sort of garden; there are sea-sonal flowers and greenery year-round, making it a peaceful refuge from both heat and cold. Here, too, you can dine without leaving the premises and do a little shopping. See Chapter 11.

Smell the Popcorn

The coldest place downtown is also one of the coolest. The **Loews Boston Common** movie theater, 175 Tremont St. (☎ **617-423-3499;** T: Boylston [Green Line]), is almost as big as an airport terminal — 19 screens — and almost as air-conditioned as the frozen-foods aisle of the supermarket. Pick the summer blockbuster with the longest running time, and don't forget your sweater.

See the World

The **Museum of Science** and the **New England Aquarium** are fascinating destinations that incorporate IMAX theaters. Before or after a visit to either institution's main building, you can explore the natural world in air-conditioned or heated comfort. The museum's **Mugar Omni Theatre** takes you everywhere from the bottom of the sea to the top of a mountain (and if you'd rather explore outer space, the complex has a planetarium, too). The **Simons IMAX Theatre** at the aquarium shows both educational films and versions of Hollywood blockbusters that take good advantage of the 3D format. See Chapter 11.

Shop 'til You Drop

Newbury Street is a peerless shopping destination, with tons of unique shops, but it's also outdoors. In inclement weather, head a couple of blocks away to the **Shops at Prudential Center.** Sure, it's a mall, but it's a really nice one. The food court has the only branch of **Krispy Kreme Doughnuts** in Boston, and the shopping is good, if a bit generic. When you've had enough, take the skybridge across Huntington Avenue to even-more-upscale **Copley Place.** Between the two shopping centers, you can easily spend half a day out of the elements. On the other side of the river, the **CambridgeSide Galleria** mall is a reasonable alternative to the Back Bay's retail megalopolis. See Chapter 12.

Feel the Wind in Your Hair

On a hot day, sightseeing and whale-watching **cruises** can liberate you from the steamy city. The water is cooler and breezier than the land (except in winter), and even a quick trip can be delightfully refreshing. You can spend as long as a half-day searching for whales or as little as ten minutes on a ferry slicing across the Inner Harbor. The one-way fare from Long Wharf, steps from the New England Aquarium, to the Charlestown Navy Yard is $1.50. See Chapter 11.

Set Sail

The Charles River is cool and wet, too. If you have the time and the money, head to **Community Boating,** 21 David Mugar Way, on the Esplanade (☎ 617-523-1038; www.community-boating.org). Two days of unlimited use of the center's watercraft (13- to 23-foot sailboats, Windsurfers, and kayaks) costs $100. Steep, yes, but in the middle of a crushing heat wave? Priceless.

Consider Pyromania

A blazing fire — in a fireplace, please — can be your best friend on unseasonably cold days (and nights) in spring and fall, as well as the depths of winter. The **Bar at the Ritz,** in the Ritz-Carlton, Boston, is home to perhaps the most famous fireplace in the city. Across the river, **Grendel's Den,** a longtime Harvard Square favorite, is a cozy bar with a just-off-the-slopes atmosphere; order fondue to preserve the illusion.

Try Bibliomania, Too

Bibliomania is an obsession with books, which is a roundabout way of suggesting that you seek out a branch of the **Boston Public Library** (www.bpl.org). All are climate controlled and offer comfortable seating. The main branch, in Copley Square, also has a cool courtyard and passable restrooms.

Get Out of Town

After a few days of 90-plus days and 70-plus nights, Boston's brick sidewalks start to feel like the walls of a brick pizza oven. When you just can't take it anymore, head to the beach. You don't even have to drive — the MBTA (☎ 800-392-6100 outside Massachusetts, or 617-222-3200; www.mbta.com) stops so close to the Atlantic that you can smell the saltwater. The cheapest road trip is by way of the subway: Take the Blue Line to Revere Beach or Wonderland, cross Revere Beach Boulevard, and wriggle your tootsies in the sand of **Revere Beach.** For a less urban experience, ride the commuter rail to Manchester-by-the-Sea. The 0.8-mile walk to gorgeous **Singing Beach** isn't much fun in the midst of a summer scorcher, but it's well worth the effort.

Appendix

Quick Concierge

Fast Facts:

Boston AAA

For road service, call ☎ 800-222-4357. For other services, call ☎ 800-222-8252. The Boston office is in the Financial District at 125 High St., off Pearl Street.

Area Codes

Eastern Massachusetts has eight area codes, and every phone number is 10 digits (11 if you count dialing 1 first). Even if you're calling next door, you must dial the area code first. In Boston proper, the area codes are **617** and **857**; in the immediate suburbs, **781** and **339**; to the north and west, **978** and **351**; to the south and east, **508** and **774**.

ATMs

ATMs are widely available throughout Boston and Cambridge at banks, on the street, in convenience stores and supermarkets, and in some subway stations. Cirrus (☎ 800-424-7787; www.mastercard.com) and PLUS (☎ 800-843-7587; www.visa.com) are the major national networks. The NYCE network (www.nycenet.com) operates in the eastern United States.

Baby Sitters

Ask your hotel's front desk or concierge for suggestions. One well-regarded local agency is Parents in a Pinch (☎ 800-688-4697 outside Massachusetts or 617-739-KIDS; www.parentsinapinch.com). It screens child-care providers and offers references to parents who request them.

The annual registration fee is $150; you also pay a per-day referral fee, an hourly rate, reimbursement for transportation, and other authorized expenses. If you're in town on business, ask whether the company you're visiting has a membership.

Business Hours

Business offices generally are open weekdays from 9 a.m. to 5 or 6 p.m. Banks are open weekdays from 8:30 or 9 a.m. to 4 or 5 p.m. and sometimes Saturday morning. Most stores and other businesses are open daily, though many stay closed until noon on Sunday. Many department stores stay open until 9 at least one night a week.

Camera Repair

Try Bromfield Camera & Video, 10 Bromfield St. (☎ 800-723-2628 or 617-426-5230), near Downtown Crossing, or the Camera Craftsman, 362 Commonwealth Ave. (☎ 617-267-5883), in the Back Bay.

Convention Centers

Boston Convention & Exhibition Center, 415 Summer St. (☎ 617-867-8286; www.advantageboston.com). Hynes Convention Center, 900 Boylston St. (☎ 617-954-2000 or 617-424-8585 for show information; www.jbhynes.com). World Trade Center, 164 Northern Ave. (☎ 800-367-9822 or 617-385-5000, or 617-385-5044 for show information; www.wtcb.com). Bayside Expo Center, 200 Mount Vernon St., Dorchester (☎ 617-474-6000; www.baysideexpo.com).

Credit Cards

The toll-free emergency number for Visa is ☎ 800-847-2911. The number for MasterCard is ☎ 800-307-7309. American Express cardholders should call ☎ 800-221-7282 for emergencies.

Dentists

Check with the front desk or concierge at your hotel or try the Massachusetts Dental Society (☎ 800-342-8747 or 508-651-7511; www.massdental.org).

Doctors

Check with the front desk or concierge at your hotel,or try a referral service. Every hospital in town has one, including Massachusetts General (☎ 800-711-4MGH) and Beth Israel Deaconess (☎ 617-667-5356). An affiliate of Massachusetts General Hospital, MGH Back Bay, 388 Commonwealth Ave. (☎ 617-267-7171), is a clinic that honors most insurance plans and accepts credit cards.

Emergencies

Call ☎ 911 for the police, a fire, or an ambulance. This call is free from pay phones.

Hospitals

Closest to downtown are Massachusetts General Hospital, 55 Fruit St. (☎ 617-726-2000), and Tufts–New England Medical Center, 750 Washington St. (☎ 617-636-5000). At the Harvard Medical Area on the Boston-Brookline border are Beth Israel Deaconess Medical Center, 330 Brookline Ave. (☎ 617-667-7000); Brigham and Women's Hospital, 75 Francis St. (☎ 617-732-5500); and Children's Hospital, 300 Longwood Ave. (☎ 617-355-6000), among others. In Cambridge: Mount Auburn Hospital, 330 Mount Auburn St. (☎ 617-492-3500), and Cambridge Hospital, 1493 Cambridge St. (☎ 617-498-1000).

Hotlines

AIDS Hotline (☎ 800-235-2331 or 617-536-7733); Alcoholics Anonymous (☎ 617-426-9444); Poison Control Center (☎ 800-682-9211); Rape Crisis (☎ 877-627-7700 or 617-492-7273); Samaritans Suicide Prevention (☎ 617-247-0220); and Samariteens (☎ 800-252-8336 or 617-247-8050).

Information

See "Where to Get More Information," later in this Appendix. For telephone directory assistance, call ☎ 411.

Internet Access and Cybercafes

The Boston area has surprisingly few cybercafes. Tech Superpowers, 252 Newbury St., third floor (☎ 617267-9716; www.newburyopen.net), offers Internet access for $5 an hour with a $3 minimum. Many businesses on this stretch of Newbury Street offer free wireless access; Trident Booksellers & Café, 338 Newbury St. (☎ 617-267-8688; www.tridentbookscafe.com), is one. Kinko's offers Internet access at its numerous locations, including 2 Center Plaza, Government Center (☎ 617-973-9000); 10 Post Office Sq., Financial District (☎ 617-482-4400); 187 Dartmouth St., Back Bay (☎ 617-262-6188); and 1 Mifflin Place, off Mount Auburn Street near Eliot Street, Harvard Square (☎ 617-497-0125). Expect to pay 10¢ to 20¢ per minute.

Liquor Laws

The legal drinking age is 21. Always be ready to show identification. At sporting events, everyone buying alcohol must show ID. Liquor stores and a few supermarkets and convenience stores sell alcohol. Sunday alcohol sales, which only recently became legal, begin at noon. Some smaller restaurants don't have full liquor licenses; they serve wine and beer or wine, beer, and cordials, but no hard liquor. If you must have a mixed drink, ask when you make your reservations.

Maps

Pick up a map at any visitor information center (see Chapter 8 for more information), at most hotels, and from the clerks in most T token booths.

Pharmacies

Nearly every neighborhood has a CVS; ask at your hotel's front desk. Downtown Boston has no 24-hour drugstore. The CVS in the Porter Square Shopping Center, off Mass. Ave. in Cambridge (☎ 617-876-5519), is open 24 hours, 7 days a week. The pharmacy at the CVS at 155–157 Charles St. in Boston (☎ 617-523-1028), next to the Charles/MGH Red Line T stop, is open until midnight. Some emergency rooms can fill your prescription at the hospital's pharmacy.

Police

Call ☎ 911 for emergencies. The non-emergency number is ☎ 617-343-4200.

Post Office

The main post office at 25 Dorchester Ave. (☎ 617-654-5326), behind South Station, is open weekdays 6 a.m. to midnight, Saturday 8 a.m. to 7 p.m., Sunday and holidays noon to 7 p.m.. Neighborhood post offices typically are open weekdays 8 a.m. to 6 p.m., Saturday 8 a.m. to 2 p.m.

Radio Stations

WBUR-FM, 90.9, is the local National Public Radio affiliate. WBZ-AM, 1030, carries news, sports, and weather, with traffic reports every ten minutes on weekdays. The local sports talk station is WWZN-AM 1510.

Restrooms

The visitor center at 15 State St. has a public restroom, as do most tourist attractions, hotels, department stores, and public buildings. The CambridgeSide Galleria, Copley Place, Prudential Center shopping areas, most Starbucks locations, and most large chain bookstores have restrooms. Freestanding self-cleaning toilets (25¢) are in several high-traffic areas downtown. Inspect these areas carefully before using them — the generous time limit makes some of the toilets popular with IV-drug users. If you're walking the Freedom Trail, especially with children, be sure to use the restrooms at Faneuil Hall Marketplace before venturing into the North End, which has no public facilities.

Safety

Boston and Cambridge are generally safe for walking. As in any city, stay out of parks (including the Esplanade) at night, unless you're in a crowd. Use common sense: Walk confidently; try not to use ATMs at night; and avoid dark, deserted streets. Specific areas to avoid at night include Boylston Street between Tremont and Washington streets, and Tremont Street from Stuart to Boylston street. Watch your step near the Big Dig aftermath (that is, most of downtown), where walking surfaces can be uneven and lighting is often poor. Public transportation in the areas you're likely to visit is busy and safe, but you should always watch out for pickpockets.

Smoking

State law forbids smoking in all workplaces, including restaurants, nightclubs, and bars. An unfortunate consequence is that outdoor seating areas at restaurants and bars tend to be extremely smoky.

Taxes

The 5 percent state sales tax doesn't apply to food, prescription drugs, newspapers, or clothing worth less than $175. The state meal tax (which also applies to takeout food) is 5 percent. The lodging tax is 12.45 percent in Boston and Cambridge.

Taxis

To call ahead in Boston, try the Independent Taxi Operators Association (☎ 617-426-8700), Boston Cab (☎ 617-536-5010), Town Taxi (☎ 617-536-5000), or Metro Cab (☎ 617-242-8000). In Cambridge, call Ambassador Brattle (☎ 617-492-1100) or Yellow Cab (☎ 617-547-3000).

Time Zone

Boston is in the Eastern time zone. Daylight saving time begins on the first Sunday in April and ends on the last Sunday in October.

Transit Info

For information on MBTA subway, buses, commuter rail, and ferries, call ☎ 617-222-3200 or visit www.mbta.com. For information on Logan Airport, call ☎ 800-23-LOGAN or go to www.massport.com/logan.

Weather Updates

Call ☎ 617-936-1234 for forecasts. Check www.weather.com or http:// weather.boston.com/?city=Boston before you go.

Toll-Free Numbers and Web Sites

Major Airlines

Aer Lingus
☎ 800-474-7424 in the U.S.
☎ 01-886-8888 in Ireland
www.aerlingus.ie

Aeromexico
☎ 800-237-6639 in the U.S.
☎ 01-800-0214010 in Mexico
www.aeromexico.com

Air Canada
☎ 888-247-2262
www.aircanada.ca

Air France
☎ 800-237-2747 in the U.S.
☎ 0820-820-820 in France
www.airfrance.com

Air Jamaica
☎ 800-523-5585 in the U.S.
☎ 888-359-2475 in Jamaica
www.airjamaica.com

AirTran Airlines
☎ 800-247-8726
www.airtran.com

Alaska Airlines
☎ 800-252-7522
www.alaskaair.com

Alitalia
☎ 800-223-5730 in the U.S.
☎ 8488-65641 in Italy
www.alitalia.it

America West Airlines
☎ 800-235-9292
www.americawest.com

American Airlines
☎ 800-433-7300
www.aa.com

ATA Airlines
☎ 800-225-2995
www.ata.com

British Airways
☎ 800-247-9297
☎ 0345-222-111 or 0845-77-333-77 in the U.K.
www.british-airways.com

Cape Air
☎ 800-352-0714
www.flycapeair.com

Cayman Airways
☎ 800-422-9626
www.caymanairways.com

Continental Airlines
☎ 800-525-0280
www.continental.com

Delta Air Lines
☎ 800-221-1212
www.delta.com

Icelandair
☎ 800-223-5500 in the U.S.
☎ 354-50-50-100 in Iceland
www.icelandair.is

Independence Air
☎ 800-359-3594
www.flyi.com

JetBlue Airways
☎ 800-538-2583
www.jetblue.com

KLM
☎ 800-374-7747 in the U.S.
☎ 020-4-747-747 in the Netherlands
www.klm.nl

Lufthansa
☎ 800-645-3880 in the U.S.
☎ 49-0-180-5-8384267 in Germany
www.lufthansa.com

Midwest Express
☎ 800-452-2022
www.midwestexpress.com

Northwest Airlines
☎ 800-225-2525
www.nwa.com

SATA
☎ 800-762-9995
www.sata.pt

Song
☎ 800-359-7664
www.flysong.com

Southwest Airlines
☎ 800-435-9792
www.iflyswa.com

Spirit Airlines
☎ 800-772-7117
www.spiritair.com

Swiss International Airlines
☎ 877-359-7947 in the U.S.
☎ 0848-85-2000 in Switzerland
www.swiss.com

TACA
☎ 800-535-8780 in the U.S.
☎ 503-267-8222 in El Salvador
www.taca.com

United Airlines
☎ 800-241-6522
www.ual.com

USAirways
☎ 800-428-4322
www.usairways.com

Virgin Atlantic Airways
☎ 800-862-8621 in the continental U.S.
☎ 0293-747-747 in Britain
www.virgin-atlantic.com

Car-rental agencies

Alamo
☎ 800-327-9633
www.goalamo.com

Avis
☎ 800-831-1212 in the continental U.S.
☎ 800-TRY-AVIS in Canada
www.avis.com

Budget
☎ 800-527-0700
www.budget.com

Dollar
☎ 800-800-4000
www.dollar.com

Enterprise
☎ 800-325-8007
www.enterprise.com

Hertz
☎ 800-654-3131
www.hertz.com

National
☎ 800-CAR-RENT
www.nationalcar.com

Rent-A-Wreck
☎ 800-535-1391
www.rentawreck.com

Thrifty
☎ 800-367-2277
www.thrifty.com

Major hotel and motel chains

Best Western International
☎ 800-528-1234
www.bestwestern.com

Clarion Hotel
☎ 800-CLARION
www.clarionhotel.com or
www.hotelchoice.com

Comfort Inns
☎ 800-228-5150
www.hotelchoice.com

Courtyard by Marriott
☎ 800-321-2211
www.courtyard.com or
www.marriott.com

Days Inn
☎ 800-325-2525
www.daysinn.com

Doubletree Hotel
☎ 800-222-TREE
www.doubletree.com

Econo Lodges
☎ 800-55-ECONO
www.hotelchoice.com

Fairfield Inn by Marriott
☎ 800-228-2800
www.marriott.com

Hampton Inn
☎ 800-HAMPTON
www.hampton-inn.com

Hilton Hotels
☎ 800-HILTONS
www.hilton.com

Holiday Inn
☎ 800-HOLIDAY
www.basshotels.com

Howard Johnson
☎ 800-654-2000
www.hojo.com

Hyatt Hotels & Resorts
☎ 800-228-9000
www.hyatt.com

Marriott Hotels
☎ 800-228-9290
www.marriott.com

Omni
☎ 800-THE-OMNI
www.omnihotels.com

Quality Inns
☎ 800-228-5151
www.hotelchoice.com

Radisson Hotels International
☎ 800-333-3333
www.radisson.com

Ramada Inn
☎ 800-2-RAMADA
www.ramada.com

Residence Inn by Marriott
☎ 800-331-3131
www.residenceinn.com

Ritz-Carlton
☎ 800-241-3333
www.ritzcarlton.com

Sheraton Hotels & Resorts
☎ 800-325-3535
www.sheraton.com

Super 8 Motels
☎ 800-800-8000
www.super8.com

Travelodge
☎ 800-255-3050
www.travelodge.com

Wyndham Hotels & Resorts
☎ 800-822-4200
www.wyndham.com

Westin Hotels & Resorts
☎ 800-937-8461
www.westin.com

Where to Get More Information

Local tourist information offices

✔ **Cambridge Office for Tourism** (☎ **800-862-5678** or 617-441-2884; www.cambridge-usa.org; 18 Brattle St., Cambridge, MA 02138) provides a free guide to Boston's "Left Bank."

✔ **Greater Boston Convention & Visitors Bureau** (☎ **888-SEE-BOSTON** or 617-536-4100; www.bostonusa.com; 2 Copley Place, Suite 105, Boston, MA 02116-6501) offers a comprehensive visitor information kit for $10.25. The kit includes a travel planner, guidebook, map, and coupon book with shopping, dining, attractions, and nightlife discounts. The "Kids Love Boston" guidebook costs $5. Smaller guides to specific seasons or events often are available free.

✔ **Massachusetts Office of Travel and Tourism** (☎ **800-227-6277** or 617-973-8500; www.massvacation.com; 10 Park Plaza, Suite 4510, Boston, MA 02116) gives free copies of the *Getaway Guide* magazine, which includes information about attractions and lodgings, a map, and a seasonal calendar. Because this office covers travel and tourism for the whole state, it distributes less Boston-specific material than the Convention & Visitors Bureau. But the information is still useful (and free!). The online "lobster tutorial" makes an excellent cheat sheet.

Newspapers and magazines

✔ **Boston.com** (www.boston.com), the *Boston Globe*'s city guide, is the most complete and up-to-date resource around, with everything from weather forecasts to movie reviews, plus enough links and listings to keep you busy for hours.

✔ *The Boston Phoenix* (www.bostonphoenix.com), Boston's alternative weekly, offers abundant arts and entertainment coverage (listings and reviews), plus excellent listings for the gay, lesbian, and bisexual community.

✔ *Boston* **magazine** (www.bostonmagazine.com) is a slick monthly that covers the arts, entertainment, and politics; gives the annual *Best of Boston* awards; and runs the city's best money-is-no-object ads.

Other sources of information

- **✓** *Frommer's Boston* gives a comprehensive look at "the Hub," with more hotel, restaurant, and attraction listings than this book can accommodate. I have this on very good authority; the author wishes you well (wink!).

- **✓** *Frommer's New England* is the perfect accessory on a multiple-state or -city visit to this appealing region.

- **✓ Frommers.com** (www.frommers.com) posts online updates to Frommer's books, as well as up-to-date deals and news, trip ideas, and message boards where you can ask and answer questions.

- **✓ Citysearch.com** (http://boston.citysearch.com) contains copious lifestyle and entertainment listings, including restaurant reviews.

- **✓ The Massachusetts Port Authority** (www.massport.com), which runs the airport, constantly updates this site with the latest weather and air-traffic information. The visitor-information area includes many useful links.

- **✓ Mayorsfoodcourt.com** (www.mayorsfoodcourt.com) offers results of restaurant inspections (and reinspections), with numerical scores and pop-up windows that explain the regulations. Gross, but addictive.

Index